DEC RSAC 1992

D1561757

July 1914

July 1914
The Long Debate, 1918–1990

John W. Langdon

BERG
New York / Oxford
Distributed exclusively in the U.S. and Canada by
St. Martin's Press, New York

Published in 1991 by
Berg Publishers, Inc.
Editorial offices:
165 Taber Avenue, Providence, RI 02906, U.S.A.
150 Cowley Road, Oxford OX4 1JJ, UK
© John W. Langdon 1991

Quotations from *War of Illusions: German Policies from 1911 to 1914*, by Fritz Fischer, translated by Marian Jackson, are used with the permission of W.W. Norton and Company, Inc. Copyright © 1975 by W.W. Norton and Company, Inc., and Chatto and Windus, Ltd.

Library of Congress Cataloging-in-Publication Data
Langdon, John W.
  July 1914: the long debate, 1918–1990 / John W. Langdon,
  196p. 216cm.
  Includes bibliographical references.
  ISBN 0–86496–880–3
  1. World War. 1914–1918—Causes. 2. World War, 1914–1918—
  Reparations. 3. Treaty of Versailles (1919) I. Title.
  D611.L225 1990
  940.3'11—dc20   90–33210

Printed in Great Britain by
Billing & Sons Ltd, Worcester

To Janice

Contents

Acknowledgments

My interest in this subject originated in a seminar conducted by Professor Vincent Confer at the Maxwell Graduate School of Syracuse University in 1967. Since 1971, I have conducted several similar seminars at Le Moyne College and have labored to keep up with the tidal wave of monographs and scholarly articles which has engulfed the study of the origins of the First World War since the publication of Fritz Fischer's work. In this unending and fascinating task, as well as in the far more limited duties involved in the preparation of this book, I have been assisted by a number of people without whose help this project could not have been completed successfully.

Professor Volker Berghahn of Brown University read the manuscript with diligence and care. His detailed suggestions, based upon his own professional expertise and his lengthy association with many of the participants in the long debate, have enriched this book substantially. Dr. Marion Berghahn, Publisher, of Berg Publishers, Inc., offered the advice, encouragement, and editorial skill so vital to the process of revision and completion. Deborah Del Gais Muller edited the copy with dexterity and with careful attention to the cadence of my prose. I was likewise guided and inspired by the counsel of several of my colleagues in the historical profession, notably Professors Joseph Curran, Douglas Egerton, Edward Judge, Robyn Muncy, and William Telesca of Le Moyne College; Professor Gerhard Weinberg of the University of North Carolina at Chapel Hill; and Dr. Samuel Williamson, president and vice chancellor of the University of the South. Williamson graciously permitted me to examine and assess his book, *Austria-Hungary and the Coming of the First World War* (New York, 1990), when it was still in manuscript form. Professor William Barnett of the Department of Religious Studies at Le Moyne College willingly shared with me his feeling for the nuances of the German language and his substantial scholarly expertise in the area of twentieth-century German religious history, enabling me to explain more fully the perspectives of Fritz Fischer and Gerhard Ritter. I am also deeply grateful to Oxford University Press for allowing me to quote passages from their translation of Luigi Albertini's *The Origins of the War of 1914* and to *The History Teacher* for permitting me to use a revised version of my essay, "Emerging from Fischer's Shadow: Recent Examinations of the Crisis of July 1914," as part of chapter 6 of this book.

My research would not have been possible without the cooperation and insight of the professional librarians at Le Moyne College and the Inter Library Loan program. The Le Moyne College Committee on Faculty Development and Research graciously funded a course-load reduction so that I might complete the revision of the manuscript. Douglas Egerton undertook the thankless chore of checking and rechecking the page proofs. My mother, Aurelia Langdon, instilled in me the desire for higher education and worked for years to make it financially possible. Her love and devotion helped shape my character and my ambitions. Throughout the entire experience, as throughout my academic career, my wife Janice provided inspiration, understanding, and love. My debt to her is registered on the dedication page.

One more person must be mentioned. My commitment to become a historian was carefully nurtured by my original mentor at Le Moyne College. The example of his meticulous and careful scholarship, his devotion to historical truth, and his love for teaching and for his students has remained with me through the past twenty-seven years. Had death been more patient with him, I would have placed this book in his hands. Instead I record with unending gratitude the name of John W. Bush, S.J., my beloved friend.

John W. Langdon
Manlius, New York
January 30, 1990

Abbreviations

BD   G. P. Gooch and Harold Temperley, eds., *British Documents on the Origins of the War, 1898–1914*, 11 vols. (London, 1926–38).

DD   Karl Kautsky, Max Montgelas, and Walter Schücking, eds., *Die deutschen Dokumente zum Kriegsausbruch, 1914*, 5 vols. (Berlin, 1919).

DDF   France, Ministère des Affaires Etrangères, Commission de publication des documents relatifs aux origines de la guerre de 1914, *Documents diplomatiques français (1871–1914)*, 3ᵐᵉ serie, 1911–14, vols. I–XI (Paris, 1929–36).

NSDAP   Nationalsozialistische Deutsche Arbeiterpartei (National Socialist, or Nazi, party)

SPD   Sozialdemokratische Partei Deutschlands (Social Democratic party)

Introduction: June 28, 1919

It was Saturday, June 28, 1919. Exactly five years earlier, in the Bosnian town of Sarajevo, Gavrilo Princip's bullets had ended the life of Archduke Franz Ferdinand, heir to the throne of Austria-Hungary, and had set in motion a series of events which would culminate in what was then called the Great War. That war had ended the nineteenth century and had come close to destroying European civilization in the process. Now, on the anniversary of the crime that had started it all, the victors and the vanquished (at least, those that still existed) met at Louis XIV's palace in Versailles, France, to sign the treaty that would, it was hoped, restore order to Europe.

Russia was absent from the councils of the victors. The empire of the tsars had collapsed in 1917 under the strain of the war and its own colossal internal difficulties. Having signed a separate peace with Germany at Brest-Litovsk in March 1918, the Soviet Union's communist leaders had, in the eyes of their former allies, forfeited their right to participation in the peace conference. Austria-Hungary, Germany's erstwhile ally, was likewise absent; the multi-national Habsburg monarchy had disintegrated into the "successor states" of Poland, Czechoslovakia, Austria, Hungary, and Yugoslavia upon its defeat in 1918. These nations were present at Versailles, but their governments bore no responsibility for the policies that had brought on the war, and they were treated with benign conde-scension by the winners.

Germany, too, was represented by a government which had played no part in the initiation of hostilities. Kaiser Wilhelm II had abdicated two days before the armistice of November 11, 1918; the Hohenzollern dynasty had been replaced by a republic led by the Social Democratic party. But Germany had remained intact as a nation, and its enemies were in no mood to be charitable. The Germans had not been invited to participate in the deliberations of

1

the peace conference. They had protested vigorously against the terms of the treaty, which they considered harsh and unfair. Now, under threat of renewed invasion, they came to Versailles to sign it.

German chancellor Philipp Scheidemann had cried, "The hand will wither that signs such a treaty!" But his government had no choice. Germany's military and naval forces would be limited in size and striking power; the nation that Bismarck had unified would lose significant pieces of territory on its borders; the land which in 1914 had been one of the world's richest would be required to pay the costs of the most devastating and expensive war ever waged, and although the final total of these "reparations" would not be decided upon until 1921, it was reasonable to expect that the sum would be enormous. All of this was justified not merely by the fact of German defeat, but by a novel departure from previous diplomatic practice – article 231 of the Treaty of Versailles, soon to become famous as the "war-guilt clause."

Article 231 had been suggested by the French, who wanted to emphasize Germany's responsibility for beginning the war as moral justification for the collection of reparations. Britain lent discreet support to the French position, and although United States president Woodrow Wilson doubted its wisdom and argued for avoiding any direct reference to "guilt," the final version of the article (largely drafted by American negotiator John Foster Dulles) blamed Germany explicitly: "The Allied and Associated Governments affirm and Germany accepts the responsibility of Germany and her Allies for all the loss to which the Allied and Associated Governments and their nationals have been subjected as a consequence of the war imposed upon them by the aggression of Germany and her Allies."[1]

Had the authors of the treaty realized the consequences of article 231, they would doubtless have omitted it. Germany exploded with indignation: they had lost the war and expected to lose the peace, but they had not expected such extensive penalties, and most Germans were unequivocal in their conviction that the war had been imposed upon them. This belief had been an article of faith in Germany since Chancellor Theobald von Bethmann Hollweg had told the Reichstag on August 4, 1914, that his government had been encircled and forced to fight. Now a new government had been

---

1. Klaus Schwabe, *Woodrow Wilson, Revolutionary Germany, and Peacemaking, 1918–1919*, trans. Rita and Robert Kimber (Chapel Hill, 1985), 287–90.

obliged to sign a document containing a frank admission of unrestricted guilt – and that confession was used to rationalize the exaction of immense sums of money from a prostrate nation. On moral as well as economic grounds, article 231 was unacceptable. Germany resolved to fight it. If it could be demonstrated that responsibility for the outbreak of war did not rest with Germany alone, then the ethical foundation for reparation payments would disappear. A parliamentary committee of inquiry was set up in the summer of 1919, charged with examining the origins and conduct of the war and the reasons for Germany's defeat. In the German Foreign Office (Auswärtiges Amt), a special branch was created – the War Guilt Section, or *Kriegsschuldreferat* – which in turn organized, financed, and directed two satellite units. One of these, the Working Committee of German Associations for Combating Lies concerning War Responsibility, disseminated arguments and literature to trade unions, employers' organizations, and clubs of all kinds. The other, more significant for our purposes, was the Center for the Study of the Causes of the War (*Zentralstelle zur Erforschung der Kriegsschuldfrage*), which from 1923 financed and published the influential monthly journal *Die Kriegsschuldfrage*, edited by Alfred von Wegerer. These organizations enlisted scholars, journalists, editors, publicists, and teachers in the cause of "patriotic self-censorship" to demonstrate the inaccuracy of article 231 and, by logical consequence, of the entire Treaty of Versailles.[2]

History, politics, and economics were now fused in the German effort to revise the treaty. That effort touched off the most famous historical controversy of the twentieth century, a dispute which continues to the present day. In the 1920s, the "revisionist school" dominated historical writing on the war in Germany and the United States. Alfred von Wegerer and Max Montgelas were supported on this side of the Atlantic by Sidney Bradshaw Fay and Harry Elmer Barnes. Fay's two-volume study, *The Origins of the World War*, a highly readable and still influential account, found a degree of guilt in all parties involved in the crisis of July 1914 and issued a forthright plea for the revision of Versailles. In France, the revisionists found few supporters (Georges Demartial, Alfred Fabre-Luce, and Victor Margueritte constituting notable exceptions); here

2. The most detailed discussion of this campaign and its effects on German historiography is the article by Holger H. Herwig, "Clio Deceived: Patriotic Self-Censorship in Germany after the Great War," *International Security* 12 (Fall 1987): 5–44.

Pierre Renouvin and Jules Isaac carried the day with their arguments in support of the overriding responsibility of Germany. Yet this "antirevisionist school" stopped short of full endorsement of the Versailles verdict, admitting that the responsibility for the calamity must be shared. Their position was echoed in the United States by Bernadotte Schmitt, whose work, as we shall see, fell short of the level of popular acceptance accorded that of Fay.

In practical political terms, the revisionists failed. The Treaty of Versailles was never revised, although the collection of reparations lapsed in the early years of the Great Depression. But in history classes in England, Germany, and the United States, the revisionist position prevailed. By the late 1930s the war-guilt controversy cooled as the impending outbreak of the Second World War came to seem more urgent than the investigation of the origins of the First. After 1945, however, scholars faced a changed situation. Did Hitler's obvious aggression point to a consistent pattern of German conduct, thereby convicting the Kaiser's government of undue belligerence in 1914? Or was Hitler a chance occurrence, a freakish, monstrous nightmare who was no more typical of German policy-makers than Caligula was of Roman emperors?

A.J.P. Taylor of Britain inclined to the former view, reinvigorating the antirevisionist position in *The Course of German History* (1945) and *The Struggle for Mastery in Europe* (1954). This standpoint was reinforced by the translation and publication in the mid-fifties of the three-volume work of Italian senator Luigi Albertini, *The Origins of the War of 1914*. German historians, on the other hand, endorsed the thesis that Hitler was a madman whose actions had no parallel in German history. This view prevailed in the United States and won numerous adherents in Britain and France. In 1952, a conference of French and German historians agreed that no government or nation had consciously desired a European war in 1914. It seemed that Versailles had finally been laid to rest and that a reassuring sense of collective guilt (which for many could be construed as no guilt at all) would dominate future scholarship on the subject.

Then came Fritz Fischer. In a massive and explosive book, *Griff nach der Weltmacht* (literally, "grasping at world power"), published in Düsseldorf in 1961, he became the first German historian to break with the doctrine of patriotic self-censorship.[3] Character-

---

3. Fischer was the first German historian to reject the traditional view in a

izing German policy as calculated to achieve domination over Europe and world-power status, Fischer and his followers (the "Hamburg school") enraged those German historians who adhered to the traditional view of Germany as an aggrieved power in 1914. More than that, Fischer's postulation of a continuity in German policy from 1897 through 1945 carried profound political implications for a West German government that was less than fifteen years old. Fischer was denounced as a traitor to his country and his profession; he was subjected to vicious personal criticism and responded in kind; the West German government cancelled funding for his 1964 lecture tour of the United States; and in the midst of all this turmoil, the revisionist position lay in ashes and the war-guilt controversy was once more a matter of vital interest to historians.

That interest continues to the present day. Recent scholarly output on the origins of the war far exceeds in volume that produced in the decades between 1919 and 1939. Keeping abreast of such extensive scholarship, never an easy task, has become truly daunting. Much of the best recent work is available only in German, a fact which precludes its comprehension by most American students of European history (to say nothing of their teachers). As a result, in most American classrooms and textbooks, the origins of the Great War are presented from a classical revisionist standpoint, as though the disputes of the past quarter century were of relevance only to specialists. Surveys of the historical literature produced in the course of the controversy are scarce and of uneven quality, leaving the educated general reader and the beleaguered teacher of survey courses in world history, Western civilization, or European history no brief, readable guide to this fascinating and important subject.[4]

---

published work. The distinguished legal historian Hermann Kantorowicz had affirmed the primary guilt of the Central Powers in his manuscript, *Gutachten zur Kriegsschuldfrage, 1914*, which was suppressed in the 1920s and was not published until 1967. In that same year, *Griff nach der Weltmacht* was published in English translation as *Germany's Aims in the First World War*.

4. Jules Isaac's *Un débat historique, 1914: Le problème des origines de la guerre* (Paris, 1933), while thorough, readable, and scholarly, has never been translated into English and is badly outdated. John A. Moses, *The Politics of Illusion: The Fischer Controversy in German Historiography* (New York, 1975), is very helpful to the student of the Fischer affair, but ignores the earlier debates and is heavily biased in Fischer's favor. H.W. Koch's introduction to his important and useful collection of scholarly articles, *The Origins of the First World War*, 2d ed. (London, 1984), likewise glosses over the first forty years of the dispute and is passionately anti-

What follows is an attempt to provide such a guide. Chapter 1 presents a brief account of the major events of the crisis of July 1914 and offers six "keys" to understanding the outbreak of the war. In the succeeding pages, the work of more than thirty historians is explained, analyzed, and placed in the context of the controversy as it has unfolded over the past seventy years. The crisis itself, beginning on June 28 and ending on August 4, is the focal point of the narrative; to have attempted to analyze all of the "underlying causes" of the war suggested and discussed in the historical literature would have taken several volumes and would have discouraged all but the most dedicated specialist from reading the account.

Similarly, the book makes no claim to be a comprehensive, complete treatment of all of the war-guilt literature. A list of books and articles on this subject written since 1919 would probably exceed twenty-five thousand items, many of which are available only in languages that I do not read. For this account I have selected the writings of those historians with whose work I feel teachers, students, and general readers *need* to be familiar in order to understand the debate. Some of these scholars broke new ground and discovered new evidence;[5] others have formulated the problem or the evidence in creative and innovative ways, restructuring the debate and capturing the imagination of the reader;[6] still others have, through their use of vivid language and their ability to synthesize widely disparate accounts, presented their positions in appealing and influential ways.[7] I am acutely aware of the existence of a large body of work which fits each of these three categories, but which, regrettably, must be excluded to limit the size of the book and to serve the needs of the nonspecialist reader.

My analysis is presented in a manner that I hope is free of prejudice and polemic. The recent stages of the debate over the war's origins have been sullied by inexcusable ad hominem attacks on the character, competence, and patriotism of the participants. Those who subject their research and writing to the judgment of the public deserve much better than this. Although my own beliefs on

Fischer. Jacques Droz, *Les causes de la Première Guerre Mondiale: Essai d'historiographie* (Paris, 1973), and Wolfgang Jager, *Historische Forschung und politische Kultur in Deutschland: Die Debatte 1914–1980 über den Ausbruch des Ersten Weltkrieges* (Göttingen, 1984), are of high quality but remain unavailable in English.
5. A partial listing includes Sidney Fay, Luigi Albertini, and Fritz Fischer.
6. A partial listing includes Paul Schroeder, James Joll, and Arno Mayer.
7. A partial list includes Joachim Remak, Harry Elmer Barnes, and Imanuel Geiss.

the merits of the contending positions analyzed here cannot, and should not, be excluded from the narrative, I have tried to offer critical reflections in a constructive manner, consistent with the respect in which I hold those who have devoted so much energy and skill to the expansion of our knowledge of this crucial five-week period.

For crucial it remains, long after its original participants have vanished from the scene. The question of responsibility for the outbreak of the catastrophic war of 1914–18 has always been more than a mere matter for academic speculation. Neville Chamberlain flew to Germany to appease Adolf Hitler in September 1938 at least in part because of his conviction (derived from reading history) that Sir Edward Grey had not made British policy sufficiently clear to Germany in July 1914. He was determined that if a second world war were to come, it would not come because of a misunderstanding – and it didn't. In 1962, John F. Kennedy said that his conduct of American policy during the Cuban missile crisis owed much to his belief that the nations of Europe had, in 1914, blundered into a war nobody wanted.[8] Those who wish to avoid a third world war often look to the crisis of July 1914 for lessons and omens. In this regard, as Holger Herwig says, "It serves no purpose to continue to believe that Europe 'slid' into war unknowingly in 1914, that no nation harbored aggressive tendencies during the July crisis, and that fate or providence alone designed this cruel course of events."[9] With the hope that this volume will help to clarify, contextualize, and explain this provocative and meaningful controversy, we now proceed to an examination of the July crisis.

It was Sunday, June 28, 1914.

---

8. Strangely, Kennedy attributed this knowledge to his reading of Barbara Tuchman's best-selling *Guns of August*, a book which holds Germany overwhelmingly responsible for the war and rejects the contention that the war occurred by accident.
9. Herwig, "Clio Deceived," 7–8.

1

The July Crisis

Archduke Franz Ferdinand, heir to the throne of Austria-Hungary, had been advised against making an official visit to Sarajevo, the capital of the Austrian province of Bosnia, on June 28.[1] It was the 525th anniversary of Serbia's defeat by the Turks at the battle of Kossovo, a day of national humiliation and mourning that would be particularly poignant in Bosnia, where Austro-Hungarian rule over a predominantly South Slav population was strongly resented. In addition, a Serb patriot had assassinated the sultan of Turkey immediately after the battle, thus earning martyrdom and preserving Serbian honor. These were adequate reasons for a prudent prince to arrange to be elsewhere on June 28, but prudence had never been the heir apparent's principal virtue. He went to Sarajevo and Gavrilo Princip, a Serbian terrorist, murdered him and his wife with a Browning revolver at point-blank range.

The archduke's violent demise left Europe appalled. It was assumed that the Serbian government was somehow involved in the crime and that the Habsburg monarchy would be justified in retaliating in some way. This is the *first key* to understanding the July crisis: was the assassination the act of a group of independent fanatics (for Princip had been one of a group of seven potential assailants), or was the Serbian government involved, either directly or indirectly? Even in Russia, self-appointed protector of all Slavic peoples, few could be found to defend Serbia publicly. Certainly Tsar Nicholas II, whose grandfather had been assassinated and whose father lived under the constant threat of equivalent mayhem,

1. This account of the crisis is derived from extensive familiarity with the published diplomatic documents of the participants and the abundance of primary and secondary descriptions written during the past seventy-five years. It traces events which are familiar to all students of the crisis and makes no pretense to originality. Perhaps the finest recent description of the events of July 1914 is chap. 2 of James Joll, *The Origins of the First World War* (London, 1984), 9–32.

could harbor little affection for anyone involved in the murder of royalty. But Russia was Serbia's defender, and if the tsar decided to oppose Austria's punitive action against Serbia (the precise form of which had not yet been determined), the Dual Monarchy must either back down or suffer military defeat.

Accordingly, the Austro-Hungarian foreign minister, Count Leopold Berchtold, decided to ask formally for the support of his country's ally, Germany. If the German government supported Austria-Hungary forcefully and publicly, as it had during the Bosnian crisis of 1908–9, Russia might dissociate itself from the Serbian cause. If the tsar's government was still resolved to support that cause, at least Austria-Hungary would have in its corner the strongest military power in the world. Germany's blessing was therefore critical, and Berchtold sent his principal private secretary, Count Alexander von Hoyos, to seek an audience with Kaiser Wilhelm II at Potsdam.

Hoyos brought with him a handwritten letter from Emperor Franz Josef to the Kaiser and a memorandum drawn up by the Ballhausplatz (the Austro-Hungarian foreign ministry). He met with Wilhelm on Sunday, July 5, and with Chancellor Theobald von Bethmann Hollweg the next day. As a result of these meetings, Hoyos returned to Vienna convinced that he had obtained the firm backing of the German government for swift, violent retaliation against Serbia. The Austro-Hungarian ambassador to Germany, Count Ladislaus Szögyény-Marich, confirmed this impression in his telegrams to Berchtold. This is the *second key* to the crisis: what were the actions and intentions of the German government when it gave the Dual Monarchy its support? Did Germany anticipate a local war, a continental war, or a European war? Did the Kaiser and his ministers envision the severity of the Austrian ultimatum to Serbia that followed, and were they informed of the contents of that document in time to have altered its nature had they wished to do so? Of the six keys identified in this chapter, it is the most significant for the historian, and has dominated the debate since 1961.

Hoyos returned to Vienna on the afternoon of July 6, and once Berchtold heard the news, he scheduled a meeting of the Common Ministerial Council for the next day. That meeting dug the grave of the Dual Monarchy. Berchtold, armed with German backing, proposed a war against Serbia to emasculate the South Slav revolutionary movement and impede Russia's ongoing efforts to expand its influence in the Balkans. He was supported by all the ministers save one, the premier of Hungary, Count Istvan Tisza, whose consent to such action was indispensable. Tisza, who feared the accumulation of Slavs in a monarchy dominated by Germans and Magyars, objected to the launching of war without giving Serbia the opportunity to comply with Austrian demands. The meeting resolved that some sort of action against Serbia was desirable, and Berchtold worked on Tisza during the ensuing week, finally convincing him by July 14 that the suggested policy was a wise one. At the Common Ministerial Council on that day, it was agreed that an ultimatum filled with unacceptable conditions was to be sent to Serbia. Tisza insisted that no Serbian territory should be annexed after the war, and the council approved this restriction.

These deliberations explain much of Austria-Hungary's lethargy in reacting to the assassination. Germany was alarmed by the delay (nearly a month passed between the murder and the ultimatum), contending that it was necessary to act quickly, while sympathy for the monarchy's position remained fresh in the minds of European governments. But Berchtold had no choice but to try to overcome Tisza's objections. He responded to the Hungarian premier's apprehension that a surprise attack would put the monarchy in the wrong by sending the legal counsellor of the foreign ministry, Friedrich von Wiesner, to Sarajevo on July 10. Wiesner was instructed to conduct an investigation on the possible complicity of the Serbian government and submit a report within forty-eight hours. On Monday, July 13, one day before the Common Ministerial Council's meeting that approved Berchtold's course of action, Wiesner reported that he could find no connection between the plotters and the Serbian government, although there was evidence to indicate the culpability of a Serbian secret society, Narodna Odbrana ("Young Bosnia"), which was tolerated by the government.[2] By the time this information was gathered and Tisza had been won over to a war policy, it was already the evening of July 14.

Now the ultimatum had to be drafted and approved by the council (a process which took five days), and even then it could not be transmitted promptly. French president Raymond Poincaré and

---

2. Wiesner unfortunately focused on the wrong society. Narodna Odbrana was in fact guiltless, and he found no evidence of participation by the real culprits, the Black Hand, an organization with direct ties to the Serbian government. In fairness to Wiesner, whose competence and honesty were above reproach, it must be pointed out that forty-eight hours was hardly sufficient time to conduct a thorough investigation.

premier René Viviani arrived in St. Petersburg for a three-day state visit to Russia on Monday, July 20. German secretary of state Gottlieb von Jagow advised Vienna to delay dispatch of the ultimatum until after the French leaders had left St. Petersburg, so that they would be unable to consult directly with the Russian government on receipt of the news. This postponed delivery of the document to Thursday, July 23, at 6:00 P.M. Belgrade time. All ten conditions were to be accepted within forty-eight hours, failing which the Austro-Hungarian ambassador, Baron Wladimar Giesl von Gieslingen, was instructed to break off diplomatic relations and leave the country.

Jagow's suggestion was accepted. The French statesmen knew nothing of the ultimatum while in St. Petersburg, although the governments of each of the powers of the Triple Entente (Russia, France, and Great Britain) had heard a variety of unconfirmed tips, some vague, some precise, of (as it turned out) varying degrees of accuracy. As Jules Isaac points out, there were two phases to the July crisis: the period between June 28 and July 23, when the crisis involved only Serbia, Austria-Hungary, and Germany, and the ensuing twelve days from July 24 to August 4, when all of Europe was affected. Poincaré and Viviani thus met with Tsar Nicholas II and Russian foreign minister Sergei Sazonov in an atmosphere of expectation, but in the absence of solid information concerning the steps to be taken by Austria-Hungary.

This is the *third key* to understanding the July crisis. What did the French and Russians discuss between July 20 and 23, and what role did the French government (and more important, the French alliance) play in the determination of Russian policy between July 24 and the proclamation of general mobilization one week later? Historians, who possess a number of excellent sources pertaining to German conduct on July 5–6, have almost nothing to guide them through the Franco-Russian conversations in St. Petersburg. The Russians apparently recorded nothing detrimental to their historical reputations; if such a document had existed, the Soviet government would certainly have published it after the war. French premier Viviani, who was also foreign minister, should have kept some sort of written record. But the editors of the French diplomatic documents could locate nothing.[3] Accurate historical assessment of the

---

3. It is possible that Viviani, who knew almost nothing about foreign affairs, wrote nothing down. Reportedly he was distracted by the Caillaux trial and French

11

situation is rendered even less likely by the fact that between July 23 and 29, the leaders of the French government were literally at sea, putting in at Scandinavian ports and receiving tantalizingly garbled messages from the radio transmitter atop the Eiffel Tower (which messages the Germans were attempting to jam). French foreign policy during this period was in the hands of the finance minister, Jean-Baptiste Bienvenu-Martin, who was not an ignoramus in foreign affairs but who, quite logically, felt unable to take decisive action in the midst of the greatest diplomatic crisis since 1870 without the presence of the duly constituted heads of government.

Poincaré and Viviani were therefore the only two leaders of a European government who were not immediately apprised of the delivery of the ultimatum to Serbia. But precise details concerning the ultimatum's contents were not so easily available. Sir Edward Grey, the British foreign secretary, and Russian foreign minister Sazonov did not obtain the text of the note until Friday, July 24.[4] The former characterized the message as "the most formidable document I had ever seen addressed by one State to another that was independent," while the latter was more direct: "C'est la guerre européene!"[5] Yet war was not viewed as unavoidable. Grey, recalling the success of his efforts at mediation during the Balkan wars of 1912–13 (and the cooperation of Germany in those efforts), suggested similar procedures to the German government now. Germany, however, disclaimed all knowledge of the note and of Austrian plans.[6] The first twenty-four hours of the time limit passed with no discernible progress.

---

internal affairs throughout the Russian visit; see Gerd Krumeich, *Armaments and Politics in France on the Eve of the First World War*, trans. Stephen Conn (Birmingham, U.K., 1984), 291, n. 153.

4. The text was officially communicated to foreign governments by the Ballhausplatz at 9:00 A.M. on July 24. The Russian government was not informed of the text by telephone from Belgrade, possibly because the Serbian government was frantically trying to reach Prime Minister Nikola Pašić, who was off campaigning in remote areas, possibly because the telephone lines from Belgrade to St. Petersburg ran through Vienna.

5. Quoted in Joll, *Origins*, 13.

6. Bismarck had adopted the same stance in July 1870, when news of the Hohenzollern candidacy to the Spanish throne had leaked prematurely. Interestingly, Sazonov appears to have believed the German assertions in this case, with regrettable effects on his mood when his illusions were dispelled. It may seem difficult to believe that he could have been so gullible, but substantial native intelligence was not one of the indispensable requirements for appointment to high office in the Russia of Nicholas II.

At 3:00 P.M. on Saturday, July 25, Serbia mobilized its army. Three hours later Pašić submitted his government's reply to Giesl, who saw that it was unacceptable and left for Vienna at once. The Serbian reply was astonishingly conciliatory, accepting nine of the ten demands (a few of them in rather equivocal language) and rejecting the tenth only in part. Because the Serbian diplomatic documents have never been fully published, it is impossible to determine the extent of Russian support for Serbia during the crucial hours in which the response was drafted. But those telegrams which have been disclosed indicate substantial backing, without which Serbia might have been obliged to accept the document in its entirety.[7] Irrespective of this, the reply was a diplomatic masterpiece which quickly swung European opinion to the side of the Serbs. Austria-Hungary's moral position began to come apart.

Europe entered its last full week of peace with the hope that the crisis could still be settled. Time was now the chief enemy of such a hope. Britain and Russia were not unwilling to see Austria chastise the Serbs, provided that this could be done without prejudice to Serbian sovereignty and territorial integrity. This certainly would have satisfied Tisza, but Berchtold was reluctant to tie the hands of the monarchy. He had Germany on his side and was ready to play his cards to the limit. For its part, Germany passed on to Vienna without comment Grey's mediation proposals and urged a rapid declaration of war on Serbia so that foreign interference in the dispute could be checkmated. At this point we encounter the *fourth key* to the crisis: Grey's reluctance to warn Germany of Britain's probable attitude in the event of a European war.

France and Russia were committed to each other in the event of an attack upon either, but Britain recognized no such obligation. The Liberal government that had been in power since 1906 operated on the assumption that Britain could not tolerate a French defeat that would leave Germany master of Europe.[8] If Russia fought Austria-Hungary and Germany intervened to assist its ally, France

---

7. This, of course, would have forced Austria-Hungary to settle for a diplomatic triumph. Joll, *Origins*, 13–14, contains a good summary of the latest research. For the texts of two revealing telegrams, see Gale Stokes, "The Serbian Documents from 1914: A Preview," *Journal of Modern History* 48 (1976): on-demand supplement, 69–83. The Serbian documents from 1914 have now been published by a Yugoslav government commission headed by Vladimir Dedijer.
8. Similar balance-of-power reasoning had led Britain to accept German unification in 1870–71 on the assumption that a French victory over Prussia would result in unacceptable French hegemony.

would be forced to back Russia or witness the destruction of the Franco-Russian alliance. Since it was quite possible that Germany and Austria could defeat France and Russia, Britain would be obliged to intervene, not owing to any written commitment but as a result of the logic of the situation. The problem for Grey was that this would split the Liberal cabinet (several of whose members would probably oppose British involvement in a European war over Serbia) and might either bring down the government or force Britain to enter the war divided. These considerations, coupled with his fond memories of Anglo-German cooperation in 1912–13, made him unwilling to issue an unequivocal warning to Germany prior to the Austrian declaration of war on Serbia. For this, as we shall see, he has been strongly criticized by historians who contend that such a warning would have led to German pressure on Austria-Hungary to defuse the crisis while there was still time.

But time was running out. Early on the morning of July 30, the German government suddenly changed course and attempted to restrain Austria-Hungary. These efforts, the *fifth key* to the July crisis, followed the receipt in Berlin of a telegram from Prince Karl Max Lichnowsky, German ambassador to Great Britain, reporting a conversation between the ambassador and Sir Edward Grey. If Grey had been evasive earlier in the crisis, he was so no longer. He informed Lichnowsky that Britain would not remain neutral in the event of a European war involving France (although his government *could* stand aside if the war involved only Austria and Russia, a conflict which Russia would probably win). Bethmann had, on the evening of July 28, already suggested to Vienna that an uncompromising attitude would swing European sympathy against the Dual Monarchy.[9] Now he dispatched two telegrams in the early morning hours of July 30, informing Berchtold that Britain would oppose the Central Powers and that direct talks with Russia and acceptance of British mediation proposals must be undertaken. The reasons for Bethmann's change of heart, the sincerity of his motives, and the eventual failure of his efforts have been the subject of extensive debate among historians.

German last-minute efforts occurred simultaneously with serious

9. This message was sent on behalf of Kaiser Wilhelm II, who had read the Serbian reply for the first time that morning and had concluded that Austria-Hungary had won a great diplomatic victory that removed any need for war. The relevant documents are printed in Imanuel Geiss, ed., *July 1914: The Outbreak of the First World War – Selected Documents*, trans. Imanuel Geiss (New York, 1967), 256–60.

events in Russia. On Tuesday, July 28, Austria-Hungary had declared war on Serbia. The following day, Belgrade was bombarded by ships of the Austro-Hungarian navy's Danube flotilla. These events exerted a profound effect on Sazonov, introducing the *sixth key* to the crisis, the general mobilization of the Russian army, which many historians consider the step that made European war inevitable.

The Russian government had immediately recognized the implications of the Austrian ultimatum. On Friday, July 24, a meeting of the Common Ministerial Council requested the tsar to authorize in principle the partial mobilization of four military districts and the Black Sea fleet.[10] The following day, a Russian Imperial Council confirmed these actions and, effective July 26, introduced the "period preparatory to war," during which actions preliminary to general mobilization could be taken throughout European Russia. Sazonov and the incompetent chief of the general staff, Nikolai Yanushkevich, appear to have believed that partial mobilization was possible; they were informed to the contrary by Quartermaster General Yuri Danilov on July 26. Nevertheless, Russian preparations went forward, and German military intelligence got wind of them. Chancellor Bethmann Hollweg on July 29 demanded the immediate cessation of Russian mobilization preparations, failing which Germany would be forced to mobilize as well, "and in that case a European war could scarcely be prevented."[11]

Bethmann's declaration may or may not have constituted an "ultimatum," but its effects on Sazonov are indisputable. In conjunction with the Austro-Hungarian declaration of war on Serbia and their bombardment of Belgrade, the German demarche convinced him that Austria had intended war from the beginning and that Berlin and Vienna had conspired throughout. He now aligned himself with those elements of the military who were pressing for general mobilization, and after a series of intricate and occasionally amusing shenanigans, secured the tsar's consent on July 30.[12]

10. The tsar added the Baltic fleet to this list, despite the council's fear that this would alarm Germany. See L.C.F. Turner, *Origins of the First World War* (New York, 1970), 93.

11. Bethmann Hollweg to Count Friedrich von Pourtalès (German ambassador to Russia), July 29, in Geiss, *July 1914*, 285.

12. The most detailed analyses of Russian general mobilization are found in Luigi Albertini, *The Origins of the War of 1914*, trans. Isabella M. Massey (New York, 1952–57), II, 528–650, and L.C.F. Turner, "The Russian Mobilization in 1914," *Journal of Contemporary History* 3 (1968): 65–88.

By now the clock compelled everyone's attention. A crisis high-lighted by an ultimatum with a forty-eight hour time limit and a precipitate declaration of war on July 28 by a nation whose chief military officer protested that his army could not begin hostilities until August 12 now entered its final, frenetic stages. Russian general mobilization did not mean war, since the Russian army could stand at ease on its own territory for weeks if necessary. Jagow had recognized this on July 27 and had declared that Germany would not feel obliged to mobilize in response. But he must have reckoned without the situation's internal logic. The German army's operational plans required an immediate thrust through neutral Belgium into northern France in the event of war between Germany and the Franco-Russian alliance, quite independent of anything done by the Russian army. Only in this way could Germany fight a two-front war successfully, by defeating France quickly and then turning to deal with the ponderous Russians. In the face of these requirements, Jagow's pronouncement was worth-less. Germany proclaimed the *Kriegsgefahrzustand* (threatening danger of war) on July 31, followed by general mobilization and a declaration of war on Russia the next day.

France's turn had finally come, and its leaders had finally gotten off the boat. The French government never hesitated in its support for Russia, but to maximize the likelihood of British intervention, it remained unwilling to declare war on Germany. Accordingly, French troops were instructed to withdraw to a distance of ten kilometers from the frontiers to avoid any provocation or staged incident. On Monday, August 3, Germany could wait no longer. With troop trains pouring men and equipment westward, the Ger-man government declared war on France.

Maddeningly, Grey had pursued his course of action to the last, refusing to reassure the French and nearly driving French ambassa-dor Paul Cambon to distraction. He had, of course, always been convinced of the necessity of bringing Britain in on the side of France. Now his policy bore fruit: only two cabinet ministers resigned rather than support war. Germany's violation of Belgian neutrality helped (Britain had guaranteed Belgium's status in 1839), but it furnished a comfortable pretext rather than a sufficient cause for war. Britain probably would have gone in any case, united or divided, Belgium or no Belgium; His Majesty's government had been trying for years to read Germany's intentions and had finally decided that those intentions threatened British security. A British ultimatum to Germany expired at midnight Berlin time on August 4, and the Great War began.

The July crisis was over, but the arguments over responsibility had only begun. From the very first, each government felt compelled to justify its conduct before its own people and the world. This led to the rapid publication of a series of "colored books" of diplomatic documents relevant to the crisis: white for Germany, yellow for France, orange for Russia, red for Austria-Hungary, blue for Britain and Serbia, gray for Belgium. Anyone who compared the books knew at once that they were designed for purposes of public relations rather than historical inquiry. Documents were selected, arranged, and edited to prove that the country issuing the book was completely blameless; in some instances, documents were fabricated, either in part or in toto.

Following the armistice, the Versailles peace conference appointed a Commission on the Responsibility of the Authors of the War and on the Enforcement of Penalties. Its members, including James Brown Scott of England, André Tardieu of France, and Robert Lansing of the United States, put together a brief diplomatic account of the crisis, using documents drawn from the colored books of the victorious powers. This narrative was used to justify article 231 and the exaction of reparations from Germany.[13] It was inaccurate, slanted, and simplistic – defects which German writers were quick to point out. But the Germans were not alone in their contempt for the rigged documentation and the one-sided verdict pronounced in the treaty. Historians in the United States, a country which had refused to ratify the treaty, took the lead in pressing for its revision.

13. The most important section of this "Report Presented to the Preliminary Peace Conference" has been reprinted on numerous occasions, including in Samuel R. Williamson, Jr., ed., *The Origins of a Tragedy: July 1914* (Arlington Heights, Ill., 1981), 1–5.

2

The High Tide of Revisionism

If the inadequacy of the colored books had not been obvious from the beginning, the shortcomings of the commission's report convinced all competent observers of the need for access to as many diplomatic records as possible. The Soviet Union had already commenced publication of the most incriminating documents that could be unearthed in the imperial archives, but the selection process was so blatantly politicized that they constituted little more than the antithesis to the *Russian Orange Book*. On December 9, 1918, the new republican government of Germany had authorized Karl Kautsky of the Independent Socialist party to undertake the publication of Imperial German documents pertaining to the July crisis; but by the time he completed his work, it was March, and the commission's report indicting Germany and Austria-Hungary was ready for submission to the conference. The Wilhelmstraße (the German chancellor's office) blocked publication of Kautsky's collection until two conservative editors, Count Max Montgelas and Walter Schücking, could be added and the collection rearranged and revised. Kautsky was denied further access to relevant archives and was obliged to return all secret documents in his possession.[1]

Publication of this five-volume collection, *Die deutschen Dokumente zum Kriegsausbruch, 1914*, came too late to affect the acceptance of the commission's report and the decision to force Germany to sign the Treaty of Versailles. The Wilhelmstraße then decided to establish the War Guilt Section (described in the Introduction) and to organize, edit, and publish documents from the period prior to 1914, in the hope that the Allies would be forced by public opinion to do the same. This assignment was entrusted to Albrecht Mendelssohn-Bartholdy, Johannes Lepsius, and Friedrich Thimme in the summer of 1919. It was anticipated that the project

---

1. The best brief account of these events is provided in Herwig, "Clio Deceived," 9–10. A detailed treatment may be found in Jager, *Historische Forschung*.

would be of limited scope (no more than three volumes) and would take about four months. The results demonstrated the dangers of relying on the self-discipline of historians, lawyers, and theologians: between 1922 and 1927, the three editors published no fewer than forty volumes of material, thereby depleting Germany's supplies of paper and creating an immensely valuable resource for researchers.[2] From those days until now, no serious scholar has been able to delve into the origins of the Great War without consulting *Die große Politik der europäischen Kabinette.*

Shamed and pressured by the appearance of *Die große Politik*, other nations quickly announced their intent to provide collections from their own archives. Great Britain produced eleven volumes, the *British Documents on the Origins of the War, 1898–1914,* between 1926 and 1938; the final volume covered the July crisis. France embarked upon a grand and excessively complicated project, the *Documents diplomatiques français (1871–1914),* which was divided into three series, volumes from each of which were published at irregular and incomprehensible intervals. By 1936, the volume on July 1914 had appeared. Austria issued the eight-volume *Österreich-Ungarns Aussenpolitik von der Bosnischen Krise 1908 bis zum Kriegsausbruch 1914* in 1930. Yugoslavia, after repeated delays, finally published the Serbian diplomatic documents (including the volumes pertaining to 1914) in 1980.[3] The Russian documents were printed in scattered sources, of which the most useful is *Mezhdunarodnye otnosheniya v epokhu imperializma,* an amazingly ambitious project intended to cover the period from 1878 to 1917. Like the French collection, it was published in three series; unlike its French counterpart, the first series never appeared at all. The third series, which deals with the July crisis and subsequent events to March 1916, was translated into German as *Die internationalen Beziehungen im Zeitalter des Imperialismus* and published in Berlin between 1931 and 1934.[4] Finally, the Foreign Office commissioned

2. Mendelssohn-Bartholdy was trained in international law, Lepsius in theology, and Thimme in history.

3. Miloš Bogičević, Serbian chargé d'affaires at Berlin in 1914 and later a paid employee of the Foreign Office, looted a variety of documents from his legation and published them in *Die auswärtige Politik Serbiens, 1903–1914,* 3 vols. (Berlin, 1928–31). Even by the subterranean standards of the worst patriotic self-censorship, this collection is worth little.

4. René Marchand translated and published some Russian documents in *Un livre noir,* 3 vols. (Paris, 1922–23). Friederich Stieve issued two collections of documents pertaining to the diplomacy of Aleksandr Isvolsky, Russian foreign minister during

the publication of documents from the Berlin ministries of Baden, Saxony, and Württemberg in 1937 (the Bavarian documents having appeared in 1922).

These collections varied widely in quality and usefulness,[5] but taken as a whole, they constituted a historical bonanza. Scholars with the linguistic facility and the time to peruse all these volumes would, if they could keep their heads from spinning, be able to acquire an unprecedented insight into the workings of the major European foreign ministries during the July crisis. Unfortunately, with the exception of the *British Documents*, the volumes relevant to 1914 were not published until the 1930s. This meant that the early stages of the controversy over war guilt were fought out by historians who had used only *Die große Politik*.[6] Their nearly exclusive reliance on German diplomatic documents gave birth to the revisionist school and made the work of later historians like Luigi Albertini, who was able to use all of the collections discussed above, indispensable to modern-day scholars who have no stomach for plowing through this forest of evidence.[7]

Regrettably, *Die große Politik* suffered from serious methodological weaknesses.[8] In scope, it was limited (if a forty-volume

---

the Bosnian crisis and later ambassador to France. But he did not explain how the documents came into his possession, and there is no means of verifying their authenticity.

5. An excellent summary of their formats, strengths, and deficiencies is provided by A.J.P. Taylor, *The Struggle for Mastery in Europe, 1848–1918* (New York, 1954), 577–83. None of the collections can be used without the realization that they were selected and edited, not by international panels, but by historians who were citizens of the nations whose documents they were reviewing. Rumors arose then and persist now to the effect that particularly embarrassing or incriminating documents were never turned over to the editors in the first place. *Die große Politik*'s omission of a large quantity of sensitive information is discussed below.

6. This caveat applies to the major works of Alfred von Wegerer, Sidney Fay, Bernadotte Schmitt, and Harry Elmer Barnes. Count Max Montgelas's *Case for the Central Powers* was published in 1925, even before the completion of *Die große Politik*; but he of course had unrestricted access to the German archives. Likewise Pierre Renouvin, head of the team of scholars sifting through the French archives, published his *Les origines immédiates de la Guerre* (Paris) in 1925.

7. For those who fall into this category, Imanuel Geiss's compilation of many of the most important documents relevant to July 1914 is a godsend despite its obvious selectivity and excessive concentration on German policy. See Imanuel Geiss, ed., *Julikrise und Kriegsausbruch, 1914*, 2 vols. (Hanover, 1963–64). The English edition is also very useful, but is considerably smaller than the original. Geiss's works are analyzed in detail in chapter 4.

8. This paragraph is adapted from the cogent summary of those shortcomings in Herwig, "Clio Deceived," 15–17, and the devastating list of omissions compiled by Geiss, *Julikrise*, I, 33–34.

compendium can be called that) by its reliance upon Foreign Office archives to the exclusion of materials from the General Staff, the Navy Office, and the Ministry of War. In reliability, it was seriously compromised by the tendency of the editors to falsify embarrassing documents and to omit large numbers of others, including a great many relevant to the July crisis. Thus this immense collection contains no records of the July 5–6 Potsdam meetings, forcing historians to rely upon memoirs and the dispatches of Austrian ambassador Szögyény; virtually no records of "talks held by the Chancellor or the State Secretary and Under Secretary of the Foreign Office with representatives of foreign powers in July 1914";[9] no records of the Kaiser's communications with German political and military figures after July 27; and (amazingly) no records of telephone calls, despite the testimony of several witnesses that Bethmann Hollweg spent long hours on the telephone on July 29 to 31.[10] Thus sanitized, *Die große Politik* provided a reliable documentary foundation for the preparation of historical accounts that the Foreign Office hoped would force revision of the Treaty of Versailles.

The German Revisionists

In 1921, the War Guilt Section of the Foreign Office had created the Center for the Study of the Causes of the War. Its journal, *Die Kriegsschuldfrage*, underwrote research and published articles on a monthly basis with the purpose of mobilizing educated opinion behind the revisionist cause.[11] The editor of this journal from 1923 until its dissolution in 1937 was Alfred von Wegerer, a former military officer who was then in the employ of the Foreign Office. Wegerer's official connection with the Foreign Office, which carried the rank of ministerial counsellor, was not disclosed to the public,

9. Herwig, "Clio Deceived," 16.
10. Ibid., 16–17, suspects that many documents were classified as private correspondence and simply returned to participants or their families, thereby resulting in their disappearance from the archives. See also John C.G. Röhl, ed., *1914: Delusion or Design?* (New York, 1973), 37. The best source for Bethmann's extended telephone conversations are the diaries of his secretary and confidant, Kurt Riezler, edited by Karl Dietrich Erdmann (see below, chapter 4).
11. *Die Kriegsschuldfrage* operated under that name from 1923 through 1929, when its name was changed to *Berliner Monatshefte*. American scholars like Sidney Fay and Harry Barnes and French authors like Georges Demartial and Alfred Fabre-Luce were frequently published in its pages.

to whom he appeared as an independent scholar and editor. From this standing he wrote hundreds of articles and two major books setting forth the principal tenets of the Foreign Office's position.[12]

Wegerer took a firm stand against Serbia and the Triple Entente. He held that the assassination of the archduke had been plotted for months by the Black Hand and was carried out with the approval of the Serbian government (our first key to the July crisis). The response of the Central Powers to the outrage was completely justifiable. Germany had no annexationist ambitions, nor any desire or plan for war; but the preservation of Austria-Hungary as a viable entity demanded the punishment of Serbia. Even so, "there is absolutely no proof that the German Government 'encouraged' Austria to declare war on Serbia."[13] England's culpability lay in its failure to act energetically to help Germany localize the Austro-Serbian conflict. Grey could have done this by withholding British support from France, thereby guaranteeing her neutrality (and incidentally guaranteeing the Central Powers an Entente-shattering military or diplomatic victory).

For Wegerer, the factor which made impossible the preservation of peace was the sixth key, the general mobilization of the Russian army. This made localization of the conflict impossible by forcing Germany to mobilize owing to "the immense numerical superiority of the forces of Russia and France."[14] In *Der Ausbruch des Weltkrieges* he argues that although Germany and Austria-Hungary had no aggressive designs, Russia was bent on acquisition of the Bosphorus and the Dardanelles, and her Balkan policy, if pursued to its logical conclusion, would have seriously destabilized the Dual Monarchy. This goal was dear to the hearts of the Russian military, which in July 1914 used Sazonov as its tool to convince the incom-

---

12. The books are *Die Widerlegung der Versailler Kriegsschuldthese* (Berlin, 1928), available in English as *A Refutation of the Versailles War Guilt Thesis*, trans. Edwin H. Zeydel (New York, 1930); and *Der Ausbruch des Weltkrieges*, 2 vols. (Hamburg, 1939), unavailable in English. Where possible, material is quoted from English editions of works cited, since those references are likely to be of more value to the English-speaking reader. The politicization of the debate is analyzed in detail in Ulrich Heinemann, *Die verdrängte Niederlage: Politische Öffentlichkeit und Kriegsschuldfrage in der Weimarer Republik* (Göttingen, 1983), and in Bernd Faulenbach, *Ideologie des deutschen Weges: Die deutsche Geschichte in der Historiographie zwischen Kaiserreich und Nationalsozialismus* (Munich, 1980).

13. Wegerer, *Refutation*, 251.

14. Alfred von Wegerer, "The Russian Mobilization of 1914," *Political Science Quarterly* 43 (1928): 228. This article was written in response to an article by Michael T. Florinsky in the same journal in 1927.

petent tsar that general mobilization must be declared. After this, there was no turning back.

Revisionism's roots can be seen clearly in Wegerer's work, particularly in the sections of *Der Ausbruch* in which he sets forth the contention that no single nation can be held responsible for the Great War. Apart from the assertion that only the Entente powers harbored aggressive designs, he broadens his vision to embrace the concept of a demonic combination of circumstances, assembled by a perverse fate, as the real "culprit" of July 1914. The war was not an eighteenth-century-style "cabinet war," planned in secret and launched for cynical and manipulative purposes. Rather, the nations involved were prisoners of chance, doomed to play their tragic roles in the absence of real control over their own destinies. Sidney Fay and Harry Elmer Barnes were already disseminating similar views in America, and as late as the 1960s the concept of a tragic destiny constituted a principal theme in the scholarship of Gerhard Ritter.

Wegerer presents his case in forceful terms and in considerable detail. His writing style is direct and unrelenting, conveying the impression of erudition seasoned liberally with righteous indignation. Yet his work has not aged gracefully. Most of his output was derived from *Die große Politik*, but even his massive *Der Ausbruch* (1939) takes little notice of the other documentary collections, except to select an occasional reference favorable to the German position. Similarly, while praising the contributions of Fay, Barnes, and other revisionist historians, he passes over the work of the antirevisionists with little more than a glance. His description of the events of the July crisis is tendentious and prejudiced, portraying Germany as a completely innocent player while assigning the crudest of motives to Entente decision makers. Had he been the sole practitioner of revisionism, it would have held the affections of few adherents beyond the mid-thirties.

But Wegerer was neither the only nor the best proponent of revisionism in Germany. Count Max Montgelas, the son of the Bavarian minister to Russia, was born in St. Petersburg in 1860 and entered the fray in 1923 with *Leitfaden zur Kriegsschuldfrage*.[15] He had served in the German army from 1879 through 1915, retiring in

---

15. Available in English as *The Case for the Central Powers*, trans. Constance Vesey (New York, 1925). Harry Elmer Barnes objected (correctly) that the English translation of the title was misleading. A better translation would have been *A Primer on the War-Guilt Question*, which would have been more accurate but less provocative and would probably have led to fewer sales.

that year (with the rank of general) allegedly because of some sort of dispute with elements of the high command. Montgelas and Walther Schücking were appointed by the Wilhelmstraße in 1919 as joint editors of the collection of German diplomatic documents originally prepared by Karl Kautsky. Conservative and unquestionably patriotic, Montgelas also possessed an instinct for balanced judgment, which animated his work.

The Case for the Central Powers, while favorable to the German cause and solidly revisionist in outlook, nonetheless goes to considerable lengths in its effort to present an objective portrait of the July crisis. Thus Montgelas, while identifying Colonel Dragutin Dimitrijević, chief of Serbian military intelligence, as the guiding force behind the assassination plot, also asserts that his involvement does not implicate the Serbian government, many of whose members were on bad terms with the Black Hand and with Dimitrijević personally. In discussing the second key (German actions and motives in early July), he stresses Berlin's willingness to give Austria-Hungary a free hand against Serbia, even should that commitment lead to war. Montgelas identifies three "mistakes" as having caused the German government to underestimate "the magnitude of the risk Austria's action against Serbia must involve": a myopic belief in monarchical solidarity as a force inhibiting action by the tsar, a failure to discern the readiness of France and Russia for war, and a misplaced faith in English neutrality.[16] Germany knew the general tone of the Austrian ultimatum and several of its conditions well in advance of its submission. The picture that emerges is of a faithful ally willing to run substantial risks in the interest of its partner, committing errors of judgment along the way yet fundamentally innocent of aggressive designs.

Montgelas criticizes the conduct of the Entente powers but is reluctant to tar them with Wegerer's broad brush. He asserts with respect to the third key that, while in St. Petersburg, Poincaré and Viviani probably received a report (dated July 20) from the French consulate in Vienna informing them of the overall tenor of the Austrian note and providing specific details on four of its conditions. Armed with this information, the French statesmen naturally would have consulted with their Russian allies and taken steps to prevent the localization of an Austro-Serbian war.[17] In a similar

16. Montgelas, *Case*, 118–19.
17. Ibid., 122–23. Unlike Wegerer, Montgelas does not impute to Poincaré and

vein, he rebukes Grey for having failed to urge moderation on Russia as energetically as Germany pressed it on Austria-Hungary. But he finds no fault with the British foreign secretary for not having warned Germany sooner and refers to German ambassador Lichnowsky's pointed telegram of July 27 and Grey's "unmistakable warning" of July 29.[18]

Moving to the fifth key to the crisis, Montgelas takes pains to characterize Germany's attitude in the final week as moderate and sincere. He quotes Bethmann's July 27 response to Lichnowsky (a document omitted from Geiss's collection) to demonstrate that Germany was not unwilling to mediate between Austria and Serbia.[19] However, he omits any reference to DD 213 (Bethmann Hollweg to Tschirschky, the German ambassador in Vienna, July 27), in which German pressure on Austria to declare war on Serbia is revealed. Montgelas was indisputably familiar with that document since it appears in the collection he edited. Rather, he deems the Austrian decision to declare war on July 28 to have had "disastrous effect" and portrays Berlin as trying to contain the damage through Bethmann's July 28 telegram to Tschirschky (DD 323).[20] Similarly, Montgelas's discussion of Bethmann's efforts of July 29–30 places the German government in a favorable light. The chancellor's early-morning telegrams to Vienna (DD 395, at 2:55 A.M. and DD 396, at 3:00 A.M. on July 30) are evidence of his willingness to exert every effort to preserve peace, even at the cost of a rupture with Austria-Hungary. DD 411, in which Bethmann stresses the necessity of placing the war guilt on Russia, is not mentioned.

Compared with Berlin's last-minute exertions, Russian general mobilization receives relatively little criticism from Montgelas. He alleges that it was the single action that made war inevitable, but his principal concern is to exonerate Austria-Hungary from the false accusation of having mobilized first (a charge made frequently during and immediately after the war). Although clearly biased on behalf of the Central Powers, Montgelas's work is not so one-sided

---

Viviani belligerent ambitions to recover Alsace and Lorraine by provoking a European war in July 1914.

18. Ibid., 135.

19. This document is assigned the number DD 277 in *Die deutschen Dokumente zum Kriegsausbruch, 1914*, ed. Karl Kautsky, Max Montgelas, and Walther Schücking, 5 vols. (Berlin, 1919). Hereafter, other documents in this collection are identified by the appropriate number.

20. Montgelas, *Case*, 138.

as to be without value to the historian. Apart from his extensive special pleading of the German position on July 27–30, he does not portray Germany as faultless and does not depict the Entente powers as bent on war. He was an amateur historian and something of a popularizer, but his assessment of the evidence available to him was not the work of a dilettante.[21]

Wegerer and Montgelas, military officers and employers of the Foreign Office, carried the burden of the revisionist cause on behalf of the Center for the Study of the Causes of the War. At this stage of the controversy, they were not joined by eminently qualified professional historians. For most members of the *Zunft* (the German historical profession, a word which bears the connotation of "guild" or "clique"),[22] the crisis of July 1914 was contemporary history or "current events." Serious historians like Wilhelm Mommsen, Hans Rothfels, Hajo Holborn, and Hans Herzfeld would for many years avoid the subject.[23] But if the German historical profession eschewed the controversy, such was not the case in the United States.

The American Revisionists: Harry Elmer Barnes

Having entered the war late and having refused to ratify the Versailles treaty, the United States carried less emotional baggage into an examination of the war's origins than did the nations which had gone to war in 1914. A policy of isolationism in the 1920s was a luxury only available to a land whose neighbors were Canada, Mexico, and a wide variety of fish. Many Americans were disgusted with European quarrels, and this feeling, coupled with a distinct predilection for fair play, made them receptive to the idea that responsibility for the war's outbreak was probably the monopoly of

---

21. Montgelas's efforts to present a balanced view may be derived from his own ambivalence about the origins of the war. In the summer of 1918, in a letter to Richard Grelling, a Berlin lawyer, he characterized the conflict as "the preventive war decided upon on 5th July. . . . [Germany] consciously brought about the war as a preventive war." The following year, when he and Schücking were appointed as coeditors of the Kautsky documents, he had changed his opinion. See the brief discussion in Fritz Fischer, *War of Illusions*, trans. Marion Jackson (New York, 1975), 446.

22. The Hamburg school applied the term *Zunft* to Fischer's conservative opponents (Ritter, Erdmann, Zechlin, and others). The term fell into disuse in the late seventies, but was used extensively at the height of the Fischer controversy.

23. Herwig, "Clio Deceived," 23.

no single nation.[24] That idea, having (as we have seen) originated in Germany, was first propagated to a wide audience in the United States by Harry Elmer Barnes, professor of historical sociology at Smith College.[25]

In the twenties Barnes was considered to be an "extreme revisionist," a judgment which he did not dispute and which defines his work to the present day. In a variety of articles appearing in journals such as *Current History* and in a major work, *The Genesis of the World War* (New York, 1925), Barnes articulated a caustic apologia for the Central Powers and an equally powerful indictment of the Entente. Written in a strident, provocative tone for which the author makes no apology, his book characterizes those who do not accept the revisionist interpretation as "die-hards," "straw-clutchers," and "bitter-enders."[26] This vitriolic, polemical style was imitated by only a few other historians in the twenties and thirties, but it was (regrettably) resurrected by both sides in the Fischer controversy of the 1960s.

The Genesis of the World War is an angry book. The author defines his inspiration in writing it as "a hatred of war in general and an ardent desire to execute an adequate exposure of the authors of the late World War in particular."[27] In discussing the first of our six keys, Barnes accepts the 1924 disclosures of former Serbian minister of education Ljuba Jovanović as proof that the Serbian government, and particularly prime minister Nikola Pašić, possessed advance knowledge of the plot and took no steps to prevent it or to warn responsible authorities. He further alleges that the crown prince of Serbia knew of the plot and bestowed gifts in advance upon the would-be perpetrators.[28] He concludes that responsibility for the immediate crisis rests entirely with the Serbian government, although the Russian ambassador and military attaché in Belgrade also knew of the plot and encouraged it. The allegations concerning

24. Perhaps this inherent inclination toward the concept of multilateral responsibility helps explain revisionism's continued appeal to historians in the United States.

25. "Historical sociology" sounds awkward to modern ears. The social sciences were, of course, originally spin-offs of history, and by 1925 sociology had not spun very far.

26. Harry Elmer Barnes, *The Genesis of the World War* (New York, 1925), x.

27. Ibid., xiii.

28. Ibid., 161. Barnes attributes this information to "reliable Serbian sources," at least one of whom was Miloš Bogičević, former Serbian chargé d'affaires at Berlin and later a paid employee of the Foreign Office.

Russian complicity are unaccompanied by citations and are attributed to "informed Serbians."[29]

Austria's response to this provocation was understandable and fully justified. A war with Serbia was vital to its national survival, and Germany, recognizing this, supported the Dual Monarchy. Barnes seems uneasy when discussing the "blank cheque" of July 5–6, mentioning it only in passing and characterizing the Kaiser's decision as having been made "hastily and in a state of unusual excitement."[30] He concedes that Germany's reversal of its established policy of restraining Austria in the Balkans was unwise; yet this was an error of judgment rather than a premeditated act of aggression, since the Kaiser was certain that no European complications would ensue. As for the Austrian ultimatum, Bethmann did not receive its text until the evening of July 22, and the Kaiser had to read about it in the newspaper! The German government believed the document too strong, but declined to cancel their "free hand" policy toward Austria. By contrast with Germany's justifiable policy, France under Poincaré had issued a similar open-ended commitment to Russia in the fall of 1912 and would do so again in 1914. These undertakings were unjustifiable and were conferred without a clear and well-balanced assessment of the political situation.

Having disposed of the blank check in one page, Barnes devotes thirteen pages to Poincaré's visit to St. Petersburg. Most of this portion of his narrative is speculative. He interprets Poincaré's rejection of Grey's July 20 proposal for Austro-Russian talks should things become dangerous as proof of the Frenchman's "inflexible determination . . . to make any diplomatic adjustment difficult if not impossible."[31] The toasts given by Poincaré demonstrated further his aggressive intent, and British ambassador Sir George Buchanan's July 24 telegram to Grey (BD 101) underlined the fact by citing a three-part agreement between Poincaré and Sazonov. This agreement, an application of the principles of the Franco-Russian alliance to the current diplomatic situation, is characterized as belligerent by Barnes.[32] Poincaré's consistent encour-

---

29. Ibid., 169–70. Jules Isaac, in *Un débat historique*, comments on p. 73: "Why then do these 'well-informed and independent Serbs' conceal themselves behind Mr. Harry Barnes? One cannot base such an accusation on these rumors, and in the last analysis, one can find nothing else to substantiate it."
30. Barnes, *Genesis*, 186.
31. Ibid., 321.
32. Identified as BD 101 in G.P. Gooch and Harold Temperley, eds., *British*

agement of Russia and his promises of French assistance in the event of European complications made it possible for Russia to take the crucial steps that made war unavoidable.

With reference to the fourth key, Barnes returns to the brevity he displayed when speaking of German policy in early July. Allotting only two pages to the controversy surrounding Grey's alleged indecision, he finds that both sides interpreted it in line with their preconceived judgments of how England would behave. The Central Powers were certain that Grey would keep England out, while France and Russia were equally confident of British support.[33] Barnes glosses over Grey's vacillation because it does not support his contention that the British foreign secretary deliberately took England into the war to destroy Germany's navy, ruin its trade, and appropriate its colonies.

Moving to Bethmann's eleventh-hour efforts to intercede with Vienna, Barnes describes them as evidence of Germany's sincere desire for peace. Bethmann was not attempting merely to place the guilt for the war's outbreak on Russia's shoulders, but to stop payment on the blank check. Why did Berchtold not take his efforts seriously? Barnes, in the 1929 edition of *Genesis*, cites a conversation he had with the former Austro-Hungarian foreign minister in 1927. Berchtold informed him that Austrian confidence in German support never wavered, and that Bethmann's warnings were not taken seriously until it became clear that they were motivated by fear of British intervention. Austria then (on July 31) agreed to consider mediation, solely because of Britain's threatening posture; but by then it was too late because Russia had already ordered general mobilization.

Russian mobilization, our sixth key, occupies twenty pages of Barnes's account. He asserts that the Russian General Staff decided on war on the evening of July 25, and Sazonov was convinced of the same by July 29, when he obtained the first order for general mobilization (subsequently cancelled and then reinstated by the

---

Documents on the Origins of the War, 1898–1914, 11 vols. (London, 1926–38), vol. 10, this telegram is printed in Geiss, *July 1914*, 196.

33. This sanguine portrayal of French confidence in English aid might have been written differently had Barnes been aware of French ambassador to Britain Paul Cambon's despair on August 1, when he told British under secretary of state Arthur Nicolson, "They are going to desert us!" But this comment was not disclosed until 1930. Harold Nicolson, *Sir Arthur Nicolson, Bart. First Lord Carnock: A Study in the Old Diplomacy* (London, 1930), 419.

tsar). The wholly unjustifiable Russian decision made war inevitable: "Austria had explicitly informed Sazonov that she 'had no intention of annexing Serbian territory, nor did she contemplate infringing Serbian sovereignty.' As Montgelas says with entire accuracy, 'This was all that Russia could legitimately ask.'"[34]

Barnes concludes that Austria's war on Serbia was fully justified and that localization was vital to Austrian security. No one should have intervened, and those who did were guilty of deliberately destroying the peace of Europe. The German government sincerely desired peace, and the German General Staff, led by Helmuth von Moltke (the Younger), was fully supportive of the government's attitude. In summation, "There is no competent and honest authority on the problem of war guilt who is not a 'revisionist.'"[35]

The writings of Harry Barnes were well received in Germany. The Center for the Study of the Causes of the War funded his trip to Europe in 1926 and put him in contact with Miloš Bogičević. His articles were translated and published in *Die Kriegsschuldfrage*, and *Genesis* was translated into both German and French. He was given all forty volumes of *Die große Politik* by the German embassy in Washington.[36] But at home, his work was greeted more cautiously. Reviewers applauded his refutations of Versailles, but questioned the intemperance of his language and the shakiness of his methodology and use of evidence. It would be left to another to bring the revisionist position to full flower and establish it as the dominant American view of the origins of the war.[37]

The American Revisionists: Sidney Bradshaw Fay

Sidney Fay was Harry Barnes's colleague at Smith College in the 1920s. Equally convinced of the simplistic and inaccurate nature of

34. Barnes, *Genesis*, 351–52.
35. Ibid., 683.
36. Herwig, "Clio Deceived," 26–27.
37. Twenty-five years later, Harry Barnes took up the cudgels on behalf of a revisionist interpretation of World War II. Contending that Franklin Roosevelt deliberately maneuvered the United States into war in 1941, he assailed the prevailing interpretations of the war's origins in books such as *Perpetual War for Perpetual Peace* (Caldwell, Idaho, 1953), and privately printed pamphlets with titles like *The Struggle against the Historical Blackout, The Bitter Fruits of Globaloney,* and *The Chickens of the Interventionist Liberals Have Come Home to Roost.* An analysis of the views expressed in these works may be found in Robert H. Ferrell, "Pearl Harbor and the Revisionists," in Esmonde M. Robertson, ed., *The Origins of the Second World War* (London, 1971), 272–92.

article 231, he attacked the Versailles verdict in a series of articles in the *American Historical Review* in 1920–21. Other articles followed in a variety of journals, including *Current History* (for which Fay served as a contributing editor until the 1950s), and his views were consolidated and refined in his major work, *The Origins of the World War*, published in two volumes in 1928 and in a revised edition in 1930. By that time he had left Smith College for Harvard University, where he taught for decades as revisionism's leading exponent.

Almost immediately, Fay distanced himself from Barnes by exonerating the Serbian government of complicity in the assassination plot. Pašić and his ministers had nothing to do with it, although Ljuba Jovanović is correct when he asserts that they learned of it after the conspirators had embarked for Bosnia and were then unable to prevent its implementation.[38] Serbia's responsibility for the events of July 1914 is therefore heavy, but not as heavy as Barnes claimed.

With reference to German conduct in early July, Fay does not absolve the German government of all guilt, but gives it the benefit of every doubt. Attempting to discredit Szögyény's telegrams of July 5 and 6, which are cited extensively by those who blame Germany, he alleges that Szögyény's advanced age casts doubt on the accuracy of his reporting, that he was a militarist who did not sympathize with Bethmann's moderation, and that Prussian minister of war Erich von Falkenhayn never mentioned Germany's wish that Austria act promptly in his letter to Moltke on July 5.[39] He

38. Sidney Bradshaw Fay, *The Origins of the World War*, rev. ed., 2 vols, (New York, 1930), II, 66, 73–74, 145. The author contends that Serbia tried to stop the border crossing, but that the frontier guards were members of the Black Hand and ignored their instructions. He states that "this is confirmed by the diary and papers of the frontier guard, Todorović, which the Austrians captured during the war," but he provides no substantiation of this claim.

39. Ibid., II, 219–20. The relevant telegrams are printed in Geiss, *July 1914*, 76–80, Fay's historical judgment here is questionable. Szögyény's assertion that Germany was pressing Austria to act with dispatch is consistent with German overall policy at least through July 25. Fay's proof for his allegation that Szögyény frequently reported inaccurately consists of a number of citations from a book by Roderich Gooß. But he does not inform the reader that Gooß held the rank of legation secretary at the Wilhelmstraße and in 1923 had been "sent to Vienna to assist the Ballhausplatz in sorting its documents" (Herwig, "Clio Deceived," 20). Gooß's impartiality in serving his governmental employers and the 1914 Austro-Hungarian diplomatic corps cannot be taken for granted. Falkenhayn's testimony also states that he did not hear the conversation between Szögyény and the Kaiser, and that the Kaiser merely read him (at top speed) the letter from Franz Joseph and the memoran-

goes on to assert that Bethmann hoped that his diplomatic scheme to win Bulgaria for the Triple Alliance would prevent a European war over the Austro-Serb crisis.

But Germany was not completely blameless. "They gave Austria a free hand and made the grave mistake of putting the situation outside of their control into the hands of a man as reckless and unscrupulous as Berchtold. They committed themselves to a leap in the dark. . . . The Kaiser and his advisers on July 5 and 6 were not criminals plotting the World War; they were simpletons putting 'a noose about their necks' and handing the other end of the rope to a stupid and clumsy adventurer who now felt free to go as far as he liked. In so doing they were incurring a grave responsibility for what happened later."[40]

Here we see why the Weimar government was so pleased with Fay's account. By placing full blame on the Kaiser and his advisers for conducting a stupid policy, he exculpated Germany as a nation and allowed the republican authorities to draw a careful distinction between the Kaiser's policies and their own. Yet he did this in a reasonable, fair-minded way which did not find Germany totally innocent and would therefore enhance the acceptability of his version.

Fay's handling of German foreknowledge of the terms of the ultimatum is even more adroit (and more historically defensible). Jagow, according to Fay, lied in his memoirs when he denied foreknowledge, although his later contention that he found the document too strong when he finally did receive it may be accepted as correct. But Germany did know some of the ultimatum's terms and much of its general tone, and the Foreign Office was surely aware that it would probably lead to war between Serbia and Austria-Hungary. The actual text reached Berlin too late for Bethmann to propose modifications, but he would not have done so even had he possessed it earlier. For "Bethmann and Jagow concluded that the more energetically they appeared to support Austria, the more likely they would be to succeed in 'localizing' the conflict and in preventing Russia and the other Powers from interfering."[41]

---

dum from the Ballhausplatz. In addition, Falkenhayn was not present in Potsdam on July 6, when Szögyény met with Bethmann, Hoyos, and Zimmermann. Fay's observation that the context of those conversations is not found in Falkenhayn's letter of the previous day is meaningless.

40. Fay, *Origins*, II, 223.
41. Ibid., II, 268.

In Fay's discussion of the third key to the crisis, the extent of French support for Russia, he approaches most closely Barnes's position. He cites the three points in BD 101 as constituting a blank check of French support for Russia in whatever methods it might choose to counteract Austrian designs on Serbia. Poincaré's motivation was to avoid a diplomatic defeat for the Entente by preventing any compromise settlement between Russia and Austria. In contrast, Fay's interpretation of Grey's conduct is far more benign than that offered by Barnes. For Fay, Grey could indeed have prevented war by warning Germany sooner or by exercising proper restraint of France and Russia. But he could not issue an early warning, not because he wanted war, but because his seriously divided cabinet might not honor such an admonition in the event that Germany called his bluff. Likewise, he was unable to restrain France and Russia because (1) such a policy might destroy the Entente; (2) he felt that England since 1912 had been morally committed to support France; and (3) he feared that German support was behind Austrian intransigence and that Prussian militarists were calling the tune in Berlin.[42]

Was Bethmann sincere in his efforts to counsel Vienna to moderation? Fay thinks so, and links those efforts directly with Lichnowsky's increasingly frantic dispatches warning Berlin against assuming that Britain would remain neutral. He cites DD 277 as proof of Bethmann's desire that Austria should accept mediation[43] and exonerates Bethmann from the charge that he deliberately sabotaged the Kaiser's *Halt in Belgrade* plan the following day. Bethmann indeed endorsed this plan in his telegram to Tschirschky (DD 323), but his language was too mild and he failed to instruct Vienna explicitly that in Wilhelm's opinion, all cause for war had vanished. For Fay, "Bethmann was too much afraid of offending Austria. He was too much concerned with preventing the odium of responsibility for a war from falling on Germany and Austria, rather than with preventing such a war altogether."[44] His efforts, while well-intentioned, came too late and were taken seriously neither by Austria nor by the Entente, "whose faith in the sincerity of Germany's desire for peace had already been shaken by her

42. Ibid., II, 557.
43. This document is omitted from Geiss, *July 1914*, but is included in the German original, *Julikrise*, II, 111.
44. Fay, *Origins*, II, 425. This language would be echoed in future years by Albertini and Fischer, although they would go beyond its implications.

apparent support of Austrian policy hitherto."[45]

That lack of faith led directly to Russian general mobilization, which was in turn attributable to the extended length of time Russia required to prepare for war and to Sazonov and the General Staff's shared conviction that such a war was unavoidable. It was this decision, in Fay's view, "made when Germany was trying to bring Austria to a settlement, which precipitated the final catastrophe, causing Germany to mobilize and declare war."[46] This saddles Russia with substantial responsibility for the outbreak of hostilities, but Fay refuses to assign such responsibility in any sort of precise mathematical fashion. It is clear that he is most severe with Austria-Hungary and least severe with England. "Austria was more responsible for the immediate origin of the war than any other power," and Germany's culpability is that of "the victim of her alliance with Austria and of her own folly."[47] But Berlin never planned for the war of 1914, did not want it, and attempted to avoid it. Russia, Serbia, France, and England were also blameworthy, in greater or lesser degrees; but there is plenty of responsibility to go around, and consequently "the verdict of the Versailles Treaty that German and her allies were responsible for the War, in view of the evidence now available, is historically unsound. It should therefore be revised."[48]

Fay's *Origins* offers a welcome contrast to Barnes's stridency. Scrupulous in its evaluation of the available evidence (and it must be recalled that Fay was unable to use any documentary collection other than *Die große Politik* and the final volume of the *British Documents*), its moderate, fair-minded tone lifted the debate beyond polemics and stamped its author as a superb practitioner of the art of writing contemporary history. In particular, the first volume's detailed assessment of the underlying causes of the war was widely praised, even by those bitterly opposed to revisionism. Ever since its publication, *The Origins of the World War* has played a significant role in the shaping of American opinion on the events of 1914. Still eminently readable today, it has endured through six decades as one of the most influential interpretations of the outbreak of the war. No one since Fay has been able to assert with a straight face

45. Ibid., II, 438.
46. Ibid., II, 555.
47. Ibid., II, 550–52.
48. Ibid., II, 558.

that Germany and Austria-Hungary bear sole responsibility – not even Fritz Fischer, although some of his critics claimed that he was simply parroting article 231.

The enthusiastic reception accorded Fay's work, both then and now, did not preclude the development of other explanations of the crisis of July 1914. Almost immediately, the revisionist school was challenged by a cross section of scholars whose interpretation would come to be known as the antirevisionist position.

3

The Antirevisionists Respond

We have seen that substantive differences in interpretation existed within the revisionist school. Wegerer and Montgelas, although employed by the same ministry and equally devoted to the destruction of the historical underpinning of the war-guilt clause, wrote from differing standpoints and assessed the keys to July 1914 in diversified ways. And on only one of the six keys can Barnes and Fay be said to have been in essential agreement. Similarly, the antirevisionist position was taken up by historians of widely divergent views and nationalities. In this chapter, we will examine the work of five of the most significant antirevisionist historians, tracing the controversy down to its transformation by Fritz Fischer in 1961.

Germany: Hermann Kantorowicz

Germany was the home not only of Wegerer, Montgelas, and the War Guilt Section, but of an antirevisionist scholar whose work was suppressed in the twenties and not published until 1967. Hermann Kantorowicz, professor of criminal law and legal history at the University of Kiel, was a member of the War Guilt Subcommittee of the Investigating Committee of the German Reichstag under the Weimar Republic. His manuscript on the subject, *Gutachten zur Kriegsschuldfrage, 1914* (Opinion on the war guilt question), was commissioned by the subcommittee in 1923. But its conclusions, based largely upon a systematic exegesis of the colored books (the only documentary collections other than *Die deutschen Dokumente* available to Kantorowicz), were unacceptable to that body, engaged as it was in the task of securing the revocation of article 231. A number of government officials, including Gustav Stresemann, succeeded in preventing the publication of the manuscript as long as the Weimar Republic endured. Its publication under Hitler was out of the question, and Kantorowicz died in 1940, his work still a secret. During the research provoked by Fritz Fischer's view in the 1960s, Imanuel Geiss, one of Fischer's students, rediscovered the manuscript, edited it, and published it in 1967.[1]

Kantorowicz brought to his assignment the combined skills of the lawyer and the historian. Those professions, of course, do not operate from the same foundations: the lawyer seeks justice, the historian seeks truth, and they are not always identical. Yet the perspective and contextual judgment of the historian can serve as a desirable complement to the precise conceptual discipline of the lawyer, and their shared devotion to close textual analysis provides grounds for cooperation and mutual reinforcement. Thus Kantorowicz states at the outset that in a legal sense, the concept of "war guilt" does not exist, since in 1914 none of the actions taken by the belligerents violated international law. Having established this, he proceeds to examine the falsifications and distortions of the colored books, following this with a careful and precisely formulated analysis of the degrees of culpability of each of the participants. In Kantorowicz, the historian's concern with things "as they happened" blends smoothly with the legal scholar's respect for principles and norms.

Although Kantorowicz's study covers only thirty-one days of the thirty-eight day crisis (from July 5 through August 4), he nonetheless alludes to earlier events. The first key to the crisis is dealt with summarily: the Sarajevo crime cannot be laid at the door of the Serbian government because no link between Pašić and the Black Hand can be demonstrated and because the Austro-Hungarian authorities themselves played an ambiguous and at least partially culpable role.[2] Germany's conduct in the first stage of the crisis was that of an associate in a scheme devised in Vienna. The Dual Monarchy seized the opportunity afforded by the archduke's murder to punish Serbia, destroy the South Slav nationalist movement, and rearrange the power structure of the Balkans. Germany

1. Hermann Kantorowicz, *Gutachten zur Kriegsschuldfrage, 1914*, ed. Imanuel Geiss (Frankfurt, 1967). For lengthier discussions of the events summarized above, see Geiss's introduction to the work (11–50) and the English-language review by Robert A. Kann in *Central European History* 1 (1968): 383–89.

2. Kantorowicz, *Gutachten*, 354–69. It should be noted that Kantorowicz's exoneration of the Serbian government is openly based on classic legal grounds. Since certain links in the evidential chain are absent, guilt cannot be proven. Those historians less concerned with legal forms have often reached different conclusions.

supported its ally, recognizing and accepting the resulting possibility of a war against Russia and France. Kantorowicz characterizes this wider war as preventive in nature, but attributes no premeditation to Germany. Bethmann was a wishy-washy politician who followed the Kaiser's lead on July 5–6 and who sincerely attempted to avert war during the last week of the crisis. The Kaiser's responsibility is graver than that of his chancellor, but Austria's is paramount.[3]

Did Poincaré and Viviani egg the Russians on? For a legist like Kantorowicz, the question answers itself. In the absence of documentation relative to their July 20–23 stay in St. Petersburg, their unconditional support for Russia cannot be proven.[4] France and Russia decided to intervene in the Austro-Serbian conflict, but Germany's precipitate initiation of hostilities absolved them of any actual aggression. Russian general mobilization, far from being determinative, was in reality a minor technicality; Germany would have gone to war in any case once Russia's determination to support Serbia became clear. To have done otherwise would have constituted a German betrayal of Austria.[5] As for Grey, his position was defensible both legally and historically, and an early explicit warning to Germany would have done no good, given the German government's preoccupation with the continental configuration of the unfolding struggle.[6]

Although Kantorowicz places the lion's share of responsibility with Austria and Germany, he does not endorse the verdict of Versailles. All countries involved in the crisis of July 1914 endangered the peace, and no one wanted or was prepared for a world war. But the Central Powers initiated the crisis, deliberately sought a localized war, and were prepared to fight a continental preventive war. It is little wonder that his manuscript was suppressed.

Hermann Kantorowicz's views had no influence upon the scholarly debate of the interwar years. His manuscript was resurrected, edited, and published as part of the Fischer controversy of the sixties, although his views support those expressed in Fischer's first book and contradict those in his second. He is included in this study because of the acuteness of his observations (most impressive in the absence of documentary verification) and his masterful blending of historical and juridical analysis. Further, his work demonstrates that

3. Ibid., 284–314.
4. Ibid., 324.
5. Ibid., 329–39.
6. Ibid., 345–53.

despite the nationalistic, indeed chauvinistic, constraints upon historians writing in Europe in the twenties (and not in Germany alone), it was possible, although unpleasant, for a principled author to refute the government's line. On this aspect of his work, Kantorowicz himself should have the last word:

> For in Germany – and indeed all over the Continent – it is by no means considered sufficient that an historical work should tell the truth in accordance with the convictions of the author. In a work dealing with higher policy it is held to go without saying that the author should enter upon his investigations in the interests of his own nation and against its antagonists, and that his work shall be "patriotic," and the outcome of "national feeling."[7]

France: Pierre Renouvin

In France, historians' views on the outbreak of the Great War were affected in part by issues of domestic politics. Raymond Poincaré, president of the republic in July 1914, was a highly controversial politician who survived the war (*and* the presidency) and returned to public life as premier in the twenties. Whenever three Frenchmen met to discuss Poincaré, at least five opinions were presented. His continuing presence in governmental affairs meant that historical analysis of the role he had played in 1914 would by its very nature be politically explosive. Other key figures in the July crisis had, in one way or another, passed from the scene: Nicholas II, Sazonov, Berchtold, Wilhelm II, Bethmann, Viviani, and Grey were no longer in positions of responsibility. Poincaré's prominence turned French scholarship on the war's origins into a judgment on his claims to present-day leadership.

This presented a two-pronged dilemma for French researchers. To convict France of culpability for the war's origins was to play the German's game and to undermine the Versailles settlement, on which French hopes for security rested. But exoneration of Poincaré in 1914 implied exoneration of his current leadership as well, even if this were unintended. It is this context in which the French polemics of the twenties must be viewed, and it is this which

---

7. Hermann Kantorowicz, *Der Geist der englischen Politik und das Gespenst der Einkreisung Deutschlands* (Berlin, 1929), 21, translated and quoted in Moses, *The Politics of Illusion*.

renders them of dubious utility (and often incomprehensible) to modern readers.

Some, like Pierre Renouvin, refused to operate within this framework. As a young historian and member of the editorial staff of the *Documents diplomatiques français (1871–1914)*, he established himself as a skillful, judicious diplomatic historian with his first major work, *Les origines immédiates de la guerre* (Paris, 1925). Translated into English in 1927, it was the first truly scholarly antirevisionist work to be published, and it exercised profound influence on the controversy. Renouvin went on to a remarkable scholarly career, becoming professor of contemporary history at the Sorbonne and later dean of the Faculty of Letters at the same institution. He also served as professor of diplomatic history at the Institut d'Études Politiques and was elected to the Institut de France. By the time of his death in 1971, he was one of the most respected historians of the twentieth century, and not in France alone.

Even more remarkably, Renouvin, unlike nearly all of the other historians discussed here, changed his views on the July crisis over time. From an antirevisionist position in 1925 based largely upon the actions of foreign ministries and statesmen, he had developed by the 1950s an outlook which took into consideration economic and social factors, as well as fundamental movements and trends operating beneath the surface of the crisis. But those views, interesting and informative as they are, played no significant role in the evolution of the debate. It was Renouvin's 1925 opinions that created a stir, and to those opinions we now turn.[8]

Renouvin's assessment of the first key to the crisis provides a balanced interpretation of Serbia's role. He points out that although there is widespread suspicion that Serbian governmental agencies inspired the plot against Franz Ferdinand, there is no objective evidence to sustain this belief. It is probable, however, that the cabinet came to learn of the conspiracy. Ljuba Jovanović's disclosures (which appeared as Renouvin was preparing his manuscript for publication) have the ring of truth, particularly since Pašić promised to publish official documents disproving his contentions, but never did.[9] In addition, the Serbian minister at Vienna, Jovan Jovanović,

---

8. Renouvin's mature reflections on the controversy may be found in a number of his later writings, especially in Pierre Renouvin, *Histoire des rélations internationales*, vol. 6 (Paris, 1955).

9. Pašić's failure to provide the documents was noted by Renouvin in the English

certainly intervened privately to suggest that the archduke's trip be cancelled, "but he did not disclose any precise information, nor did he reveal the existence of a conspiracy."[10] Even had he done so, the Austrian government, which may have received other, more explicit warnings, knew the risks and would have sent the archduke anyway so as not to appear intimidated by the South Slav national movement.

In response to the outrage, the Central Powers consciously risked a European war. Ambassador Szögyény's testimony concerning the events of July 5–6 at Potsdam is confirmed by Hoyos's memoirs; there was no misunderstanding based on age or incompetence, and no words were put into Bethmann's mouth (an action which would have been extremely foolish, since Berchtold would soon have discovered the duplicity in conversation with Tschirschky). The Kaiser informed Captain Zenker of the Navy Staff and War Minister Falkenhayn that war was a distinct possibility and preparations for it should be made. But there was no preference for a military solution: "The Government at Berlin had pronounced itself in favor of immediate political action, and had urged its ally to make some move, without asking either what it wanted or where it was heading."[11]

There are, however, no grounds for believing Germany ignorant of the thrust of the Austrian ultimatum. It is true that the Foreign Office had no hand in its drafting, but Germany was informed of Austrian intentions from a number of sources independent of each other.[12] Renouvin alleges that the Kaiser's written notes and messages from July 20–25 prove that he did not believe that localization could succeed. If Germany considered the note excessively harsh, it nonetheless placed no obstacles in the path of its transmission and endorsed it in separate communications to the chanceries of Europe.

---

edition of his book published in 1927, but not in the French original (which was published two years earlier).

10. Pierre Renouvin, *The Immediate Origins of the War*, trans. Theodore Carswell Hume (New York, 1927), 30.

11. Ibid., 43. Note both the similarities with and differences from Fay's interpretation of the same events.

12. The eventual publication of so many diplomatic documents demonstrated that the basic demands contained in the Austrian note constituted one of the most open secrets in history prior to July 23. So many ambassadors, chargés, attachés, and well-informed citizens speculated on the contents with such consistent accuracy that one is led to suspect the presence of a leak in the Ballhausplatz that approached the Danube in size.

Our third key, the role played by Poincaré and Viviani in encouraging Russia, is the most vexing area for French historians for reasons already discussed. Renouvin, in his work on the editorial staff of the DDF, searched in vain for documents from the July 20–23 visit to St. Petersburg.[13] In the absence of concrete evidence and with Poincaré in power, it would have been easy for Renouvin to assert that the French statesmen were innocent of the charges leveled against them. Instead, he discusses the matter briefly and stands on the three points of agreement cited in Buchanan's telegram (BD 101), speculating no further concerning Poincaré's possible understandings with Sazonov. Unable either to convict or acquit on the basis of the evidence, he states what is known and leaves perusal of the unknown to others. Many historians can sympathize with his position and identify with the attitude he adopted.[14]

With reference to the attitude of Sir Edward Grey, Renouvin felt on firmer ground. He dismisses the notion that Grey was merely attempting to entice Germany into war by refusing to disclose England's true intentions. Rather, the divided cabinet precluded any effort by the foreign secretary to clarify a position which seems clear only in retrospect. There can be no doubt, however, of German hopes for British neutrality. Renouvin's analysis of the fifth key ties Bethmann's last-minute efforts to the opinion that

> as far as Germany was concerned, the fear of England was the beginning of wisdom. . . . What the Chancellor feared most of all was not war. . . . What he did desire above all was that, if war should become necessary, it should not be started under favourable conditions. . . . What was uppermost in the Chancellor's mind was that the war should be a struggle of the Central Powers against Russia and France, and not against the Triple Entente.[15]

Thus Bethmann's reaction to Grey's proposal for mediation of

13. He describes the preparation of the DDF in Pierre Renouvin, "Les documents diplomatiques français, 1871–1914," *Revue Historique*, 226 (1961): 139–52.

14. Despite the antirevisionist nature of Renouvin's work, reaction to it by revisionists was mixed. Harry Elmer Barnes simply ignored it, despite the fact that his *Genesis* was published after *Les origines* appeared. But the French revisionist Georges Demartial referred to Renouvin's "honorable . . . example of professional conscience" in his "L'état de la question des responsabilités en France," *Current History* 13 (1926): 787–93.

15. Renouvin, *The Immediate Origins*, 343–44.

July 26 is, for Renouvin, evidence that he wanted only to furnish England with a reason to believe in his good will; he did not expect Vienna to cave in. By the same token, his telegram of 10:15 P.M. July 28 (DD 323) watered down the Kaiser's peace initiative and emphasized that responsibility for the war must fall on Russia – the best approach to insuring English neutrality. Finally, his desperate dispatches of July 30 (DD 395, 396) reflect his deepening conviction that England will come in after all; they are sincere, but they do not indicate a sudden conversion to the desirability of peace for its own sake.

Moving to Russian general mobilization, Renouvin spends ten pages disproving the allegations that the tsar's decision was influenced by reports of German military preparations, a threatening telegram from the Kaiser, and advice from Paris. He holds that "the sole motive . . . in the decision in favor of general mobilization, was the technical military argument."[16] Partial mobilization in the southwest against Austria-Hungary alone would have rendered general mobilization hopeless. Besides, since Russian mobilization was so much slower than its German counterpart and since Germany would certainly intervene on Austria's behalf to save it from defeat even if Russia mobilized *only* against Austria, what could possibly be gained by waiting?[17] Russian mobilization *was* important, but it was, in the last analysis, only a reaction to decisions and events initiated by others. And it did not mean war, whereas German mobilization *did*.

Renouvin concludes by finding Germany innocent of planning to provoke a general war regardless of the circumstances or the consequences. He contends that "Germany would have been satisfied, on 27th July as on the fifth, with a diplomatic victory."[18] But the Central Powers bear the lion's share of the guilt. They had good reason to fear South Slav nationalism, and Germany was just as entitled to stand by its ally as Russia was to defend Serbia, a country to which it was not allied. But Germany and Austria, while hoping

---

16. Ibid., 210.
17. This, of course, is the reasoning that prevented the preparation of a plan for partial mobilization of the Russian army. It is difficult to dispute the logic of the conclusion, but those who (quite correctly) criticize German military planning for the inflexibility of the Schlieffen Plan should not entertain the opposite notion that flexibility therefore characterized the war plans of other countries. On this, see the valuable study by Paul Kennedy, ed., *The War Plans of the Great Powers, 1880–1914* (London, 1979).
18. Renouvin, *The Immediate Origins*, 354.

to avoid a European war, were absolutely resolved upon a local war between Austria and Serbia to redraw the power structure of the Balkans. "They had agreed upon the program after careful deliberation, having coolly considered all the possible consequences of their actions."[19] This was the indispensable element in the outbreak of the Great War.

Renouvin's book was quickly translated into English, appearing in booksellers' windows in the United States simultaneously with the accounts produced by Barnes and Fay. Soon these contributions to the burgeoning controversy would be supplemented by the two provocative volumes of a University of Chicago professor.

United States: Bernadotte Everly Schmitt

Schmitt, like Sidney Fay, earned his doctorate at the University of Chicago; but while Fay left for the northeast, Schmitt stayed in Illinois to embark upon a career that would not only make him one more in a seemingly endless list of American historians bearing tripartite names,[20] but would juxtapose his name forever to that of Fay at opposite poles of the war-guilt issue. In the early 1930s, the debate between Fay and Schmitt assumed heroic proportions, with the former's contention that all powers were guilty (and Germany less so than Serbia and Austria) contradicted by the latter's argument that German guilt outweighed all others and validated the basic premise, if not the actual simplistic language, of article 231 of the Treaty of Versailles.

For generations of American students and scholars, this has remained the most familiar aspect of the long controversy. The immense works of Albertini and Fischer, to say nothing of the apparently interminable bickering of German historians during the past twenty-five years (much of which has never been translated into English), have been thoroughly digested by few on this side of the Atlantic. This fact underscores the importance of Schmitt's work not only in our discussion but in American historiography. Indeed, the fact that Fay was widely perceived to have gotten the better of the dispute (in part because of the greater readability of his

---

19. Ibid., 355.
20. Harry Elmer Barnes, Sidney Bradshaw Fay, Bernadotte Everly Schmitt, Archibald Cary Coolidge, Charles Homer Haskins, Lacey Baldwin Smith, Robert Howard Lord, and countless others attest to this peculiar custom.

work) has colored American perceptions of the July crisis down to the present.

Schmitt, like Fay, employs a two-volume format; but while Fay made Sarajevo the dividing line between the two, Schmitt breaks the narrative at the delivery of the Austrian ultimatum. He is concerned solely with the July crisis itself, leaving to Fay and others the discussion of the underlying causes of the war. After a detailed assessment of the situation in the Balkans, he evaluates the evidence pertaining to Serbian complicity in the Sarajevo crime. To Schmitt, the provocative assertions of Ljuba Jovanović and others remain unproven. They are filled with discrepancies and inconsistencies, and it is impossible for the historian to determine accurately the motives of their authors. Certainly, if the Serbian government became acquainted with the existence of the conspiracy, it was derelict in its duty in failing to warn Austria vigorously. But the available evidence does not indicate that the Serbian government approved of the plot, let alone initiated it. Schmitt is far less ready than Fay to indict the Serbian authorities, demonstrating a sympathy for their position stronger than that of Renouvin.

With reference to the second key, Schmitt continues to take issue with Fay. It is not true that the Kaiser was ignorant of the sort of action Austria intended to take; Falkenhayn, von Müller, and Szögyény independently confirm his knowledge and the fact that he endorsed the Austrian proposals with the full weight of his position. In particular, Szögyény's evidence is thereby validated from German sources. Wilhelm II not only approved the principle of Austrian action against Serbia, but urged that such action take place at once. If Russia intervened, Austria could count on Germany's firm support.

The Kaiser and Bethmann faced the possibility that a European war might easily result from the Austrian measures. Schmitt reminds the reader that even the *German White Book* of August 1914 conceded that Germany was well aware that they might be called upon to assist their ally. In this concept of loyalty, of course, Germany was not alone in Europe.

> It had a perfect right to adopt such a policy, for war was a legitimate instrument of national policy, and every other government was equally prepared to fight rather than submit to a threat to national interests or to diplomatic humiliation. But Wilhelm II and Theobald von Bethmann-Hollweg were the *first* responsible statesmen to take decisions which

45

might have the most dire consequences.[21] They had no intention of touching off a European war, but they gambled on the willingness of Russia and France to accept a diplomatic defeat without fighting and lost the wager.

Did Germany know the terms of the ultimatum in advance? Schmitt observes that this is of little consequence since, by granting unconditional support to any action which Austria-Hungary might care to take, the German government had on July 5–6 sacrificed any control it might otherwise have exercised over its ally. But to set the record straight, he notes that Tschirschky informed Berlin of the general substance of the note on July 11, including the intention of the Ballhausplatz to formulate demands which Serbia could not accept. Berchtold himself solicited Germany's opinion on the same day, but Jagow adopted an attitude of detachment. When the actual text was communicated to Berlin on the evening of July 22, no objections were raised, despite the fact that the ultimatum was not delivered in Belgrade until 6:00 P.M. the following day. Schmitt's account of the second key is therefore unfavorable to the German position and, although critical of Austria's attitude, less condemnatory than the description provided by Fay.

Schmitt moves on to the question of French influence on Russia by quoting the three provisions of BD 101 and placing them in the context of the visit. He asserts that these expressions of solidarity and mutual support are given in the normal diplomatic language one would expect to read following a state visit at the highest level. The first provision, community of views on the maintenance of the general peace, was so innocuous that it was published in a communiqué as the visit ended; the second, that action should be taken at Vienna to prevent Austrian intervention in Serbian internal affairs, was forthwith transmitted to the French ambassador to Austria-Hungary and was hardly conspiratorial; and the third,

---

21. Bernadotte Everly Schmitt, *The Coming of the War, 1914*, 2 vols. (New York, 1930), I, 329. Here Schmitt makes a cogent observation which all students of the July crisis must bear in mind. War was indeed a legitimate instrument for settling quarrels (a fact which those born since 1945 sometimes forget), and the statesmen who began the Great War could not have known that they would nearly destroy European civilization in the process of settling this particular dispute.

The name of the German chancellor was often spelled with a hyphen prior to 1939; since then, it has usually been spelled without one. Since Bethmann died in 1920, he had nothing to do with the change. I have used the modern spelling, except in the case of direct quotations such as the above.

"solemn affirmation of obligations imposed by the alliance of the two countries," was publicly affirmed in the speeches and toasts delivered by Poincaré and the tsar.[22] Far too much has been read into this document by the revisionists. The presence of such language is to be expected; only its absence on such an occasion would cause speculation. In reality, the tsar and the French president said much stronger things to the Austrian and Russian ambassadors during the diplomatic receptions and dinners that accompanied the visit. These warnings fell on deaf ears, possibly because of the way in which they were reported to Berlin. The German ambassador to Russia, Count Friedrich von Pourtalès (who was Bethmann's cousin), informed the Foreign Office that the French had received a cool reception in Russia and that their warnings were bluffs. For several days the German government apparently believed this nonsense.[23]

So far, Schmitt's antirevisionism had been strong and consistent. The fourth key, however, gave him pause. He grants the merit of Renouvin's (and, for that matter, Fay's) contention that Grey could not have committed himself earlier in the absence of solid backing from his cabinet, to say nothing of the House of Commons and the nation. But it is nonetheless regrettable that Grey did not convey some sort of warning earlier than July 27 – and it is, in Schmitt's opinion, a criticism which may be valid. "At least it is possible that a clear-cut declaration of solidarity with France and Russia would have induced the German Government to modify its course and to restrain its ally."[24] Having conceded this, he hastens to add that such a caution would have had little positive effect unless it were issued prior to the rejection of the Serbian reply on July 25; and paradoxically, "quite conceivably it might have had the opposite effect from that desired, of rousing the German Government to instant action."[25] It is clear that Schmitt was troubled by Grey's conduct, yet was unable to propose an alternative line that would have answered all the objections that stood in the path of an early warning.

This ambivalence over Grey's actions does not carry over into Schmitt's interpretation of Germany's attempts to restrain Austria-Hungary during the final week of the crisis. Bethmann's telegram of

22. Ibid., I, 450 and n. 1.
23. Ibid., I, 456.
24. Ibid., II, 409.
25. Ibid., II, 409.

July 27 passing along England's mediation proposal (DD 277) was not intended to impede Austria, but to cast the blame on Russia and, incidentally, to deceive London: "There is strong reason for thinking that the *démarche* was only a slippery trick to throw dust in the eyes of Sir Edward Grey."[26] Bethmann did not recommend acceptance of the British proposal, a fact which is underscored by Szögyény's telegram of the same evening to Berchtold. But the increasing evidence of the British intention to stand by France was becoming difficult to ignore. Bethmann's telegram of July 28 (DD 323) discloses the awkwardness of his position. Obviously, says Schmitt, he hoped that Austria would proceed with its war against Serbia, provided that England would remain neutral; but Lichnowsky's telegrams and Grey's slowly toughening language were beginning to make this prospect appear less likely. "Yet if he really put the screws on his ally, he would not only create consternation in Vienna and Budapest, but the Potsdam promises could and doubtless would be flung in his face."[27]

Faced with this dilemma, the chancellor advised Berchtold to act in such a way that Russia would be blamed for any intervention on Serbia's behalf and that this blame would provide England with a justification for staying out of the war. It did not work. Austria's declaration of war on Serbia affected the Russians profoundly and shocked Grey into making a forceful, unambiguous declaration to Lichnowsky. Bethmann looked into the abyss and drew back. He fired off his early-morning telegrams to Vienna on July 30 and tried to restrain Russia with assurances that Berchtold would negotiate. But Schmitt isolates and identifies the central contradiction of these admittedly sincere steps: "After having given Vienna to understand that the motive of his mediation was to put Russia in the wrong, . . . the chancellor now had to insist that the new *démarche* be taken seriously, in order to prevent a European war (to which he had previously consented)."[28] Who could blame Berchtold for being confused, particularly when a stand-fast message arrived from Moltke later that same day? Who *did* rule in Berlin? The answer, for Schmitt, is simple yet maddening: Bethmann's July 30 policy was not consistent with his earlier efforts, and in the context of rapid-fire military timetables and concern over the comparative speed of

26. Ibid., II, 71.
27. Ibid., II, 129–30.
28. Ibid., II, 167.

various nations' mobilization procedures, it is not surprising that his last desperate moves were fruitless.

For both the Austrians and the Germans were indeed concerned over Russian mobilization, and Schmitt, while not defending the Russian action, argues vigorously that the outcome would have been the same in any event. Sazonov's behavior was convoluted and erratic; it was unfortunate that a man of these characteristics happened to be Russian foreign minister at such a dangerous juncture in history. Certainly general mobilization need not have been embarked on so precipitately. Another twenty-four hours would have made no military difference and might have given Bethmann's efforts more of a chance to sway Vienna (although Sazonov could not know that Bethmann was trying to call off Austria, and much of the available evidence pointed the other way). But for Schmitt, the central issue remains imposing. The Central Powers did not wish merely to chastise Serbia, but to alter the balance of power in the Balkans. To attempt to do this without consulting the Russian government, which had played a major role in that region for more than a century, was foolhardy at best. What did Berlin and Vienna think Russia was going to do – sit back and let Serbia be swallowed whole?

Unfortunately, says Schmitt, the Central Powers gambled that Russia would not intervene militarily. Even after Russian partial mobilization, when it was clear that they had guessed incorrectly, they could still have salvaged the situation by agreeing to negotiate. Sazonov may have behaved erratically early in the crisis, but he had made it clear from the outset that Russia could not accept an invasion of Serbia, and he carried that policy through. "This was the logical and the only reply possible to the policy of surprise with which the Austro-Hungarian and German Governments sought to overawe and even to terrorize Europe."[29]

Strong words indeed. Schmitt will have none of Fay's explanations of German conduct, none of his nuanced exonerations.[30] German policy appeared belligerent because it *was* belligerent. The Central Powers attempted to change by force a European balance of power which they saw as unfavorable but which the Entente perceived them as dominating. The fact that the Entente reacted

---

29. Ibid., II, 256.
30. Jules Isaac called Fay "l'homme des nuances," and Schmitt would not have disagreed.

strongly to this provocation was to be anticipated, and to the extent that Germany did not anticipate it, its policy was not only foolish, as Fay concludes, but dangerously aggressive.

Now the lines were neatly drawn. The revisionists had their champions, the antirevisionists theirs. For Americans, the debate became personalized between Fay and Schmitt; Germans like Wegerer and Montgelas and Frenchmen like Renouvin were obviously parties at interest, and Barnes's work, although stimulating, bordered on defamation and handled evidence in a cavalier fashion. Fay and Schmitt were top-of-the-line historians, careful of their contexts, respectful of their sources, and bent on the creation of sensible and fair accounts of the July crisis. They dominated the controversy throughout the thirties.

As the decade grew old, however, the debate seemed less immediately significant. Adolf Hitler came to power in Germany in 1933, proclaiming to all who would listen that the Great War had never ended and that the armed truce would soon be terminated. He led Germany toward a renewal of hostilities with nations whose leaders had been appalled by the carnage of 1914–18 and could not conceive of a situation in which a great power would be led by someone who had enjoyed that bloodshed and wanted to renew it. In such circumstances, the causes of the war of 1914 began to seem less important than the prevention of the next conflict. When that proved impossible, when the Treaty of Versailles lay in ruins, the battle over its fairness and possible revision lost its immediate relevance for many scholars.

Italy: Luigi Albertini

Some, of course, continued to study the Great War undistracted by the approach of Hitler's revenge. For more than a decade, an Italian journalist had been painstakingly preparing what he hoped would constitute the definitive treatment of the background and events of the July crisis. Luigi Albertini, for many years editor of the great Milanese daily *Corriere della Sera* and later a member of the Italian Senate, had withdrawn from public life rather than bow to Benito Mussolini. Turning to the study of contemporary history, he utilized his mastery of European languages to examine all of the great documentary collections, becoming the first historian of the war's origins to do so. He prepared translations of the most significant telegrams and news accounts of the period and eventually published them in his books.[31] Capitalizing on his broad range of contacts with major political and diplomatic figures of previous years and adding to that a journalist's persistence in the pursuit of sources, he was able to interview or correspond with nearly every living participant in the July crisis. Many of these statesmen expressed themselves with unusual frankness; others replied to Albertini's probing, relentless questions with preposterous prevarications or embarrassed silence. The result was a huge reservoir of previously untapped source material which he carefully transformed into a tour de force of diplomatic history.

Albertini's three-volume masterpiece, *Le origini della guerra del 1914*, was published in Milan in 1942–43 as Italy's experiment with fascism ended. The author himself died as the first volume was appearing, leaving unwritten a concluding chapter in which he had intended to summarize his findings and assess the comparative degrees of responsibility borne by the chief participants in the July crisis. For this reason, his work has been omitted from most of the major anthologies of historical writing published on the subject.[32] But Albertini's three volumes, totaling more than two thousand pages, examined every stage of the thirty-eight-day diplomatic ballet in very close detail. For a full decade, they remained unknown to all historians save those literate in Italian; an English-language translation was finally prepared and released in stages between 1952 and 1957. Since their publication in English, students of the crisis have found them to be an indispensable storehouse of information and sage appraisal, vigorously yet elegantly written, and not entirely free from prejudice (Albertini had been one of the most vocal proponents of Italy's entry into the war on the side of the Entente, and his chapters on Italian policy must be read with caution). In Albertini's work, the antirevisionist position attained its apotheosis.

Condensing Albertini's massive compendium is a perilous undertaking, and I beg the reader's indulgence of the inevitable oversimplifications. He presents a detailed survey of the background and results of the Sarajevo atrocity, perusing the complex

31. The translations of documents provided by Albertini are generally of high quality, but inaccuracies and improper choices of words occasionally crept into his work. Where possible, these translations should be compared with the originals or with the translations rendered by Imanuel Geiss.
32. From most, but not from all. Samuel R. Williamson Jr. prepared a useful three-page encapsulation of Albertini's views and published it in his anthology, *The Origins of a Tragedy*.

story with remarkable patience and endeavoring to separate fact from opinion from fabrication from slander. Although the exact sequence of events may never be known, he finds it likely that Ljuba Jovanović told the truth in his 1924 article and that Pašić instructed the Serbian minister at Vienna, Jovan Jovanović, to warn the Austrian authorities. But if Jovan Jovanović delivered any warning at all (and Albertini is not certain that he did), it was delivered not to Count Berchtold but to the Austrian finance minister, Leon Ritter von Bilinski, in whose jurisdiction Bosnia was placed, and it was expressed in the most vague and generalized terms. Pašić's responsibility lies not in helping to hatch the plot (he did nothing of the sort), but in the failure of his ineffectual actions to prevent the murder. For he dreaded war, knowing that Serbia would be conquered by Austria, and the effect of his policy was to expose his country to that which he most deeply feared. In such circumstances, he should have "pounded on the door and cried out not ceasing" in order to defend properly the interests of his country.[33] These findings differ in no significant way from those of Schmitt and Renouvin, but Albertini's mastery of the intricate plots and subplots of this Balkan morality play far exceeds theirs. No better assessment of the context and implications of Sarajevo would exist until Vladimir Dedijer published *The Road to Sarajevo* in 1966.

Albertini's analysis of the second key to the crisis reveals a significant distinction between his interpretation and those of Fay and Schmitt. Fay sees Berchtold as an unprincipled adventurer who ruthlessly tightened the noose that the German government had been unwise enough to place about its own neck. Schmitt considers the Austro-Hungarian foreign minister a clever manipulator who maneuvered Berlin into proposing a course of action that he had had in mind all along. But for Albertini, "Berchtold was incapable of an adroit move. All he had done was to don his armour and leave it to his ally to decide whether he was to keep it on or doff it. . . . It is not impossible that at the bottom of his heart Berchtold would have liked Germany to prevent Austria from acting rashly and silence the war party."[34] The Potsdam interviews thus played a crucial role in the creation of a warlike attitude in the Austrian government through German pressure.

33. The reference is to Alan Paton, *Too Late the Phalarope* (London, 1953).
34. Albertini, *The Origins*, II, 133. If this interpretation is accurate, then what a surprise Berchtold must have gotten! Berlin's course of action was the reverse of their counsels of moderation in November 1912 and July 1913.

Szögyény's account of those interviews is, in Albertini's opinion, accurate. Fay uses negative proof in his contention that Bethmann never stated in his telegram of July 6 to Tschirschky that Austria should attack Serbia at once; it is true that Bethmann wrote no such thing, but this does not mean that no such suggestions were made. Szögyény, far from being the bumbling, senile fool that Gooß, Wegerer, Montgelas, and Fay portray, was held in high esteem by the Ballhausplatz. His telegram of July 6 to Berchtold, "one of the most damning documents on German responsibility for the war, was published in 1919, a year before Bethmann Hollweg died and its authenticity was never called in question by him. How, indeed, could Szögyény possibly have invented a whole speech of this tenor if it had never been made? All that he would have achieved by so doing would have been a disavowal from Berlin and the loss of his own credit."[35] Indeed, Count Hoyos revealed to Albertini in an interview in 1933 that Szögyény's telegram had really been drafted by Hoyos himself, who was admittedly a member of the "war party" at Vienna but who was far from senile and who likewise had nothing to gain by putting words into the mouths of German officials.

This did not mean, however, that Germany was determined to unleash a European war. They were not convinced that the Dual Monarchy would take the forceful action which they felt was necessary on this occasion; and even if Vienna did act, France and Russia would not, and the conflict would be a cakewalk for the Austro-Hungarian army. Albertini is skeptical of German utterances which indicate preference for a "preventive war" on favorable terms now rather than under less propitious conditions later. He doubts that they would have so strongly encouraged Austria had they been certain that Russia would intervene at once. German policy in early July was based on a gamble that the Entente would stay out of a purely Balkan quarrel; it was this miscalculation that launched the Great War, rather than, as Fay alleges, the blunder of putting Germany's destiny in Berchtold's unworthy hands. Albertini sums it up: Berchtold was not an unprincipled adventurer, and there was no noose around Germany's neck. The Kaiser and Bethmann wanted Austria to finish off Serbia, and if they had counseled peace instead, no one at Vienna would have pursued matters further.

---

35. Ibid., II, 146–47. The best proof of the telegram's authenticity is that German policy until July 29 paralleled it.

This interpretation persists through Albertini's discussion of German foreknowledge of the ultimatum. He echoes the judgments of Renouvin and Schmitt that Tschirschky's July 10 telegram to Jagow (DD 29) conveyed the vital components of the note: the forty-eight-hour time limit, the establishment at Belgrade of an organ of the Dual Monarchy to conduct the investigation, and the fact that the document was being designed in such a form that Serbia could not accept it. Berchtold *was* tardy in sending a copy of the finished product to Berlin, but not for the reason given by Fay, that he feared Germany might object to its stringency. Rather, Vienna was concerned that Bethmann would think the note *too lenient* and would demand stronger language! Jagow had implied as much in his letter to Tschirschky on July 17 (DD 61), urging Austria to cash the blank check.[36] Late transmission would avoid this impasse by presenting Germany with a fait accompli. As for Jagow's postwar assertion that he and Bethmann thought the note too stiff, the evidence points the other way. The toughest provisions were known in Berlin by July 11; Germany made no request for changes; Jagow did not complain to Tschirschky at the time that the demands were unreasonable; and Szögyény wired to Berchtold Jagow's statement that the German government endorsed everything in the note. The picture that emerges is one of consistent German support for a strong Austrian posture against Serbia.

What about French support for Russia? Here Albertini departs from the classic antirevisionist viewpoint. While Renouvin notes the absence of documentation from the St. Petersburg visit and refrains from speculative comment, Albertini lays it on the line: it was Viviani's duty as premier and foreign minister to compose some sort of minutes of the top-level discussions. Poincaré had done this when he had visited Russia in 1912 as premier. "If it was not done, there must have been good reasons for this," and Albertini leaves us in no doubt as to what they might have been.[37] The visit produced a "heated atmosphere" and certainly contributed to Russia's willingness to accept quickly the Austrian challenge. French ambassador Maurice Paléologue unquestionably egged the Russians on and delayed reporting vital information to Paris; but he and Poincaré had been close friends since their lycée days, and it is inconceivable that he would have adopted a policy profoundly different from that of the president.

36. Ibid., II, 262–64. Fay omits the relevant passage from DD 61.
37. Ibid., II, 196.

Nevertheless, Barnes's assertion that Poincaré was the chief architect of the Great War is preposterous. He is less culpable than the German and Austrian leaders, less culpable even than Sazonov. "The French President's share was in availing himself of the mistakes committed by Austria and Germany to carry through the *revanche* and restore to France Alsace and above all his own Lorraine."[38] Opportunistic he was, but he did not plan war, and in the absence of the policy agreed upon by the Central Powers he would have had no chance to wage it.

If Poincaré is treated sternly by Albertini, at least he comes off as a shrewd leader who missed no chance to advance the interests of his country. Sir Edward Grey is not so fortunate. Basing this portion of his narrative on *Die große Politik*, Albertini asserts that Germany counted on English neutrality from the very moment of the issuance of the blank check. Grey's behavior between then and July 29 gave Berlin no reason to change its assessment; indeed, the infamous request for a guarantee of English neutrality in return for a German promise to respect the territorial integrity of France could never have been made had Germany not been misled seriously. If Grey had spoken on or before July 27 with the language and emphasis he used on July 29, "Germany would very likely have restrained Austria from declaring war on Serbia and the European war, at least for the time being, would have been averted."[39] No ultimatum was necessary or even desirable; a plain, straightforward admonition would have sufficed.

Albertini is contemptuous of the argument so frequently advanced by Grey's supporters that a divided cabinet ruled out any possibility of forceful intervention. The cabinet was no less divided on July 29 than it had been three weeks earlier, and Grey's frank and explicit conversation with Lichnowsky on July 31 took place without his having consulted either the cabinet or Parliament. If he could take this sort of initiative at the end of the crisis, when its utility was dubious, why could he not have acted in the same vein earlier with greater hope of success? Indeed, why did Grey wait so long to do *anything*? Why did he proclaim his and his government's indifference to the fate of Serbia, rather than warning both sides "not [to] resort to forceful methods and mobilization, warning

---

38. Ibid., II, 197. In contrast to Poincaré, Viviani is handled with approval and respect by Albertini, whose attitude some recent treatments find difficult to understand. See in particular Krumeich, *Armaments and Politics*, 221.
39. Albertini, *The Origins*, II, 514.

them that the political and moral strength of Britain would be thrown in against the aggressor, and that, if war came, his decisions would be influenced by the conduct, peaceful or aggressive, of the two sides"?[40]

In this appraisal there is no implicit approval of German conduct. "Elementary political common sense" should have shown Bethmann that English neutrality in a German war against France and Russia was an impossibility. But Grey did nothing to dispel this illusion and everything, albeit inadvertently, to reinforce it. Perhaps because no one in London had yet concluded that intervention was likely, he permitted events to control the Foreign Office when he should have taken the reins himself. "For fear of forcing the public opinion, [he] did his best to save the peace, but made bad use of the powerful position he was in to stop war."[41] The thrust of Albertini's argument conforms to the antirevisionist interpretation, but his analyses of the third and fourth keys to the crisis indicate that he is hardly an apologist for the Entente.

Grey may have been feckless in his efforts to enlist the cooperation of Germany, but he certainly received no assistance in this quest from Bethmann. Albertini, in his discussion of German final-week efforts, contradicts the position of German historians that Bethmann's July 27 telegram (DD 277) passing along the English mediation proposal to Vienna was a good-faith effort to preserve peace. In reality, as Szögyény's telegram of the same date proves, it was plainly and simply an attempt to gain the good will of London through duplicitous methods. As Fay admits, Bethmann's paramount goal in these days was to keep England neutral by insuring that blame for the war would fall on Russia.

When Bethmann learned that England would oppose Germany in a war involving France, he sent the two famous telegrams (DD 395, 396) in the early morning hours of July 30. These Albertini deems entirely sincere, in agreement with all other historians we have discussed. But Berchtold ignored the dispatches, and Albertini is not surprised. Bethmann, in his view, could have stopped payment on the blank check at this late date only by employing the strongest possible language. He would have had to tell Austria that it had all

---

40. Ibid., II, 518.
41. Ibid., II, 645. John F.V. Keiger, *France and the Origins of the First World War* (New York, 1983), 156, points out that Albertini denounces Poincaré's repeated admonitions to Viviani to treat Germany firmly while berating Grey for not realizing that Germany should be treated firmly.

been a terrible mistake, that a war of two Central Powers against the entire Entente would destroy the Dual Monarchy rather than save it, and that Germany's earlier promise of unconditional support was no longer valid. This would assuredly have attracted Berchtold's attention and might yet have saved the day. But Bethmann may have thought he had more time; after all, Austria could not commence hostilities until August 12, and by that time the pressure on Vienna, supplemented of course by additional conversations in the intervening days, would have had the desired effect. "But he counted without the paroxysm which the Austrian declaration of war had evoked in Russia and which drove Sazonov into making an irreparable mistake."[42]

This mistake, the Russian general mobilization, consumes fifty-four pages of Albertini's narrative. It was the most detailed and accurate description of that confusing sequence of events at the time of its publication, and in those respects remains unsurpassed today. What appears in those pages is no confirmation of Kantorowicz's unpublished belief that Russian general mobilization was a minor technical matter. But those who read it or read this brief condensation of its chief arguments must bear in mind that Albertini insists that "the main obstacle to a peaceful solution of the conflict" was not Russian mobilization, but what provoked it – the Austrian declaration of war on Serbia.[43]

Sazonov's role in the final days of the July crisis was in Albertini's eyes an unfortunate one. Emotional, erratic, and not particularly bright, he alternately soothed and raged at the Austrians, hoping to call their bluff through a partial mobilization of thirteen army corps. The virtue of this approach was that it was directed solely against the Dual Monarchy and presumably would not alarm Germany. The problem with it was that no provision for it had been made by the Russian General Staff. Sazonov apparently did not realize this, and the chief of the General Staff, Yanushkevich, did not either, having been appointed for his talents as a courtier and flatterer rather than for his skills as a military planner.

In any event, partial mobilization was in Albertini's eyes a poorly selected response. "Sazonov would have done better to remind Pourtalès of Jagow's having agreed [on July 27] that Russia might mobilize against Austria. It is, indeed, incomprehensible that he

42. Albertini, *The Origins*, II, 527.
43. Ibid., II, 531.

never availed himself of that argument."[44] And partial mobilization failed to deter Austria while provoking a sharp rejoinder from Germany. Two events on July 29 pushed Sazonov over the edge: the news of the bombardment of Belgrade by ships of Austria-Hungary's Danube flotilla and an abrupt demarche from Germany (DD 342) which Sazonov later characterized as an ultimatum. Bethmann denied that charge and followed the message the next day with DD 380, a more moderate and conciliatory telegram (omitted by Geiss from his collection); but this communication did not arrive in St. Petersburg until the morning of July 30, and by then Sazonov had reached a decision. He was now convinced that Austrian behavior was the result of a conspiracy between Berlin and Vienna and that war with Germany was therefore unavoidable. If this were true, then Russian partial mobilization would hopelessly dislocate the call-up, a procedure which under the best conditions resembled controlled chaos. General mobilization was therefore the only possible option.

Albertini does not fault Sazonov's logic in rejecting partial mobilization; indeed, he should never have considered it in the first place. But proceeding to general mobilization at this point in the crisis was a grave blunder. He was not averse to some sort of punishment of Serbia, providing that its sovereignty and territorial integrity remained intact. Such a solution was at hand through the Kaiser's *Halt in Belgrade* proposal, although Austria had not yet shown any willingness to negotiate on such a basis. Sazonov could tell from the messages arriving from Count Alexander Benckendorff, his ambassador in London, that England was gradually closing ranks with Russia and France. It would be reasonable to anticipate that Germany would shrink from such a confrontation and would urge moderation on Vienna. Sazonov, says Albertini, should have recognized this and held the military in check until it was clear that diplomacy had played its last card. Had he done so, "probably, if not certainly, some agreement could have been found on a formula in the nature of the *Halt in Belgrade*."[45]

Why, then, did Sazonov go to the tsar and demand general mobilization? Albertini finds the answer in his ignorance of what general mobilization implied for powers other than Russia. For many historians of the July crisis, the phrase "mobilization means

44. Ibid., II, 549.
45. Ibid., II, 578.

war" imparts to the events of those days a fatalistic, mechanistic tinge reminiscent of Greek tragedy. Once the armies had begun to prepare, there could be no turning back. For Albertini, this is more than preposterous; it is bad history. Mobilization of the Russian army was equivalent to war from the time of the conclusion of the military components of the Franco-Russian alliance in 1892 until November 1912, when this understanding was explicitly revoked by the tsar. Sazonov knew that the Russian army could remain behind its own frontier in a fully mobilized state for weeks, if necessary. So could the armies of France, Italy, and even Austria-Hungary (which declared war on Serbia on July 28 but told its ally Germany that hostilities could not possibly commence prior to August 12). But for Germany, mobilization *was* equivalent to war because of the inflexibility of the timetable laid down in the Schlieffen Plan, a product of the desperation born of contemplating a war on two fronts.

Should Sazonov not have known that German mobilization would quickly result in the invasion of Belgium and Luxembourg, thereby (at the very least) complicating the situation immensely? In response, Albertini notes that not even Grand Admiral Alfred von Tirpitz knew this in Germany, and it is arguable that the Kaiser was equally uninformed. Russian mobilization was precipitate and catastrophic, but it was a step that was taken not in the certainty that it would lead to war, but in the mistaken belief that it was simply a more dangerous diplomatic maneuver. "Had [Sazonov] known as a mathematical certainty that to order mobilization was to decide irrevocably on war, most probably he would have hesitated yet awhile longer before advising the Tsar to take the step." For this reason, "the final, definite responsibility for the outbreak of the war lies with the German plan of mobilization."[46]

This misunderstanding plagued Sazonov to the end, and Germany did nothing to dispel it. On July 31, when Germany proclaimed the *Kriegsgefahrzustand*, Bethmann, in his own handwriting, drafted the final ultimatum to Russia. Even in this crucial document, he failed to tell Sazonov that for Germany, mobilization was equivalent to war, although it was known in Berlin that such was not the case in the Russian army. "By not making the point plain, Bethmann ran the risk that Sazonov would argue with the Tsar: "But Germany is mobilizing too; we can go on negotiating

---

46. Ibid., II, 581.

and discussing just the same.' And, indeed, . . . that is exactly how he did argue."[47]

This, to Albertini, is an indication that Bethmann had lost all hope of controlling the conflict. He cast his lot with the military on July 31 despite favorable news from Lichnowsky, who was reporting (DD 489) that England was not irrevocably committed to the Russian position and that the *Halt in Belgrade* remained a viable alternative to European war. Albertini criticizes Bethmann severely for having failed to recognize this opportunity to split England off from France and Russia and in the process gain acceptance of Austria's right to punish Serbia. But if these had been his intentions at one time, they were so no longer. German mobilization brought the timetables into play and rendered diplomacy superfluous.

Concluding his labors, Albertini assigns the lion's share of responsibility for the outbreak of war to the Central Powers. Germany wanted a localized war from the beginning and urged the Austrians forward; Bethmann undercut Grey's mediation attempts and his own emperor's peace plan; the German military, with its rigid expectations embodied in the Schlieffen Plan, deprived the diplomats of the flexibility necessary to work out a reasonable compromise. Austria, for its part, was not a reluctant partner. Berchtold used German pressure to convince doubters in his own government, framed an unacceptable ultimatum, and resisted all efforts to settle the dispute peacefully, even when Germany itself urged compromise. But the Entente is not without its share of the blame. Sazonov may be excused for not knowing the implications of German mobilization, but not for remaining ignorant of the specific details of his own, particularly for failing to understand that partial mobilization was impossible. He panicked on July 29 and escalated the crisis irreparably through general mobilization. In England, Grey misunderstood the entire crisis, neglecting to warn Germany in time and simultaneously failing to restrain St. Petersburg and Paris. Poincaré, of course, was no help either. He gave the Russians as much slack as possible and did nothing to lead them to believe that France would be anything less than an enthusiastic participant in whatever European complications might ensue. As for Serbia, although its responsibility is not paramount, it balked at any sign of remorse for the archduke's murder and refused to cooperate with Vienna in any meaningful way. Belgrade probably should have

47. Ibid., III, 41.

accepted the ultimatum in toto, although here Albertini sees the fine hand of St. Petersburg in stiffening Serbia's will to resist.

This all too brief condensation does no justice to the richness of Albertini's work. His insights, precision, erudition, and prejudices must be experienced at first hand if the reader is to appreciate the full flavor and scope of his accomplishment. *The Origins of the War of 1914* represents the zenith of the antirevisionist school, useful not only for what it does, but for what it does *not* do. For Albertini, "The fact is that the question of the origins of the war is an entirely different one from that of the rights and wrongs of the war. The latter is an immense problem which we do not set ourselves to solve. All that we can affirm . . . is that even if one or both of the Central Powers had sufficient reasons for starting a war, it would always have been a wrong decision on their part to do so in conditions unfavorable to themselves, throwing the world into chaos only to bring about their own defeat and ruin."[48] It is here that Harry Barnes goes wrong, confusing the two questions and clouding his judgment with passion. Luigi Albertini elevated the study of the July crisis to a higher plane while providing a marvelous historical resource for which all scholars of the period remain in his debt.

England: A.J.P. Taylor

Albertini, of course, did not have the last word. By examining and distilling the documentary evidence in such detail, he absolved future historians of the necessity of retracing his steps. His work came to constitute a quasi primary source, frequent citation of which freed scholars to delve more deeply into other areas of the crisis and to concentrate on interpretation rather than itemization. This did not take place at once. The conclusion of World War II, the failure of Hitler's dreams, and the consequent destruction of the work of Bismarck left Germany fragmented and weak, no longer a threat to its neighbors and no longer a nation to which the Treaty of Versailles had any practical relevance. The meeting between Soviet and American troops on the Elbe settled the argument between revisionists and antirevisionists and relegated the study of the origins of the Great War to a less passionate context.

For German historians, this was a welcome development. Hitler's monstrosity, fully revealed only after 1945, made it possible for

48. Ibid., II, 136–37.

them to defend German policy in 1914 by contrasting it with Nazi racism and megalomania. Gleefully they joined scholars from other nations in an orgy of Hitler bashing that continues in full flower today, half a century after the invasion of Poland. For scholars in West Germany, the study of the Nazi era could be undertaken with no sense of obligation to defend a man and a party who were obviously outside the realm of ordinary human experience,[49] while those in the German Democratic Republic could denounce the Third Reich in complete ideological respectability. The contrast between 1914 and 1939 seemed so apparent that few paid much attention to it.

One who did concern himself with it was A.J.P. Taylor, fellow of Magdalen College, Oxford, and a diplomatic and political historian of considerable stature and liveliness.[50] In *The Course of German History* (London, 1945), his brilliant *The Struggle for Mastery in Europe, 1848–1918* (New York, 1954), and *War by Time-Table: How the First World War Began* (New York, 1969), he articulated the antirevisionist position in pungent language, simultaneously placing it at the center of what he viewed as a consistent pattern of aggressive conduct on the part of Prussia/Germany from Bismarck's day through 1945. A master of aphorisms ("No war is inevitable until it breaks out"; "Serbia's real crime in Habsburg eyes was to exist"; "Austria-Hungary went to war in 1914 to prove that it was still alive"), he caught the attention of those with an eye for a well-turned phrase as well as those who simply lacked the time or the patience to read Albertini.

Taylor disposes in short order of much of the argumentation surrounding the July crisis. Serbian complicity in the Sarajevo crime is irrelevant to the course of events: Berchtold was determined to have it out even in the absence of any indication of culpability. The fact that such indications were later found has nothing to do with his policy in July 1914. On July 5–6, the Kaiser and Bethmann

---

49. From this grew the oft-repeated obervation that Hitler was insane: he committed insane acts, and if he was insane, then normal, sane people are absolved from any responsibility for his crimes. This concept, while psychologically fascinating, is historically meaningless but nonetheless comforting to many. Congruent to it, and more defensible, is the assertion of Dehio, Meinecke, Ritter, and numerous others that Hitler possessed demonic qualities and acted in ways foreign to traditional norms of human conduct.

50. His full name, Alan John Percivale Taylor, is initialized in keeping with the British custom (a tradition no less unusual than the American custom of tripartite names).

reacted in a purely predictable manner. Their unconditional support for Berchtold seems shocking today, but at the time "no crowned head, the German Emperor least of all, could have told the Austrians that they should disregard the Archduke's assassination."[51] This being said, the fact remains that Germany prodded the Austrians into starting a war with Serbia in full knowledge of possible complications. "They did not decide on war; but they did decide on 5 July to use their superior power either to win a war or to achieve a striking success."[52]

Taylor has little respect for Bethmann's policy. Despite Germany's immense strength, he had developed the idea that his country was declining and that a preventive war would improve its position. But this was attributable not to careful reflection, but to instinctive reaction. Bethmann assumed that Russia would not stand up to Germany (it had, after all, backed down in 1909), and he had "no means of knowing whether Russian resolution or the state of Russian armaments might have changed. He guessed blindly in the void."[53]

Little responsibility rests with France and Britain. Poincaré and Viviani encouraged Sazonov with their reassurances of French support for the Russian alliance, but there is in the record no trace of any intent to precipitate war; their policy was purely reactive. The acrimonious dispute over Grey's ambivalence, on the other hand, is a waste of ink. Grey had no effect whatever on the designs of the continental powers. Germany's war plans required an invasion of Belgium irrespective of the British position. "Indeed they had always assumed that Great Britain would enter the war; they did not take her military weight seriously, and naval questions did not interest them. . . . On the other side, France and Russia decided on war without counting firmly on British support."[54]

What of Bethmann's attempts to restrain Vienna? By July 29 it was clear to him that the crisis was not evolving in a favorable fashion. The localized war had been started, but Russian behavior was not pacific. Now he decided to endorse the *Halt in Belgrade* proposal, which might have worked had he passed it along without prejudice two days earlier. But Berchtold responded, not with

51. A.J.P. Taylor, *War by Time-Table: How the First World War Began* (New York, 1969), 63.
52. Taylor, *The Struggle for Mastery*, 522.
53. Taylor, *War by Time-Table*, 65.
54. Taylor, *The Struggle for Mastery*, 525.

63

compliance with Germany's new wishes, but with general mobilization. With Russia and Austria-Hungary both mobilizing, the German General Staff could wait no longer, and they convinced Bethmann that war was now unavoidable and Germany must think of nothing other than winning it. This explains the decision that Taylor considers crucial: the July 31 proclamation of the *Kriegsgefahrzustand*, a decision made urgently and "almost without debate."[55] Russian and Austrian mobilization had been, in essence, diplomatic moves; but German mobilization meant war. "When cut down to essentials, the sole cause for the outbreak of war in 1914 was the Schlieffen plan. . . . Yet the Germans had no deliberate aim of subverting the liberties of Europe. No one had time for a deliberate aim or time to think. All were trapped by the ingenuity of their military preparations, the Germans most of all."[56]

Taylor's prose is delightful and his interpretation compelling. Certainly the statesmen of July 1914 reacted inadequately to a very serious diplomatic situation, and in so doing wrecked the peace of Europe. Yet his work is not as impressive as his writing makes it sound. "Silly" and "foolish" are overused adjectives in Taylor's lexicon, and his own cavalier disregard for evidence which either does not fit his interpretation or is merely inconvenient leads one to suspect that on occasion those adjectives should be applied to him rather than by him. He simplifies a very complex situation to the point of monocausation, in some ways doing to the antirevisionist position what Harry Barnes did to revisionism. Taylor was the most prominent writer on the July crisis during the 1950s, but the serious student should look elsewhere for a balanced, detailed overview.

Taylor's version of the events of July 1914 was the last major interpretation written before the publication of Fritz Fischer's work (initially in the pages of *Historische Zeitschrift* in 1959 and two years later in monographic form). Methodologically it is thoroughly consistent with all previous stages of what had already become a very long debate. Taylor, like the other historians mentioned to this point, concentrated on political and diplomatic history to the almost complete exclusion of domestic economic and social factors. This emphasis on the primacy of foreign policy in the crisis of July 1914 would soon be challenged by an entire school of historians who would attempt to reorient this debate, and many others, in a

---

55. Taylor, *War by Time-Table*, 96.
56. Ibid., 121.

direction that emphasized the primacy of *domestic* policy. In 1954 this development still lay in the future, but the future was not far off.

In 1961, Taylor continued his pursuit of the theme of continuity in German history by publishing his most controversial work. *The Origins of the Second World War* raised a firestorm of criticism in Britain and America because of Taylor's characterization of Adolf Hitler as "a traditional German statesman" and of Munich as "a triumph for all that was best and most enlightened in British life." The possibility that these assessments might have been unfair to traditional German statesmen and British life rather than favorable to Hitler and Munich occurred to few; most saw in them an exculpation of the Nazi past, astonishing in such a staunch British patriot and anti-appeaser as Taylor. In the same year, across the North Sea, Fritz Fischer published *Griff nach der Weltmacht*, the reaction to which would by comparison trivialize the opposition to Taylor's book.

4

The Hamburg School

Fritz Fischer was an unlikely candidate for the role of disturber of the historical peace on the war-guilt question. Fifty-three years old in 1961, he had spent most of his academic career specializing in early modern European history. He had taken his doctorate under the church historians Erich Seeberg and Hans Lietzmann at the Theological Faculty of the University of Berlin between 1927 and 1934. Named professor of history at the University of Hamburg in 1942, Fischer had produced several articles on Reformation history and German Protestantism, as well as a book entitled (ironically, as it turned out in later years) *Moritz August von Bethmann Hollweg und der deutsche Protestantismus* (Berlin, 1937).[1] His reputation was that of a solid if not particularly distinguished historian.

After the war, Fischer's horizons expanded. He studied in England and the United States and spent the spring of 1955 as a visiting professor at the University of Notre Dame. Becoming interested in questions of objectivity and subjectivity in historiography, he read with interest the writings of Americans like Barnes, Fay, and Schmitt on the outbreak of war in 1914. Upon his return to Hamburg in the fall of 1955, he held seminars on the history of the Great War and interested several of his doctoral students in his work. Shortly thereafter, he was granted permission to consult the German Central Archives (including the archives of the Imperial Chancellery and the Foreign Office's commercial department) and

---

1. Fischer's appointment at Hamburg later became a subject of controversy. His chief antagonist, Gerhard Ritter, called him "an old Nazi" who had gained his chair through party loyalty. Prior to moving to Hamburg, Fischer had held a position as a researcher at Walther Frank's Historical Institute, and his appointment at Hamburg in 1942 could not have been bestowed upon anyone devoid of loyalty to the National Socialist party. Ritter used Fischer's past as a weapon against the latter's interpretation of German foreign policy, although he never succeeded in defining a link between Fischer's previous membership in the NSDAP and a subsequent desire to distort history in a manner unflattering to Germany.

the Prussian State Archives. These deposits are located in Potsdam and Merseburg in the German Democratic Republic, and in the mid-fifties it was virtually impossible for a West German scholar to be admitted to them. Fischer's access to these materials infuriated other West German historians like Gerhard Ritter (although Ritter's student, Hans-Günther Zmarzlik, was later granted entry). He was able as a result of these years of research to locate and publish for the first time significant quantities of previously secret material pertaining to Germany's role in the Great War.

Fischer released portions of his findings in the form of articles, the most noteworthy of which appeared in *Historische Zeitschrift* in 1959.[2] Placing his work in the historiographical perspective created by Hans Gatzke, Erich Volkmann, Gordon Craig, and others, he depicted Germany's war aims as overtly aggressive in nature and drew disturbing parallels between his country's objectives in the two world wars. His views attracted considerable attention within the *Zunft* and led to a rather pointed exchange of correspondence with Gerhard Ritter in 1960. But provocative as his opinions on continuity in German history were, they appeared to be confined to the period covered by the Great War itself (1914–18). Those who held conflicting viewpoints contended with good reason that the objectives of a nation engaged in a major war may bear little resemblance to the aims with which it began the war. Once hostilities have been joined and blood spilled, pressure groups within the government, the military, and civilian society insist that the spoils of war be of a magnitude commensurate with the sacrifices necessary to earn the victory.[3] Fischer, whose reading of the evidence at his disposal led him to believe that these cogent observations did not apply to Wilhelmine Germany, was thereupon forced to delve into the background to the Great War to justify his assertions. He did this in the opening two chapters of his book.

Griff nach der Weltmacht (1961)

For many Germans, *Griff nach der Weltmacht* was one of those rare books which forever alter the perspective and outlook of the

2. Fritz Fischer, "Deutsche Kriegsziele: Revolutionierung und Separatfrieden im Osten, 1914–1918." *Historische Zeitschrift* 188 (1959): 249–310.
3. This had happened to Bismarck, who had not initiated the Franco-Prussian War in order to annex Alsace and Lorraine, but found at the end of the conflict that such annexation was unavoidable.

reader. Most of it dealt with Germany's aims in the First World War
– and that, indeed, would become the English translation of its title.
The original title, "grasping for world power," is of course much
more eye-catching. Yet it was mainly the first two chapters that
proved to be the most controversial: the first discussed the development of German imperialism from a quest for great-power status to
one for world-power standing, while the second analyzed the July
crisis of 1914.

For generations of scholars and educated general readers who had
been brought up on the revisionist gospel of Wegerer and Montgelas, supplemented by foreigners like Barnes and Fay, Fischer's
sledgehammer prose was devastating. Even more intimidating was
the avalanche of evidence, much of it never before published, which
threatened to bury the reader of Fischer's book.[4] Nearly all of this
evidence concerned the work's central theme – the war aims of
Imperial Germany – which may help to explain why much of the
initial criticism of Fischer's thesis centered on the first two chapters.
It would take time and a great deal of additional research to assess
the merits of the war-aims material, but Fischer had written his
initial chapters as an explanatory introduction and had provided a
provocative interpretation based not on new information, but on a
reevaluation of previously disclosed material. For those steeped in
the literature of the July crisis, that material covered familiar
ground.[5]

Fischer's emphasis on German policy is obvious from the outset.
He analyzes the July crisis with scant regard for the actions of any
other country except (to a limited extent) Austria-Hungary. Thus
he provides no assessment of the complicity of the Serbian government in the Sarajevo murders, moving directly to the events of July
5–6 at Potsdam. Here he presents a powerful indictment of German
conduct. The Kaiser and his military and diplomatic advisers urged
the Austrians to act swiftly against Serbia, so swiftly that Serbia
would not have time to evaluate the situation and offer compensa-

4. The quantity of evidence amassed by Fischer led to some amusing incidents on
West German television during the furor concerning his theses. Often one of his
opponents would challenge his interpretation of a particular document. Whenever
this happened, Fischer would simply rummage through his files and pull out another
document which confirmed his original point. This meant that the entire debate took
place on territory laid out by Fischer's research.
5. Fischer's methodology was likewise familiar, consisting of an Albertini-style
arrangement of scores of diplomatic documents, extensive quotations from which
were tied together by transitional paragraphs.

tion to the Dual Monarchy. Such an offer would deprive the Central Powers of the major success which Germany hoped to obtain – at the very least, a huge diplomatic victory not only over Serbia but the Entente also, and perhaps a huge military victory as well. There was no reason to fear the Entente's reaction, for "one of the basic assumptions of German policy in these weeks [was] that Russia and France were still militarily weak enough to enable Germany to weather the crisis, however it developed."[6]

Wilhelm II, of course, could not commit Germany to such a path without the concurrence of his chancellor. The blank check could only be cashed if it bore Bethmann Hollweg's countersignature, and this was provided on July 6. Bethmann echoed Wilhelm's admonition to act speedily, using advantageous international conditions as a warrant for such haste. Fischer joins battle with Fay on this point: Germany was not dragged along behind irresponsible Austria; the emperor hoped for a localized war in which the fate of Serbia was inconsequential. The purpose of the conflict was to split the Entente, thereby bringing about a new alignment in the Balkans that would favor Germany and Austria. It would also implement by force the grasp for world power that Germany had pursued for more than a decade but had thus far failed to attain.

Fischer grounds his interpretation of German policy on his conviction that the German government was convinced of British neutrality in any Austro-Serb war. His chapter on the July crisis is entitled "Germany and the Outbreak of War: The Miscalculation on British Neutrality." The Kaiser was unwilling to be confused by the evidence: when Pourtalès transmitted Sazonov's remark that Britain would object to Austria's policy toward Serbia and that British intervention in such a dispute was likely, Wilhelm's marginal notes on the document indicate a refusal to entertain the notion that Sazonov might be right. Yet, says Fischer, Germany knew all too well that Russia could not remain indifferent to the fate of Serbia. Hopefully Russia would make a fuss and then back away, as had happened during the Bosnian crisis in 1909; but if not, then Germany could contemplate a war against Russia and France with equanimity, provided that Britain stood clear.

German policy thus followed a consistent path from July 5 until the delivery of the ultimatum. Jagow pressed the Austrians for full

6. Fritz Fischer, *Germany's Aims in the First World War* (New York, 1967), 54. All quotations are taken from this English-language edition, reduced by about one-third from the original edition.

details of the ultimatum, not with a view toward moderating them but with the intention of assuring Berlin that the terms were unacceptable. Count Hoyos obligingly confirmed this on July 18, and when the actual text arrived on the evening of July 22, Germany made no protest. Once Belgrade's reply had been rejected, Bethmann set to work to localize the conflict and prevent British attempts at mediation. Only very late in the crisis did he come to realize that British intervention was likely. As late as July 27–28 he consciously accepted the risk of continental war, trying to gain the most advantageous possible position for Germany by putting Russia in the wrong and keeping the British out.

Bethmann's policy broke down on July 29. In a late-evening conversation with British ambassador Sir Edward Goschen, the chancellor made his famous attempt to secure British neutrality in return for Germany's promise to respect the territorial integrity of France. Goschen's telegram outlining this proposal shocked Grey into the realization that Germany was willing to fight both France and Russia over the Serbian question. This confirmed the wisdom of the warning he had issued earlier that day to Lichnowsky, whose telegram to Bethmann was deciphered and handed to the chancellor just after Goschen had left. "Its contents for the first time shook the whole structure of Bethmann Hollweg's diplomacy, the cornerstone of which had been the hope of British neutrality."[7]

Now Bethmann was up against it. As Jagow had told French ambassador Jules Cambon on July 26, the Foreign Office was certain that Britain would remain neutral. Lichnowsky's telegram, by calling this belief into question, destroyed what had been the foundation of German policy since July 5. Bethmann panicked and sent DD 395 and 396 to Tschirschky in the early morning of July 30, calling on Vienna to change course and negotiate. Fischer notes that many German historians have used these telegrams to demonstrate that German policy was pacific, but he is skeptical: "The significant thing about them is not so much Bethmann Hollweg's urgent attempt to get Vienna to accept the British proposals as the fact that they find no parallel among the documents of the night of July 29–30 or of July 30 itself. . . . [T]hey are the products of the shock born of the unexpected information about Britain's attitude."[8]

7. Ibid., 78.
8. Ibid., 79.

Even at this desperate hour, Bethmann remained reluctant to alter course completely. Berlin had pressed Vienna so consistently since July 5 that it would have taken more than two midnight messages to Tschirschky to convince Berchtold to reverse himself now. Neither the foreign minister nor Count Tisza was anxious to accommodate this sudden, drastic shift in German policy, which was urged on the Ballhausplatz in a less than convincing manner. "The essential point was that although the premises of Bethmann Hollweg's policy . . . had collapsed, he could not steel himself to change his policy, to talk unambiguously to Vienna and to force it to obey him."[9] If Bethmann really wanted Austria to climb down, he would have to threaten to withdraw German support in the event of Russian intervention. This would have gotten Berchtold's undivided attention and probably would have prevented a war that Germany would have to wage in highly unfavorable circumstances. But Bethmann did nothing of the sort, and once he recovered his nerve on the morning of July 30, he resumed his previous course, this time emphasizing Russian guilt not for the purpose of securing British neutrality but to neutralize the German Social Democrats and obtain their support for the war. The late-night telegrams to Tschirschky were the product of momentary panic rather than any profound alteration in strategy.

Bethmann's attitude toward the Social Democrats is central to Fischer's argument. The German government, like the French, feared possible socialist sabotage of any war effort and had considered the possibility of arresting prominent socialist leaders and opinion makers should hostilities break out.[10] Wilhelm II and some of his more belligerent military associates favored the use of the state-of-siege regulations to effect this, but Bethmann and his staff feared that such action would make martyrs of the socialist leadership and split German society on the eve of a major war. To avoid this, on July 24 he authorized State Secretary Clemens von Delbrück to prevail upon the appropriate civilian and military

9. Ibid., 80. This at least is Fischer's interpretation of the available documents. There were, of course, other channels of communication between Berlin and Vienna. Kurt Riezler, Bethmann's personal secretary, noted in his diary that the chancellor spent long hours on the telephone in those days. Did he talk to Berchtold directly? What did they talk about? How forcefully did Bethmann express himself? We have no way of knowing.

10. For French plans in this respect, centering on the notorious *Carnet B*, see most recently Philippe Bernard and Henri Dubief, *The Decline of the Third Republic, 1914–1938* (Cambridge, U.K., 1985), 3–7.

authorities to exercise restraint. Four days later, the chancellor himself met with Albert Südekum of the SPD's right wing and urged him to impress upon the socialist leadership the importance of their support for the government, failing which the military elements would gain the upper hand in the crisis and Russian belligerence would be buttressed. The seeds of the *Burgfrieden* were being sown.[11]

In these circumstances, Russian general mobilization was indeed important, but not in the sense usually advanced by historians. Resigned to British intervention and a world war, Bethmann had now capitulated to the General Staff, which after noon on July 30 demanded immediate proclamation of the *Kriegsgefahrzustand*. The chancellor fobbed off Moltke until the morning of July 31, when it was agreed that the appropriate orders should be given upon confirmation that Russia had, as rumored, ordered general mobilization. When such confirmation arrived at noon, "Bethmann Hollweg's courage in waiting for Russia to order general mobilization had thus reaped its reward: the German people was [sic] ready for war in the conviction that it had been gratuitously assailed. Sazonov had put this trump into his hand."[12]

Fischer's conclusions are as straightforward and uncompromising as his narrative.

As Germany willed and coveted the Austro-Serbian war and, in her confidence in her military superiority, deliberately faced the risk of a conflict with Russia and France, her leaders must bear a substantial share of the historical responsibility for the outbreak of general war in 1914. This responsibility is not diminished by the fact that at the last moment Germany tried to arrest the march of destiny, for her efforts to influence Vienna were due exclusively to the threat of British intervention and, even so, they were half-hearted, belated and immediately revoked.[13]

Berlin's decision to run the risk of a continental war was taken by the Kaiser, the Foreign Office, and the General Staff in early July; but beyond this, it was endorsed wholeheartedly by the imperial chancellor, who bore sole responsibility for such action according to the German Constitution and who persevered in his policy even when the emperor himself weakened. The arguments of earlier

11. Fischer develops this argument more fully in *War of Illusions*.
12. Fischer, *Germany's Aims*, 86.
13. Ibid., 88.

German historians that Germany was pursued in July 1914 by fate, destiny, tragedy, and doom are untenable. The entire German government consciously embarked upon a path which it knew might lead to war with Russia and France, hoping along the way for British neutrality but resolved to run the risk anyway.

This is Fischer's *first interpretation* of the July crisis, published in 1961. To anyone familiar with the literature we have already examined, it is at first glance unexceptional. Imanuel Geiss later wrote that Fischer came to his conclusions "just by picking up Albertini and reading the documents published since 1919" – elementary steps that few German historians had taken.[14] His contention that Germany bears "a substantial share of the historical responsibility for the outbreak of general war in 1914" surprised no one conversant with Albertini's arguments and is not substantively different from the conclusions reached by Renouvin and Schmitt. Why then did this chapter cause such an uproar in Germany?

The Controversy over Fischer's Views

A generation after the argument began, it is tempting to characterize it as "Fischer and his students (the so-called Hamburg school)" versus "traditional German historians." Tempting, but inaccurate. Fischer's work received favorable reviews from a number of prominent German publications, including *Der Monat*, *Die Zeit*, and *Der Spiegel*. And even though most members of the *Zunft* sided against him, they did so with varying degrees of disagreement. A few, like Hans Rothfels, declared flatly that the traditional interpretation of July 1914 had survived Fischer's challenge and needed no revision. Others, led by the venerable and highly respected Gerhard Ritter, agreed with Fischer that patriotic self-censorship and apologetics were historically invalid; Michael Freund went so far as to characterize such versions as *Unschuldlüge*, "the not-guilty lie," a play on *Kriegsschuldlüge*, "the war-guilt lie."[15] Having conceded this, they defended most of the components of the traditional approach. Finally, historians like Karl Dietrich Erdmann and Egmont Zechlin (in work we shall discuss in chapter 5) scrapped the revisionist line

---

14. Imanuel Geiss, "The Outbreak of the First World War and German War Aims," in Walter Laqueur and George L. Mosse, eds., *1914: The Coming of the First World War* (New York, 1966), 75.

15. Ibid., 75.

entirely in favor of a synthesis that adopted some elements of Fischer's analysis.

Lack of a unified opposition did not prevent those opposed to the Hamburg school from engaging in vitriolic personal attacks against Fischer. Gerhard Ritter was not the worst offender here, but because of his professional stature his remarks were widely disseminated and quoted as authoritative. He referred to Fischer as "an old Nazi" who had gained his chair at Hamburg through the NSDAP apparatus.[16] At the Congress of the German Historical Association in West Berlin in 1964, Ritter accused Fischer of fabrication of sources and deliberate misreading of evidence. Fischer struck back, contending that "Ritter's intellectual tradition [is] the tradition of apologetic journalism and historiography which began in 1914 or 1918 and which regarded it as a national duty not to clarify and analyze but to justify, or at least 'understand,' the evolution and the actions of the Prusso-German national state."[17] This was clearly unfair because, since 1945, Ritter had been a persistent critic of that tradition and had modified many of the positions that he himself had held before the Second World War. This increasingly strident character assassination was mirrored in exchanges between Fischer and other less prominent historians. The results were a poisoning of the entire debate and a radicalizing of Fischer's own position on the July crisis that would be elaborated in his second book.

Students of the crisis must not, however, succumb to the temptation to view the debate in terms of personal vilification; in such circumstances "it is hard not to feel obliged to take sides with one or the other party."[18] This would be a mistake, not least because it would obscure rather than clarify the substantive issues at stake in the debate over Fischer's work. Six of the most frequently discussed areas of dispute are analyzed below.

1. Errors and Exaggeration in Fischer's Work

Ritter, Zechlin, Hans Herzfeld, Golo Mann, and others identified a number of mistakes and overstatements in the second chapter of *Griff nach der Weltmacht.* Some of these were obvious blunders which Fischer promptly corrected in subsequent German editions

16. See above, chapter 4, n. 1.

17. Fritz Fischer, *World Power or Decline*, trans. Lancelot Farrar, Robert Kimber, and Rita Kimber (New York, 1974), 96.

18. James Joll, "The 1914 Debate Continues: Fritz Fischer and His Critics," *Past and Present* 34 (1966): 110.

prior to the release of the English version quoted here. Others involved mistakes in judging sources and were changed in Fischer's second book, *War of Illusions*. Still others were depicted as errors but were really interpretations with which the critic could not agree. This was particularly true with reference to Bethmann Hollweg, as Fischer and Ritter examined documents which could be read two ways, depending on the reader's view of the motives, aims, and character of the chancellor. These Fischer refused to "correct," asserting that he was as entitled to his interpretation as Ritter was to his.

Fischer's defenders were quick to point to errors and apologetics in Ritter's four-volume *The Sword and the Scepter*, in which he sets forth his own interpretation of the July crisis. A number of such mistakes do exist, and Ritter, who died in 1967, was unable to correct them prior to the publication of the English edition of his work. Hansjoachim Koch, editor of an extremely valuable collection of excerpts and full-length articles relevant to the dispute and himself a bitter critic of Fischer, points out that Fischer's and Ritter's errors stem at least in part from defects "inherent in the German university system where it is quite customary for a professor to send his assistants and/or PhD candidates into the archives to carry out the basic research for 'their professor's work.'"[19]

Such mistakes, although regrettable and certainly avoidable, invalidate neither Fischer's nor Ritter's work. Despite their personal animosity, neither was immune to the reasoned arguments of the other. Fischer corrected the errors which Ritter and others pointed out, while Ritter (had he lived longer) would surely have done the same and indeed did make substantial modifications in his interpretations in light of Fischer's research.

2. Fischer's Exclusive Concentration on German Policy

Chapter 2 of *Griff nach der Weltmacht* is written with scant reference to the other powers involved in the July crisis. German historians denounced this preoccupation with German responsibility as evidence of Fischer's feelings of guilt for Germany's role in 1914 and as a serious methodological distortion bound to lead to a slanted view of the crisis. British and American historians joined the *Zunft* in the latter criticism, which Fischer himself had anticipated

---

19. H.W. Koch, "Introduction," in Koch, *Origins*, 9. This procedure is not unheard of in American graduate schools, and there is no basis for smugness on the subject among American readers.

in the introduction to the first (German) edition of his book: "Some may regret the absence of continued reference to the war aims of Germany's enemies. But, firstly, the British, French, and Russian archives have not yet been opened to the public for the period after 1914; secondly, the war aims of each of these states would require a separate book."[20] What he implied here, but did not state explicitly, was that the chapter on the July crisis was incidental to the purpose of his book and had been included solely to provide background information essential to his interpretation of the war aims of Imperial Germany. The archives of Britain, France, and Russia *were* open for the period covered by the July crisis, but a full-scale reinterpretation of that crisis was not Fischer's intent.

Fischer's critics stated with justification that his chapter did not present a balanced portrayal of the crisis. His defenders asserted that this was a task best left to others and that Fischer should not be criticized for *not* having written a different book. James Joll, Fischer's most influential supporter in England, went so far as to depict such criticism as "a silly line of attack."[21] A useful approach might be to recognize that within the context of Fischer's book, his chapter on July 1914 is helpful and appropriate. Standing by itself, as it was never meant to do, it would present a thoroughly inadequate portrayal of the July crisis.

3. Fischer's Alleged Use of Marxist Analysis

This might appear a strange criticism of someone whom Ritter had reproached for his activities in the Third Reich; but the allegation reflected the charged atmosphere of the Fischer controversy during the 1960s when most West German historians still believed that German foreign policy before 1914 had been determined by the country's exposed geographic position and external pressures exerted by hostile neighbors. Fischer, by contrast, had turned more and more to explaining German *Weltpolitik* in terms of domestic pressures and conflicts. But the Hamburg historian did not adopt a

---

20. Fischer, *Germany's Aims*, xxii. A generation after Fischer's disclaimer, only a few works of any significance on the war aims of other powers have appeared. See in particular V.H. Rothwell, *British War Aims and Peace Diplomacy, 1914–1918* (Oxford, 1971); D. Stevenson, *French War Aims against Germany, 1914–1919* (Oxford, 1982); Pierre Renouvin, "Les buts de guerre du gouvernement français," *Revue Historique* 234 (1966); and Horst Günther Linke, "Russlands Weg in der Ersten Weltkrieg und Seine Kriegsziele, 1914–1917," *Militärgeschichtliche Mitteilungen* 2 (1982): 9–34.
21. Joll, "The 1914 Debate Continues," 108.

Marxist class conflict model or even speak of a capitalist ruling class struggling to deal with the contradictions of an advanced (monopoly) capitalism. Instead he stressed the influence of the powerful agrarians and, if anything, operated with elite-group theory. All this did not prevent the Marxist label from occasionally being applied by his opponents.

Nor did it help that Fischer's case *was* unusual. He had been the first West German historian to be granted access to a number of archival deposits located in the East.[22] The information he culled from those sources proved highly embarrassing to those who believed in Germany's innocence in 1914, a group that included the West German government. In the spring of 1964, at the urging of a number of prominent historians, Foreign Minister Gerhard Schröder withdrew funds that had already been committed by the Goethe-Institut, the German Cultural Institute, for a scheduled lecture tour by Fischer in the United States.[23] Wolfgang Mommsen, whose trenchant criticism of Fischer's work has proved highly valuable to historians, registered his disgust in 1966 at the reprinting in an official government bulletin of Eugen Gerstenmaier's denunciation of the Fischer thesis.[24] Why *was* Fischer admitted to the East German archives, if not to undermine the "official" West German view of Germany's innocence in 1914?

Beyond these suspicions, Fischer's opponents pointed to the very nature of his methodology. His emphasis on structural analysis at the expense of the history of great personalities seemed profoundly Marxist in orientation. Karl-Heinz Janssen, a pupil of Gerhard Ritter, remarked that at the aforementioned Congress of the German Historical Association in 1964, Fischer and his associates were received enthusiastically by young historians and their students. These onlookers viewed Fischer's thesis less as a contribution to the ongoing controversy over war guilt than as a revolutionary act. They "believed like the conservative Ritter that Fischer was basically applying a Marxist approach to German history, although not

22. See above.

23. The decision evoked a wave of criticism, and the trip was eventually funded by the American Council of Learned Societies. Volker Berghahn, in a letter to the author on November 15, 1989, points out that the cancellation of the trip had nothing to do with Fischer's use of East German archives, but with the use he made of them to (according to Gerhard Ritter) blacken the image of Germany abroad.

24. Wolfgang J. Mommsen, "The Debate on German War Aims," in Walter Laqueur and George L. Mosse, eds., *1914: The Coming of the First World War* (New York, 1966), 68.

admitting he was a Marxist, as this would have denied him any prospect of success in West Germany from the outset."[25]

The Hamburg school, which did not remain silent on the question of Fischer's alleged Nazi connections, countered these assertions vigorously. And a careful reading of Fischer's work indicates that he is hardly a Marxist. As Wolfgang Mommsen has pointed out, Fischer lays the blame for Germany's imperialistic policy not merely at the feet of the great industrialists and the ruling classes, but on the doorstep of the German people as a whole. The extreme left of the SPD either supported government policy or exercised scant influence on what occurred in 1914. And Fischer's controversial contention that Germany bears the lion's share of responsibility for the outbreak of war – a conclusion that, as we shall see, was later extended to imply *sole* responsibility – contrasts sharply with the Marxist-Leninist view that "all capitalist states are inexorably driven to war."[26] If Fischer's work is juxtaposed with a classic of Marxist historical exegesis, Fritz Klein's *Deutschland im Ersten Weltkrieg*, the inconsistencies are inescapable. This collaborative work is based on Leninist theories of imperialist behavior, which hold that Germany's responsibility for the outbreak of war derives from the unusually aggressive character of German imperialism. All states were in some respect guilty, but Germany's lack of desirable colonies and its inbred Junker militarism made her variant of imperialism particularly rabid.[27]

Based on this comparison, Fischer's work seems no more Marxist than that of Sidney Fay, which also considers social and economic factors (although in a more rudimentary manner than *Griff nach der Weltmacht*) and which at least assigns a share of responsibility to all parties. Fischer's use of Marxist analysis in some portions of his work is undeniable, but it would be difficult to find a modern social historian whose scholarship is free from such a debt. The salient point is that Fischer's writings are not those of a scholar shackled to an outdated and dogmatic worldview by preconceived notions.[28]

25. Karl-Heinz Janssen, "Gerhard Ritter: A Patriotic Historian's Justification," in H.W. Koch, ed., *The Origins of the First World War*, 2nd ed. (London, 1984), 294.

26. Mommsen, "The Debate," 69.

27. Fritz Klein, ed., *Deutschland im Ersten Weltkrieg*, 3 vols. (Berlin, 1968).

28. Nor would this be a fair criticism of many Marxists today. Geoff Eley, for instance, presents in his writings a "flexible Marxist" approach to structural problems of Wilhelmine Germany. In such a framework, not only historians like Fischer, but also Hans-Ulrich Wehler and Fritz Klein are methodologically suspect. See Geoff Eley, *From Unification to Nazism: Reinterpreting the German Past* (Boston, 1986).

4. Fischer's Interpretation of Bethmann Hollweg

For Gerhard Ritter, this issue and the one that follows were the most galling of Fischer's distortions. Bethmann Hollweg had always been protrayed as an enigmatic, Hamlet-like figure, a philosopher-statesman in a world dominated by strutting militarists and an overly emotional emperor. After 1945, historians as diverse as Ritter, Meinecke, Herzfeld, Rothfels, and Zechlin had united in their characterization of Bethmann as "an honourable German statesman who was conscientiously trying to preserve the security of his country and was genuinely concerned to preserve world peace."[29] He had played a shadowy but in no way sinister role on July 5–6 and had attempted to restrain Austria-Hungary when general war threatened. During the war itself, he had opposed the militarists on a variety of issues, including the resumption of unrestricted submarine warfare and had finally been ousted in favor of the military dictatorship of Hindenburg and Ludendorff in 1917. Germany's two twentieth-century defeats and all its modern crimes and blunders were attributable to men like *them* and not to decent, upright civilians like Bethmann.

Fischer's book blew this traditional interpretation into very small pieces. Bethmann emerges from its pages not as a peace-loving statesman trapped and eventually destroyed by Germany's tragic destiny, but as a chief architect of that destiny, a calm, dispassionate planner who was resigned to the necessity of war as the only way out of Germany's encirclement by the Entente. Thus Bethmann was a key player on July 5–6 rather than a bystander; he egged the Austrians on and urged them to declare war on Serbia more than two weeks before they could possibly invade it; and his last-ditch efforts to initiate negotiations were never intended to succeed, but were motivated solely by the desire to put Russia in the wrong so that England would remain neutral and the Social Democrats would support the government's policy.

So far, all this is familiar to readers of Renouvin, Schmitt, and Albertini as well as Fischer. But Fischer goes much farther. "He . . . solved the problem . . . of why the 'moderate' Bethmann made such frequent and seemingly unaccountable concessions to the 'extremists,' by the simple device of showing that Bethmann was something of an extremist himself."[30] Here Fischer's chapter on the July crisis

29. Moses, *The Politics of Illusion*, 116.
30. Klaus Epstein, "German War Aims in the First World War," *World Politics* 15 (1962): 171.

cannot be separated from the rest of his argument. By presenting an imposing array of evidence, much of it never before published, in support of his contention that Bethmann was an enthusiastic proponent of Germany's annexationist schemes between 1914 and 1917, he locates the chancellor's actions of July 1914 in a consistent pattern of activity designed to expand Germany's territorial boundaries and make it a "world power" equivalent to Great Britain, Russia and the United States.

It was this depiction of Bethmann as a coldly calculating expansionist that so dismayed Ritter, Zechlin, and others. Fischer's constant repetition of what he perceived as continuity in German policy in the twentieth century (part of the sixth issue, to be discussed below) blended with his portrayal of Bethmann to suggest to them that he was equating the Reich chancellor of 1909–17 with his successor of 1933–45. They accused Fischer of conjuring up a deliberately falsified image of Bethmann as a man who consciously provoked a world war for atrocious, indefensible purposes. Why had Fischer done this? According to Ritter, to assuage his own feelings of guilt over Hitler's crimes (and, by implication, over his own complicity in those crimes as an alleged Nazi), he had willfully distorted the German past and located roots of Nazism in the Wilhelmine Reich. This colossal deception had been conceived and carried out for the ignoble purpose of permitting Fischer to salve his own conscience. A man like Ritter, who considered his own anti-Nazi credentials impeccable (he had belonged to the Confessing Church, had hidden Carl Goerdeler in his own house after the failure of the plot to kill Hitler, and had been spared conviction and execution as a conspirator only because an Allied bomb blew up the courthouse and the examining magistrate charged with judging his case), could never condone such action.[31]

Fischer's assessment of Bethmann goes much too far, as we will see in chapter 5. His interpretation is grounded in a tendency to see deliberation and consistency where less committed scholars often see confusion and uncertainty. He cannot accept the possibility that Bethmann felt obliged to support Austria or risk losing Germany's only ally, although such motives are by no means incompatible with

31. Ritter and Goerdeler, of course, came to their anti-Nazi stances only *after* Hitler had been in power for several years. Ritter's assessment of Fischer's motives misses the point that Fischer, like many other Germans, changed his mind about National Socialism and learned a number of bitter lessons from the experience of the Third Reich.

the contention that Bethmann pressured Austria to act swiftly and aggressively against Serbia. His conclusions are defensible and arguable, but so are Ritter's, and those of Zechlin are for many analysts more plausible than either of the foregoing. Yet Fischer was not as harsh with Bethmann as Ritter contended; his "point was really much more subtle, and less dependent on personalities."[32] He was willing to concede that Bethmann may not have been a committed imperialist and may have had profound misgivings about Germany's course of action. But for Fischer, Bethmann's personal feelings are irrelevant; only his conduct as a public figure can be judged by the historian (the rest constitutes material for the biographer).

Ironically, Fischer's effort to revise the traditional interpretation of Bethmann by concentrating on events rather than personalities was widely viewed as an effort to vilify Bethmann's character. It is on his analysis of the events of July 1914 that the reader's judgment of this issue must turn, and while that analysis is defensible, it cannot be proven conclusively for the available evidence can easily be read to support other, less drastic positions.

5. Who Supported Aggression in 1914?

Germany's defeat in 1945, combined with Hitler's emasculation of the General Staff and the officer corps, had thoroughly discredited Prussian militarism. Patriotic German historians henceforth felt free to delineate fully the negative effects of militarism on Germany, a congenial task for those who, like Gerhard Ritter, had long despised it. It became an article of faith within the *Zunft* that prior to 1914 a gulf had existed between the objectives of the German political leadership and general public, on the one hand, and the Great General Staff on the other. Bethmann was in many ways the victim of this dichotomy, and when Fischer presented his revisionist view of Bethmann's role in July 1914, its implications for the prevailing interpretation of the civilian/military split were immediately understood.

Fischer demonstrated, relentlessly and implacably, that Germany's policy during the July crisis was not divided into two parts – a defensive orientation form July 5–30, followed by reluctant acceptance of belligerency once Russian general mobilization

---

32. Norman Stone, "Gerhard Ritter and the First World War," *Historical Journal* 13 (1970): 166.

occurred. Instead, he outlined a coherent, consistently offensive strategy directed by the civilian authorities from the outset. Moltke's infamous intervention on the afternoon of July 30, when he pressed the Austro-Hungarian military attaché to urge Vienna to mobilize at once, and his follow-up telegram to Austrian chief of staff Franz Freiherr Conrad von Hötzendorf along the same lines at 7:45 A.M. the following day, are portrayed by Fischer as consistent with the spirit of the strategy employed since July 5. Far from being an attempt to override the chancellor's policy, as even Albertini thinks, Moltke's action was easily understandable in light of his concern with the rigid scheduling required for the implementation of the Schlieffen Plan. It was not opposed in any way by Bethmann (who forced Moltke to delay the *Kriegsgefahrzustand* for purely tactical reasons rather than any profound disagreement over strategy), and it had no significant impact on the course of events.

Beyond this (which was bad enough from Ritter's perspective), the entire thrust of Fischer's account not only posits an identity between civilian and military objectives in July 1914, but between their shared goals and the hopes and dreams of German society. Wolfgang Mommsen saw in this the most striking aspect of the Fischer thesis: "The most important part of the argument is the attempt to prove that the views of the political leaders did not differ significantly from those of the military leaders but that, on the contrary, their common aim of fighting for German world power was in complete harmony with the desires of the overwhelming majority of the German people."[33] Ritter could not control his rage. If Fischer's argument held, then what would become of the conviction, which Ritter shared with millions of Germans, that Germany went to war in 1914 for purely defensive reasons out of fear of encirclement by the Entente? The General Staff may have broken the leash in late July, but this was no justification for an indictment of the civilian authorities, who had lost control of the situation by that point but who had never planned for such a catastrophe. Yet that was exactly what Fischer was doing.

Ritter struck back in a highly charged review of Fischer's book in *Historische Zeitschrift*. "But was our goal really [splitting the Entente and expelling Russia from the Balkans] rather than the maintenance of our Austrian ally as a great power? In other words, is the German policy of 1914 to be understood as aggressive or

33. Mommsen, "The Debate," 53.

defensive?"[34] Fischer knows that it was defensive, yet he quotes documents selectively in support of a preconceived, dastardly distortion. The civilian government in Berlin was not motivated by militaristic ambition, but by the perfectly understandable desire for self-defense. Ritter charges Fischer with an attempt to warp the views of younger generations of Germans, concluding his review on a lachrymose note. Fischer, in response, notes Ritter's use of the word "our" when referring to German actions in July 1914 and accuses him of demonstrating "a constant personal involvement, a constant desire to understand and forgive every action of the Germans, who seem to him to need understanding and forgiveness."[35] In Fischer's opinion, Ritter's emotional involvement with Bethmann's position dates from his military service in the Great War and his innate patriotic-conservative standpoint, a perspective that Fischer rejects.

This issue is central to a proper understanding of Fischer's impact on German historical thought. In rejecting the traditionally conceived dichotomy between military goals and those of civilian society, he held before German eyes the appalling possibility that their faults lay not in their stars but in themselves. If Fischer's interpretation held, then civilian elites[36] were just as guilty as Moltke, Falkenhayn, and Ludendorff in acting belligerently in 1914. And the evidence he presented in defense of this position, while not absolutely conclusive, was so extensive and internally consistent that it could not be wished away. In the last analysis, each reader must judge this issue on an individual basis, since the evidence can be read in many ways. But however one ultimately decided, the fact that Fischer had raised the question in the first place was emotionally devastating.

6. The Political Implications of Fischer's Work
Growing out of the previous issue, this concern led to the aforementioned involvement of the Bonn government in the debate.

34. Gerhard Ritter, "Eine neue Kriegsschuldthese?" *Historische Zeitschrift* 194 (1962): 657.
35. Fischer, *World Power or Decline*, 114.
36. Fischer employs sociological categories in much of his work. Whereas a Marxist scholar would use the term "ruling class" to refer to officials like Bethmann, Jagow, Zimmermann, and their associates, Fischer uses the term "elites," a far broader category which also encompasses members of the right-wing patriotic and conservative associations whose impact on German policymaking he indicts so vigorously.

Fischer's book destroyed the revisionist position in Germany for all but a few scholars; Ritter, Zechlin, Herzfeld, and others quickly abandoned it, although refusing to admit that Fischer's evidence had forced them to do so. This meant that the Adenauer government's oft-stated position on German reunification had become untenable. If the Versailles treaty was in fact correct, or at least essentially correct, in its view of German responsibility for the outbreak of the Great War, then German claims that the treaty was unfair were obviously without foundation. Now the government had tacitly endorsed the assertions of Ritter and others that the Nazi period represented an inexplicable aberration in German history and that the Bismarckian Reich should someday be restored, since Germany should not be punished eternally because of the atrocities perpetrated by an unrepresentative gang of thugs. But if the Second Reich was just as guilty as the Third of imperialistic, aggressive expansionism, the moral arguments for German reunification lacked validity. Gerhard Schröder's denial of funds for Fischer's 1964 lecture tour was obviously motivated by more than academic concerns: the Bonn government had no interest in seeing Fischer's views propagated in the United States.

Thus in a very genuine sense, Fischer undermined the anti-Versailles cause which had long been espoused by various German governments and by the *Zunft*. It is, however, permissible to inquire, so what? Given the Cold War and the balance-of-power requirements of NATO and the Warsaw Pact, what chance did German reunification have anyway? Fischer may have betrayed this cherished ideal, but it would never have been achieved in 1961 in any case. True enough, but Fischer's crime transcended these considerations. Continuity was his watchword, and continuity was a concept the mention of which sent many Germans screaming into the night.

Obviously, any suggestion that Bismarck's work found its fulfillment in Hitler would be repudiated by historians who looked on German unification as a sacred achievement, as well as by an educated general public which had grown up revering the Iron Chancellor as the father of his country. Additionally, any suggestion that Imperial Germany was primarily responsible for the Great War would make it difficult to maintain that the Nazis were unprincipled barbarians who had warped and perverted a cultured, refined, and peace-loving nation. But Fischer went beyond even this. *Griff nach der Weltmacht* never mentioned Hitler's name, but the massive documentation presented there virtually compelled the reader to suspect that Nazi ideas and ambitions were deeply rooted in the German past. This would have been intolerable had Fischer merely attributed such ideas to the German elites; but he held before the eyes of the public the appalling possibility that those ideas had been endorsed enthusiastically by a large number of Germans prior to 1918.

If Fischer's contentions were true, there was nowhere to hide. Hitler was not some kind of monster utterly divorced from German culture, some sort of bohemian Austrian who had mesmerized Germany and imposed upon it a vicious, demagogic, un-German dictatorship. Instead, he was what he had originally claimed, a drummer for nationalistic and imperialistic ambitions long accepted in Germany, the frustration of which in 1918 had left Germans brokenhearted. This, if true, would explain much of Hitler's appeal to the German people: he was giving them what they had long desired. He was not a Martian after all, not an Austrian, but a German.

This was strong medicine, and the reluctance of patriotic German historians to swallow it is not to be wondered at. For Ritter, Zechlin, and Erdmann, to say nothing of extreme right-wingers like Erwin Hölzle, Fischer was more than a mistaken historian: he was a dangerously misguided man who cared nothing for his own country. The Hamburg school, of course, disagreed profoundly. In their view "it is possible for a dissenter still to be a patriot. Fischer's historiographical aim is directed at cementing democratic values among his countrymen by pointing to the catastrophic results of earlier anti-democratic values."[37] This of course helps to explain Fischer's popularity in Great Britain, where many had long contended that Germany must come to grips with its authoritarian past in order to build a stable democracy in the aftermath of war.

These six issues, in conjunction with other subsidiary concerns which space does not permit me to mention, opened a gaping chasm between the Hamburg school and its opponents. The latter felt that they had been left orphans by an unscrupulous propagandist who, not content with denouncing the evil portions of their nation's history, had defamed its achievements as well. The former saw themselves as knights on horseback, just as German as their opponents and anxious to build a new, egalitarian democracy on the ruins of imperialistic ambition. Sebastian Haffner, author of the

37. Moses, *The Politics of Illusion*, 71.

provocative synthetic interpretation *The Meaning of Hitler*, spoke for them in 1969:

> Unfortunately the anachronistic illusions upon which these wars were based have still not died out. That Fischer has ruthlessly exposed them is his greatest merit. The reading of his book causes the scales to fall from one's eyes: the entire body of ideas on which the two German wars rested was wrong; sixty million people died because of an error of logic. In revealing this error Fischer's book not only relates history; it *makes* history.[38]

The Hamburg School: Imanuel Geiss

Fischer's disciples, imbued with a sense of mission, now entered the *Zunft* and applied their *Doktorvater*'s techniques to other aspects of German history. Many of them, like Dirk Stegmann, Barbara Vogel, and Peter-Christian Witt turned to analysis of Wilhelmine Germany, seeking a deeper understanding of the roots of the disaster of 1914. Hans-Ulrich Wehler, who was not a student of Fischer but was influenced by his writings and those of Eckart Kehr, published widely in this area and became in many ways more controversial than Fischer himself. As for Fischer, he too continued to search for antecedents to the Great War, and the period 1911–14 would form the framework of his second book. Only one of his pupils, Imanuel Geiss, stayed with the crisis of July 1914, taking up the cudgels on behalf of the Hamburg school and in the process creating a reference source of immense value.

Geiss, currently professor of modern history at the University of Bremen, sought to make the vast documentary collections on the July crisis accessible to ordinary readers. He selected more than 700 of those he considered most significant, arranged them in chronological sequence, and published them with lengthy commentaries in *Julikrise und Kriegsausbruch, 1914* (1963–64). This two-volume work in German was reduced to a one-volume English translation containing 188 documents (*July 1914: The Outbreak of the First World War – Selected Documents*, 1967). Now it was no longer necessary for historians and general readers to go to the original massive compendiums or to seek fragments of documents in Albertini's volumes. One had only to pick up Geiss and locate the

---

38. Sebastian Haffner, quoted in ibid., 105.

relevant documents in their proper chronological context and all in one language.

Valuable though these volumes are, they are not without limitations. Geiss selected the documents which he considered most important and his selection proved controversial. Omissions include Yanushkevich's telegram to Warsaw of 7:20 A.M. July 29 announcing July 30 as the first day of Russian general mobilization (drafted before the tsar countermanded the order and restored partial mobilization), as well as Bethmann's July 27 telegram to Tschirschky (DD 277) in which the chancellor urges mediation on Vienna. A number of scholars, in particular the Australian L.C.F. Turner (whose work on Russian mobilization will be discussed in chapter 6), accused Geiss of bias in the selection process. They held that the documents had been chosen and arranged in support of the Fischer thesis and that telegrams injurious to the Entente had been omitted. Others observed that nearly all of the documents concerned *German* policy in July 1914, perpetuating a tendency for which Fischer had been severely criticized. These criticisms were particularly applicable to the English edition, which is 75 percent smaller than the original German work and therefore excludes many documents contained in those volumes.

Certainly the English-speaking historian should use Geiss with a combination of appreciation and caution. His collection, convenient as it is, cannot replace the original volumes on the July crisis published by England, France, Germany, and Austria-Hungary. His German-language, two-volume edition is much more complete and should be used by anyone who can handle German; but even this version is somewhat tendentious. Geiss defended himself by saying that "it would be a distortion to create an artificial balance in the documentation when none existed. . . . [I]t is a reflection of the events, not of personal bias."[39] But this is unconvincing. Other nations *were* involved in the crisis and not merely as reactors to German policy. It is difficult to escape the conclusion that the Hamburg school's concentration on Germany's role is politically as well as historically motivated.

This does not mean that *July 1914* cannot be used with confidence. The translations are excellent, and the chronological arrangement provides precise narrative context which the individual volumes of the twenties and thirties lack. Geiss uncovered a number

39. Geiss, *July 1914*, 15.

of documents omitted from *Die große Politik* because they weakened the revisionist case; these are published for the first time in *July 1914*. (One could only wish he would have been equally energetic with respect to Entente diplomacy.) Even Geiss's commentaries, although written from the perspective of the Hamburg school, are of considerable value so long as the historian realizes that they are interpretive in nature. To those commentaries we now turn.

Geiss, unlike Fischer, analyzes each of our six keys to the July crisis. With respect to Serbian complicity, he goes farther than any of the other historians we have studied in exonerating the Pašić government. Citing the attempt of Pašić to prevent the crossing of the border by Princip and his confederates, Geiss asserts that when Colonel Dimitrijević heard of this, he attempted to terminate the plot through one of his agents at Sarajevo. Princip and his band, however, refused to scrap the undertaking and succeeded in assassinating the archduke. "In the last analysis, the murder at Sarajevo was thus primarily the deed of Princip himself and can only indirectly be charged to the 'Black Hand,' and virtually not at all to the Serbian Government (let alone the Serbian people)."[40]

As might be expected, Geiss hammers the policy of the German government in early July. Wilhelm II told Szögyény on July 5 that he would have to consult with Bethmann Hollweg, who was at Hohenfinow. But after lunch he assured the Austrians that Germany would support Vienna regardless of the possibility of Russian intervention. When Bethmann confirmed this to Hoyos the following day, neither of the Austrians was aware that the chancellor had been in Potsdam the previous day and had conferred with the Kaiser on several occasions between June 29 and July 5.[41] Germany assumed that Russia and France would not intervene and encouraged Vienna to strike quickly. "The German Government thus consciously took upon itself the risk of a conflict with Russia and of the continental war which would ensue. All these resolutions were taken in such secrecy that no official minutes are to be found among the German documents – an extraordinary omission in view of the otherwise pedantic exactness of Prusso-German bureaucracy."[42]

40. Ibid., 52–53. No evidence is offered for the assertion that Dimitrijević tried to cancel the attempt.
41. Ibid., 61. Geiss gives incorrect dates for Bethmann's conferences with the Kaiser prior to July 6, and Fischer corrected him in *War of Illusions*. See below.
42. Geiss, *July 1914*, 74.

After the Potsdam interview, Berlin was kept closely informed of the development of the Austrian ultimatum. Geiss cites the evidence produced by previous historians (Tschirschky's July 10 telegram and July 11 letter to Jagow and the telegram from Hans von Schoen, Bavarian chargé d'affaires in Berlin, to his government in Munich on July 18) and adds a further nail in Germany's coffin – a telegram from Koester, the Badenite chargé d'affaires at Berlin, to his government on July 20. This document delineates "the principal clause and points 1–7 (out of a total of 10) of the ultimatum."[43] Geiss criticizes the *Zunft* for having accepted and propagated the "official line" that Germany had no knowledge of the ultimatum's terms "despite the fact that documents which have been made known since 1919 unequivocally prove the contrary."[44] Germany, after all, could hardly have protested the ultimatum since its text accorded perfectly with German suggestions to Austria between July 5–18.

France's understandings with Russia are dealt with next, and Geiss is on firm ground in noting that no documentation exists from the St. Petersburg meetings (an omission attributable not to his selection procedures, but to the French government). He points out that Poincaré and Sazonov must have discussed the situation in the Balkans, but denies flatly the contention of Harry Barnes and Karl Dietrich Erdmann that France issued a blank check to Russia similar to the one issued by Germany to Austria. (Joachim Remak would repeat this charge four years later.) "However, Russia and France were not disposed to tolerate a violation of Serbian sovereignty," as indicated by the telegrams dispatched to the Russian and French ambassadors at Vienna following the conclusion of the visit.[45]

So the French do not come off too badly, and as for England, Sir Edward Grey is in the clear. Geiss holds that the British foreign secretary did everything possible to warn Berlin; to substantiate this, he cites two interviews with Lichnowsky. On July 20, Grey informed the German ambassador that "everything would depend on the form of the satisfaction demanded, and whether moderation would be exercised, but especially on whether the accusations made

43. Ibid., 94. Albertini mentions this telegram (*The Origins*, II, 159), but does so in a different context and fails to note its similarity with the actual text of the ultimatum.
44. Geiss, *July 1914*, 93. Gerhard Ritter perpetuated this myth in *Staatskunst und Kriegshandwerk: Das Problem des Militarismus in Deutschland*, 2d ed., 4 vols. (Munich, 1965), II, 312. The English edition, *The Sword and the Scepter* (Coral Gables, Fla., 1970), vol. II, omits it.
45. Geiss, *July 1914*, 138.

against Serbia could be made on convincing grounds." Two days later, he declared that England would be prepared to exert influence on Serbia to accept the Austrian conditions "in case they are moderate and are made reconcilable with the independence of the Serbian nation."[46] Geiss to the contrary, these communications are clearly inadequate. The July 20 statement, couched in normal diplomatic parlance, could easily be misconstrued by Berlin, where (in the opinion of the Hamburg school) layers of wishful thinking on the subject of British neutrality blanketed the brains of the Foreign office. Grey's declaration of July 22 was even less likely to influence Germany since (again according to Hamburg) Bethmann was interested neither in Serbian acceptance of the Austrian terms nor in the preservation of Serbian independence. Quickly Geiss drops the matter, having proven nothing.

Geiss is on more familiar territory when dealing with the fifth key (German last-week efforts). He fails to mention Bethmann's July 27 telegram to Tschirschky concerning mediation proposals (DD 277), portraying the chancellor as consistently bent on undercutting such offers, whether they came from Grey or from his own sovereign. Thus on July 28 Bethmann distorted Wilhelm's *Halt in Belgrade* proposal by dropping the conclusion that war was no longer necessary before transmitting the plan to Vienna. The following day, Lichnowsky informed Berlin that Grey had issued a clear-cut warning of British intervention in a war between Germany and France. Bethmann now panicked and urged moderation on Vienna, but only so that the blame for the conflict might fall on Russia. "It would have been sufficient for the Chancellor to declare: 'We have made a miscalculation, the war cannot be localised, Britain will not remain neutral, so we must call off the war; the Reich can no longer offer protection to the Danube Monarchy if she persists in the war against Serbia singlehanded.' Yet at no point did he speak the decisive words."[47] Why not? Because he did not want to stop Austria's war against Serbia, but preferred to improve Germany's chances in a European conflict. Here, as in his discussion of the second key, Geiss closely follows Fischer's line.

Russian general mobilization, which Fischer barely mentions, is handled in some detail by Geiss – but exclusively from the standpoint of German policy as a precipitant. The internal deliberations

46. Ibid., 138.
47. Ibid., 269.

of the Russian government and military are not covered; admittedly, the Soviet government never published a comprehensive volume of evidence pertaining to July 1914, but enough telegrams and internal records were published sporadically to warrant the inclusion of some of that material in a compendium of this nature. Geiss draws the unfavorable parallel between Jagow's July 27 assurance that Russian mobilization against Austria-Hungary would not mean war with Germany and Moltke's July 29 memorandum to the Wilhelmstraße stating the precise opposite. Unlike Fischer, who views Moltke's intervention as understandable in light of the military timetables, Geiss considers it an unwarranted overruling of the civilian government by the military.

Russian attitudes are mentioned briefly and in most cases only indirectly. Geiss provides one piece of titillating evidence when he publishes a report from Count Karl Kageneck, the German military attaché at Vienna, to the German General Staff on July 18. Kageneck disclosed the possibility that Belgrade would be bombarded during the opening days of the forthcoming war; the actual bombardment was one of the two events of July 29 that had such a profound effect on Sazonov (the other being the German "ultimatum"). The document in question was one of those unearthed by Geiss in the files of the Foreign Office and published for the first time in *Julikrise und Kriegsausbruch, 1914*. But even this information is treated from the German standpoint. Geiss emphasizes that the German military brought undue pressure to bear on the civilian government and gives the controversy over Russian general mobilization a unique twist: "German general mobilization in answer to Russian partial mobilization made continental and world war virtually inevitable."[48] For Geiss, Russian mobilization was merely a pretext for Germany to mobilize while putting the blame on Russia, just as the assassination at Sarajevo had been a pretext for the implementation of a policy which Austria-Hungary and Germany had wanted to carry out anyway. "At 11:55 [A.M. on July 31], only five minutes before the self-imposed deadline, the eagerly awaited telegram from Pourtalès [announced Russian general mobilization]. The alibi for German mobilization had finally been provided."[49]

Thus Bethmann's first objective in putting the blame on Russia, the assurance of British neutrality, did not succeed; but in his

48. Ibid., 267.
49. Ibid., 271.

second objective "he succeeded only too well. The social-democrats supported the German war effort, and the Russians are still blamed in Germany today for having started the war."[50] Who therefore is to blame for these regrettable events? In Geiss's mind, there is no doubt. Germany is primarily responsible since it willingly ran the risk of local and European war. Germany did not want a world war and hoped that Britain would remain on the sidelines; but it egged Austria on, and even if it had not done so, its responsibility would still outstrip Vienna's because one word from Berlin would have restrained the Dual Monarchy. Germany was certain of victory in a European war and contemplated the possibility with . equanimity. Austria is secondarily responsible since it wanted a localized war with Serbia, but Vienna did not want a European war and desired to avoid one if Germany could overawe Russia (as in 1909).

What of the Entente? All three powers hoped to avoid European war and urged mediation on Vienna in the belief that preventing the local war was the surest way of forestalling its spread. Nonetheless, they are not without responsibility. Russia mobilized too early, thus providing Germany with a pretext for its own mobilization. France did nothing to restrain St. Petersburg in this matter. England should have clarified its position from the outset, although in Geiss's opinion it is doubtful that Germany would have altered its behavior in any case. Here Geiss ensnares himself in a contradiction, since if the German government was truly counting on British neutrality (and this is a principal contention of the Hamburg school), then why would an early declaration by Grey not have modified German conduct? If, as Geiss and Fischer assert, Bethmann panicked upon receiving irrefutable evidence of British intentions, why would he not have panicked had such evidence been available several days earlier? Here the Hamburg school tries to have it both ways, with unimpressive results.

Clearly, however, the Entente powers are far less responsible than the Central Powers for the outbreak of hostilities in 1914. Geiss places himself behind the Fischer thesis, provides the documentary evidence to back it up, and in his commentaries supplies a coherent narrative of the July crisis which is more substantial than chapter 2 of *Griff nach der Weltmacht*. Fischer himself, in response to the critiques of his book, his thesis, and his personal sincerity,

50. Ibid., 84.

spent the 1960s researching and writing a second book that would tell the story of German imperialistic pretensions from 1911 to September 1914. This book, published in 1969, contained a significant radicalization of the Fischer thesis.

War of Illusions (1969)

Griff nach der Weltmacht, while hinting at the social and economic factors affecting German foreign policy, nonetheless emphasized the traditional politico-diplomatic perspectives on the July crisis. *War of Illusions* broke new ground here. Under the influence of students like Dirk Stegmann and Peter-Christian Witt, Fischer took a deeper interest in socioeconomic questions and traced the roots of Germany's policy in July 1914 back to the attitudes and behavior of German elites as early as the turn of the century. The application of such factors to the immediate prewar period would be developed much more extensively by Hans-Ulrich Wehler, Volker Berghahn, and others.

In *Griff nach der Weltmacht*, Fischer had endorsed Albertini's contention that Germany bore chief responsibility for the outbreak of the Great War. His critics claimed that these were weasel words, that Fischer really believed that Germany was *solely* responsible for the catastrophe but was afraid to say so openly. What else, they asked, could explain Fischer's refusal not merely to examine the war aims of the Entente powers, but even to concede the possibility that some of their actions in July 1914 might have been less than pacific? Fischer might allow, in a theoretical sense, the possibility that other nations shared the blame; but, like his student Geiss, he cast that responsibility exclusively in terms of the improper reactions of Entente countries to aggressive German initiatives. Given this attitude and given the avalanche of evidence of German culpability arranged tendentiously in *Griff nach der Weltmacht*, how can the reader regard Fischer's limitation of German responsibility as anything other than a non sequitur?

Fischer appeared intent on confirming his critics' belief when he published his second book. *War of Illusions* revised *Griff nach der Weltmacht*'s contention concerning German responsibility. This time Fischer concluded, as the result of his exploration of the 1911–14 period, that Germany had planned the war at least since the "War Council" of December 8, 1912, at which Wilhelm II instructed his chief military advisers to prepare for a war within

eighteen months.[51] He radicalized the thesis which he had advocated so compellingly in 1961 – that the German government
planned a major war from the outset of the July crisis – by contending that the German decision for war could be traced to decisions
made at least eighteen months *before* July 1914. Germany deliberately initiated a war which cannot be termed "preventive" because
what it would have been intended to "prevent," an attack by the
Entente upon Germany, was never in the cards and the German
government knew it.

Fischer notes, with his customary ethical rigorism, that although
it is a positive development for historians to have agreed that
Germany in 1914 risked a major war, that position remains fraught
with apologetic tendencies. At least we have advanced beyond the
famous statement by Lloyd George that the European powers
"slithered into war." That contention was meretricious from the
beginning, having been articulated solely to "pour oil on troubled
waters and to give defeated Germany moral support against French
power politics."[52] But to believe that Germany embarked on a
preventive war implies that it feared defeat at the hands of the
Entente if it waited for Russia to complete its rearmament program
in 1917. How could Germany fear such a thing? No plans for such
an attack existed. It is true that many German politicians, including
Bethmann himself, believed in 1914 "that a few years hence the
Empire would simply no longer have the necessary military superiority to impose its political and economic conditions on the Entente
and on Russia in particular, i.e. it could not have its way by
threatening with armed forces and if necessary using it."[53] This,
however, does not mean that the Wilhelmine Reich launched a
preventive war in 1914 out of hopelessness or in the belief that only
such drastic measures could prevent the imminent destruction of
Germany at the hands of its enemies. Rather, "it was an attempt to
defeat the enemy powers before they became too strong, and to
realise Germany's political ambitions which may be summed up as

51. Fischer, *War of Illusions*, 161–64. This interpretation of the minutes of a
previously little-known meeting occasioned a tremendous furor, discussion of which
lies outside the scope of this book. See Adolf Gasser, "Der deutsche Hegemonialkrieg von 1914," in Imanuel Geiss and Bernd Jürgen Wendt, eds., *Deutschland in der
Weltpolitik des 19. und 20. Jahrhunderts* (Düsseldorf, 1974), 307–39; Wolfgang J.
Mommsen, "Domestic Factors in German Foreign Policy before 1914," *Central
European History* 6 (1973): 3–43; and Rohl, *1914*, intro.

52. Fischer, *War of Illusions*, 462.
53. Ibid., 470.

German hegemony over Europe."[54]

Thus the term "preventive war" carries too much irrelevant baggage for Fischer's taste. What Germany feared was not defeat, but the frustration of its overweening and ultimately irresponsible ambitions. To forestall that eventuality, the Kaiser's government embarked on an aggressive path which culminated in the Great War. This goes far beyond the original "Fischer thesis" expounded in 1961, and as we shall see, it drew a line which many of Fischer's defenders found impossible to cross.

In other respects, the account of the July crisis presented in *War of Illusions* differs little from that found in chapter 2 of *Griff nach der Weltmacht*. Substantial new evidence is presented and some mistakes and misinterpretations are cleared up, but no more attention is paid to the Entente powers than was paid earlier. When discussing German conduct in early July, Fischer straightens out Geiss's misunderstanding of Bethmann's whereabouts by demonstrating that the chancellor spent every day between June 29 and July 6, with the exception of June 1 and 3, at Potsdam in conference with the Kaiser. Fischer discovered this during his research at Potsdam, when he came across Bethmann's account of expenses incurred while traveling between Berlin and the Kaiser's residence at the Neue Palais. Wilhelm obviously deceived Hoyos and Szögyény when he told them on July 5 that Bethmann would have to be summoned the next day from Hohenfinow; in reality, he was already at Potsdam, which probably explains the Kaiser's abrupt readiness later that afternoon to back the Austrians with full vigor.

This is not all that Fischer unearthed at Potsdam. He reveals that, between July 18–20, Bethmann consulted ranking officials of the Prussian government and the Imperial ministries concerning measures to be taken upon mobilization. After these conferences, the secretary of state for the interior scheduled a meeting on July 24 "on the limitation of the declaration of the state of war and other measures preliminary to mobilisation."[55] On Sunday, July 26, Moltke returned to Berlin and immediately sent a draft ultimatum to Belgium to the Foreign Office for perusal. Simultaneously, "mobilisation orders for the civil authorities were also prepared for signature by the Emperor."[56] These disclosures, and many others

54. Ibid., 470.
55. Ibid., 483.
56. Ibid., 486–87.

like them throughout his books, give Fischer's arguments imposing force and power. It is difficult to read these pages and still maintain that German general mobilization was never seriously contemplated before the news of Russian preparations began to trickle into Berlin on July 29. For his opponents, this is a further indication of Fischer's selective assembly of evidence and his eagerness to misinterpret it in a manner unfavorable to Germany. Zechlin, Erdmann, and others see in these actions the regrettable yet perfectly understandable contingency plans of a great power encircled by a hostile alliance.

War of Illusions contains four pages on Russian general mobilization, probably in response to Ritter's complaint in "Eine neue Kriegsschuldthese?" that Fischer made no reference to the responsibility borne by non-Germans. But his formulation would scarcely have satisfied Ritter, who died before this book was published; nor would it have persuaded other historians who believe in the more or less equivalent responsibilities of all the powers. For even after nearly a decade of fending off criticism of his leniency toward Russia, Fischer gives no quarter here. "Russia's responsibility cannot therefore be said to lie in the fact that on 30th July the Russian government decided to transform the partial mobilisation into a general one; it can be held responsible because it refused to stand by while Serbia was destroyed and it was itself completely pushed out of the Balkans, that is forced to give up hope of the Straits. Russia's share of responsibility for the outbreak of war . . . lies in the fact that it adhered to this principle of Russian policy, not in the fact that it decided on 30th July to proclaim a general mobilisation."[57]

Fischer deals with Russia in a favorable manner and uses Bethmann's own words to justify his position. He exonerates the tsarist government of any desire or intent to fight a European war and states furthermore that Sazonov tried throughout the crisis to avoid such a conflict. "Bethmann Hollweg himself said at the Prussian Ministry of State [on July 30]: 'Although Russia had proclaimed a mobilisation its mobilisation measures could not be compared with

---

57. Ibid., 491. In one respect, of course, this represents a concession by Fischer. From a position of denying by omission any Russian culpability, he has conceded that Russia was indeed at fault for refusing to abandon its traditional Balkan policy. Readers who view Russian claims to the Straits as indefensible would find this admission congenial. Fischer, however, finds no fault with Russian policy in that portion of Europe and implies forcefully that this culpability is really a form of innocence.

those of the west European [powers]. . . . Russia did not want a war, it had been forced by Austria to take this step.'"[58] This was damning evidence indeed, made more effective by two facts: it had been a matter of public record since 1919, and Fischer's critics, both before and after 1969, did not attempt to impugn its veracity.

Germany's efforts to restrain Austria during the last week of the crisis are assessed in greater detail in Fischer's second book than in his first. And here he showed that he had not remained impervious to criticism. In *Griff nach der Weltmacht*, he had alleged that Bethmann had cancelled DD 441, a telegram sent to Tschirschky at 9:00 P.M. on the evening of July 30, because of the arrival of a telegram from George V to Prince Henry of Prussia that seemed to hold out some small hope for British neutrality. Fischer had argued that this had encouraged Bethmann sufficiently to persuade him to rescind a new, more potent admonition that Berchtold must negotiate seriously with St. Petersburg. Gerhard Ritter had ridiculed this contention, characterizing the telegram as "unimportant" and attributing Bethmann's undisputed change of mind to "the tragic turning point of the whole July crisis," the evening meeting with Moltke and Falkenhayn at which the military convinced the chancellor that Russian preparations made it negligent to delay the *Kriegsgefahrzustand* beyond noon of the following day.[59]

Ritter's point was well taken, and Fischer altered his interpretation to reflect it (without, of course, admitting that he had adopted a different explanation and without acknowledging Ritter's objection). In *War of Illusions* he describes George V's telegram as "innocuous" and attributes Bethmann's nullification of DD 441 to his conference with Moltke and Falkenhayn and to the rumors of Russian general mobilization which reached Berlin at 11:00 P.M. on July 30. This revision in no way affected Fischer's interpretation of German behavior. "With this decision [to proclaim the *Kriegsgefahrzustand* by noon on July 31], taken before news of the Russian general mobilisation was received, Berlin had fixed the beginning of the war for the first days of August even without the government being driven to this by Russia's general mobilisation."[60] Indeed, Ritter's explanation of the circumstances of the cancellation only buttressed Fischer's critique of Bethmann. In the mid-1960s, he found in the Political Archives of the Foreign Office in Bonn

58. Ibid., 492.
59. Ritter, "Eine neue Kriegsschuldthese?" 665.
60. Fischer, *War of Illusions*, 498.

Tschirschky's own reference to the incident (recalled on November 11, 1914): "I was personally requested by telephone [by Wilhelm von Stumm, political director at the Foreign Office] immediately to cease all mediation activity in Vienna *because* news of the Russian mobilisation had just been received."[61]

Thus Russian mobilization did not destroy the peace, and it was not, as is often alleged, the decisive step which made war inevitable. Germany would have mobilized even had partial mobilization remained in effect. As chapter 6 will demonstrate, L.C.F. Turner, one of Fischer's critics, makes precisely this point in very explicit terms, but draws from it the very different conclusion that even Russian *partial* mobilization constituted an unacceptable provocation to Germany and hence made war unavoidable. Fischer uses the same set of facts to exonerate Russia and convict Germany.

In one other respect, Fischer and Ritter are in accord, although neither would admit it and each would assign ultimate blame to different parties. Bethmann's efforts to persuade Berchtold to negotiate suddenly bore fruit in Vienna. "On 30th July the Austro-Hungarian Foreign Ministry became for the first time fully conscious of the danger that Britain, contrary to German assurances, would join in the European war on the side of France and Russia."[62] But Berchtold's new-found interest in an agreement with Russia was frustrated by Germany's military actions consequent upon the Bethmann/Moltke/Falkenhayn conference on the evening of July 30. Ritter blamed the military for bullying the civilian government into submission, while Fischer held all parties responsible and saved his strongest blows for Bethmann; but they were equally convinced that but for the rush to military measures on July 31, hostilities might yet have been averted.

Thus in 1969 Fischer, having earlier demolished the consensus that had existed prior to 1961 among historians in Germany, now exploded the new consensus that his own writings had helped to create. Germany had not engaged in a preventive war, but in a cold-blooded power play to dominate Europe by force. "Going beyond Renouvin, Schmitt, and Albertini, Fischer's new thesis is the most uncompromising assertion of Germany's guilt by any major Western scholar."[63] Germany's elites consciously set out to

---

61. Ibid., 498.
62. Ibid., 505.
63. Konrad H. Jarausch, "World Power or Tragic Fate? The *Kriegsschuldfrage* as Historical Neurosis," *Central European History* 5 (1972): 78.

use war to submerge social tensions at home, and Germany's war aims, far from developing over the course of the conflict (as Fischer's critics had consistently asserted), actually constitute the principal cause of the war.

So the lines were drawn, and the curse was cast. Historians, not only in Germany but throughout the world, were not slow to respond.

5

Opposition to Fischer

Griff nach der Weltmacht and *War of Illusions* made news around the world. Fischer found both defenders and antagonists in France, Great Britain, Scandinavia, the German Democratic Republic, the Soviet Union, and Poland. His work was translated into a number of languages, including Japanese. In the United States, where historians had long been influenced by the revisionism of Fay and Barnes, his impact was less profound. Antirevisionists found little to distinguish his initial thesis from Albertini's conclusions, and most found it difficult to credit his 1969 revisions. Most undergraduate students of European history or Western civilization continued to be taught from textbooks espousing the revisionist standpoint by professors who likewise believed that the outbreak of the Great War was a terrible accident for which every power was responsible. Few in United States followed the course of the scholarly debate in Germany over Fischer's views, principally because it was conducted in German.[1]

Nowhere, however, were Fischer's contentions disputed more energetically than in West Germany. The *Zunft* reacted to his early publications with a mixture of outrage and professional curiosity. Few agreed with Hans Rothfels that the traditional revisionist approach had survived Fischer's assault unscathed; few likewise

---

1. Regrettably, H.W. Koch is correct when he sneers in the Introduction to the second edition of his *The Origins of the First World War* that he "has met British and American experts on German history who can neither read nor speak a word of German." The lack of English translations of basic German historical works of the past thirty years (pertaining not only to this controversy but to many other areas) is deplorable and is unlikely to be remedied in the near future. Faced with this dilemma, most American professors of European history are forced to fall back on reviews and snippets, either because their grasp of German is inadequate or because they have time to read foreign-language publications only in their principal area of research. This accounts for much of the ignorance of the Fischer controversy prevalent among historians in this country, as well as for similar ignorance of most of the work of Hans-Ulrich Wehler, Andreas Hillgruber, and others.

were ready to abandon it completely. Most expressed some degree of reservation or opposition while quietly modifying their own opinions to conform to those of Fischer's findings they considered indisputable. In this chapter, we will examine the most creative or influential writings of the West German opponents of the Hamburg school, beginning with the man who was widely recognized in the 1960s as the outstanding living figure in the German historical profession.

Gerhard Ritter (University of Freiburg)

To call Ritter the dean of German historians (as many did) was to understate his influence. A veteran of the German army in the Great War and of the Resistance in World War II, he blended passionate patriotism, scholarly detachment, and high professional standards in an attractive combination. Like Fritz Fischer, whom he grew to despise, he started out in church history and later studied political and diplomatic affairs. In the United States, his biography of Luther remains a widely used supplementary reading in many religious studies courses, while his biography of Frederick the Great is still considered the finest treatment of that fascinating figure.[2] Ritter emerged from 1945 a hero because of his role in the Resistance. Quickly he used those enviable credentials to legitimize his contempt for the patriotic self-censorship of earlier generations of historians.

This was only one of many ironies permeating the Fischer controversy: Gerhard Ritter was anything but an apologist for German policy in 1914.[3] A harsh critic of the military establishment, his *Schlieffen Plan: Critique of a Myth* (1956) heaped opprobrium on the militaristic mindset which had devised an inflexible, intrinsically absurd battle plan and had then bullied the civilian authorities into following it without sufficient consideration of the consequences. But if, as Norman Stone wrote, Ritter considered Hitler to be a second-generation Ludendorff, then Carl Goerdeler was a latter-day Bethmann. Ritter, like many other German historians, placed Bethmann on a pedestal as a weak but well-intentioned

2. The preface to this book, written in 1933, was authoritarian in tone and did considerable damage to Ritter's reputation in the English-speaking world. The book remains in print and is still used in some undergraduate surveys of German history, albeit with a preface modified after the war.
3. This is not to deny his apologistic stance concerning the Second Reich as a whole, in which he had grown up and for which he fought in the Great War.

philosopher-statesman who heroically resisted military pretensions as long as he was able to hold out. In the chancellor's conduct there was neither malice nor aggression – only sincere love of country and a decent respect for the legitimate rights of all nations.

Fritz Fischer shattered this image of Bethmann, and Ritter never forgave him. Fischer, after all, was an upstart: twenty years younger than Ritter, he was a boy during the Great War and had accepted a university appointment under the Nazi regime in 1942. Now he was applying to recent German history techniques that Ritter found foreign and, in the process, fouling his own nest. Ritter shared "the prejudices of the German Resistance with which he was associated – anti-Nazi, of course, but also anti-republican, anti-Socialist, anti-Versailles, and anti-Catholic as well."[4] Since Fischer appeared to fit all those categories except the religious one and had criticized Bethmann in rather severe terms, Ritter was bound to be critical of his contentions.

Ritter's response to Fischer did not take the form of a self-contained account of the July crisis. Instead, it was threefold and disparate. He denounced Fischer in public and professional gatherings, most notably at the October 1964 Congress of the German Historical Association in Berlin and in several interviews on West German television. He took issue with Fischer's theses and interpretations in a number of written reviews, of which "Eine neue Kriegsschuldthese?" in the *Historische Zeitschrift* was the most widely disseminated.[5] Finally, he addressed Germany's role in July 1914 in the second volume of his classic four-volume treatment of the problem of militarism in Germany, *Staatskunst und Kriegshandwerk (The Sword and the Scepter)*; he evaluated Bethmann Hollweg's character and motivations in volume 3. But *The Sword and the Scepter* deals primarily with German militarism, and its discussion of July 1914 is oriented towards this problem rather than toward a chronological analysis of the crisis. Its account of the crisis also contains a number of factual errors which render some of its interpretations suspect and which Ritter might well have corrected had he lived beyond 1967.

4. Stone, "Gerhard Ritter," 161.
5. This, the most famous of Ritter's written comments on Fischer's work, captures admirably the flavor and emotion of his reactions. A highly charged essay, it was written in a mind-set of passion, annoyance, and despair; its fervor recalls the indignation of Harry Elmer Barnes rather than the controlled, careful analysis of Pierre Renouvin or Sidney Fay.

Serbian culpability in the Sarajevo murders is for Ritter beyond question. He states correctly that upon hearing the news of the killings, 'Almost instinctively everyone was convinced that Serbia was guilty.'[6] Evidence assembled since that time has only confirmed this initial impression.[7] As for German policy in July 1914, it was by no means as bellicose as Fischer seems to think. True enough, Austria could not have acted aggressively without German support; even Conrad realized that. But the issuance on July 6 of an unconditional pledge of assistance was not a decision to launch a preventive war, but a terrible blunder, a disastrous misstep attributable to military eagerness and civilian shortsightedness. Fischer deliberately misconstrues German intentions through misinterpretation of a number of innocuous occurrences and outright invention of nonexistent sins.

One of the most curious examples of this kind of interpretation is the assertion that Under Secretary of State Zimmermann on July 5 had "given Count Hoyos to understand" that Germany, in case of a Russian-French intervention, was able alone, because of its military position, to take on both, so that Austria-Hungary could concentrate entirely on the Balkans. To credit Zimmermann with such stupidity is to underrate his intelligence considerably; there is not the slightest support for it in the sources.[8]

6. Ritter, *The Sword*, II, 235.

7. In *The Sword*, II, 235, n. 23, Ritter writes that Albertini "oddly enough overlooks the hand-written confession of Colonel Dimitrijević, which the German military authorities found in Belgrade during the Second World War," and which was published in July 1943. Albertini's ignorance of this document is no doubt attributable to his death in 1942. Vladimir Dedijer, in *The Road to Sarajevo* (New York, 1966), explains that Dimitrijević was forced to sign the confession during his trial for treason in 1917. His personal guilt, of course, is accepted by nearly all historians, but the degree of governmental complicity that such a verdict implies remains a disputed question.

8. Ritter, "Eine neue Kriegsschuldthese?" 661. It should be noted that in 1917, then-Secretary of State Zimmermann dispatched the "Zimmermann Note" to Mexico, asking for Mexican support in the war against the United States in exchange for the return of the Mexican Cession. This action, which helped bring the United States into the war, may have some bearing on an assessment of Zimmermann's intelligence. Ritter's second contention is only partially accurate. A telegram from Tschirschky to Jagow (DD 18) mentions Hoyos's conversation with Zimmermann and refers to a memorandum which could not be found in the Austrian archives when the Austrian documents were begin published in the late 1920s. Its absence may be imputable to the presence in Vienna in 1919 of Legation Counselor Dr. Roderich Gooß, who was sent by the Foreign Office to assist the Austrians in organizing their archives.

Did Germany know the details of the ultimatum in advance? Ritter says that the government did know that Vienna intended the terms to be unacceptable. He fails to mention the July 10 and 11 dispatches from Tschirschky to Jagow containing explicit references to several of the clauses, and asserts that "the German foreign ministry had vainly tried to secure information in time on the precise wording and date of delivery of the proposed ultimatum."[9] But it is Fischer's portrayal of Bethmann Hollweg's character that exercises Ritter the most. "A completely new picture of Chancellor Bethmann Hollweg is put before us. In place of a very conscientious, honest, but in his decisions changeable official who was always beset by fresh doubts and was lacking in a sure political instinct, there appears a tough and crafty power politician who plays with the fate of Germany with unscrupulous flippancy."[10] For Ritter, Bethmann was not an adventurer, a man who could gamble the fate of millions on a single throw of iron dice. Fischer's assessment of his character was more than a profound misunderstanding; it was pure character assassination, the willful distortion of the public record of a good and decent man.[11]

Ritter, like Fischer, spent little effort on the deciphering of French, Russian, and British intentions, concentrating instead on German policy in July. His disapproval of Fischer's portrayal of Bethmann did not end with the dispatch of the ultimatum, but carried over into the chancellor's final efforts to hold Berchtold back. Here the fault was exclusively Austria's, and Fischer misreads the evidence so consistently as to cast doubt on his sincerity. He reads DD 272 (Bethmann to Tschirschky, July 27) in a manner decidedly unfavorable to Bethmann, while Ritter characterizes it as

9. Ritter, *The Sword*, II, 250. Ritter is mistaken here. Tschirschky informed Bethmann on July 14 that the note would not be delivered until the 25th (DD 49); three days later Bethmann was notified that the displeasure expressed by Jagow at this delay had led to a decision to transmit the note on July 23 (DD 65).

10. Ritter, "Eine neue Kriegsschuldthese?" 667–68.

11. As we shall see below, the diaries of Kurt Riezler, Bethmann's chief political and administrative assistant, came to light as a result of the Fischer controversy and now constitute a valuable source for the evaluation of Bethmann's personal opinions and actions. It must be remembered that Ritter knew nothing of these diaries until 1964, when he was working on the third volume of *The Sword*. Since the diaries were still privately held and were being prepared for publication, Ritter (like Fischer) was able to see only fragments of them in manuscript form. But what he saw did not impress him. In *The Sword*, III, 495, n. 4, he comments that "It is true . . . that [Riezler's entries] bear a strongly emotional tinge and on that account alone must be used with care. Riezler was not really a 'political animal' and his sense of objective realism fell far short of Bethmann Hollweg's."

"a serious warning to Berchtold not merely to reject the British proposals."[12] Ritter argues that Fischer is unduly favorable to Berchtold's policy and unfairly harsh to Bethmann's. Is it logical to assume that the chancellor was *never* sincere in his instructions to Tschirschky when those instructions appear pacific, but only when they seem bellicose?

Ritter makes a telling point. Fischer's analysis of DD 323 (Bethmann to Tschirschky, 10:15 P.M., July 28) finds Bethmann guilty of gross duplicity in asking Berchtold to negotiate while really urging Tschirschky to convey the opposite intention. "The possibility that the additions [watering down the instructions] were intended to spare the sensitivity and mistrust of the Vienna government (which always so easily felt itself patronized) and to make its compliance somehow more palatable is not once considered."[13] Why not? Because such a reading does not coincide with Fischer's opinion that Bethmann's policy was cynical and aggressive. If Bethmann meant what he said when he admitted trying to throw culpability onto Russia, why is it impossible for him to have meant what he said when he urged negotiations between Vienna and St. Petersburg? Once again, such language can be read in more than one way. Historians must keep in mind that honest disagreement is not equivalent to deliberate misrepresentation, and they must recognize the possibility (or likelihood) that neither Fischer nor Ritter is correct in every instance.

When Ritter turns to the role of the military in the final days of July, his disagreement with Fischer becomes even more stark. He calls attention to Bethmann's persistent opposition to the demands of the chief of the General Staff and the Imperial war minister that Russian mobilization must be answered at once. In so doing, he rejects categorically Fischer's assertion that DD 395 and 396, Bethmann's early-morning telegrams to Tschirschky, were intended solely to assure that guilt would rest on Russia's shoulders in order to keep Britain neutral and induce the SPD to support the war. But he offers no evidence that would validate his interpretation over Fischer's, and his implication that at 3:00 A.M. on July 30 Russian mobilization would have to be responded to is simply incorrect. According to his own account, Moltke supported Bethmann's

---

12. Ritter, "Eine neue Kriegsschuldthese?" 663. In this instance as in others, the document can be interpreted either way. In such circumstances, charges of willful distortion by either party are simply wrongheaded and deplorable.
13. Ritter, "Eine neue Kriegsschuldthese?" 664.

cautious policy toward Russia until the *afternoon* of July 30, and it was not until the late evening of that day that the General Staff could present evidence that Russian general mobilization was in progress.[14] This came too late to influence Bethmann's earlier telegrams.

Fischer's version of these events was not without impact on Ritter. He blames Berchtold for ignoring Berlin's pleas that British mediation not be rejected out of hand, but concedes that the Austro-Hungarian foreign minister might have had cause to behave as he did: "Not without the complicity of Bethmann Hollweg and his foreign minister von Jagow, Vienna at first chose to interpret these pleas as meaning that the Germans wished not so much to avoid a great war as to shift the odium of aggression to the Russians."[15] Five years earlier he would never have written such a thing. Yet for Ritter, the crucial events were dictated not by the civilians but by the military. Moltke and Falkenhayn, prisoners of the illogical Schlieffen Plan,[16] were not eager for war but were almost neurotically anxious to begin it as soon as they became convinced that Russian preparations were in earnest. Ritter went to great lengths both before and after *Griff nach der Weltmacht* to explain the technical military considerations that impelled the generals to force the unwilling Bethmann into war; he was both personally and professionally annoyed at Fischer's apparent unwillingness to understand such factors.

Ritter and Fischer read the same material, but they read it from vastly different perspectives. Ritter "emphasizes the differences between generals and statesmen where Fischer had shown the unity between them."[17] The former sees German history in the twentieth century as a classic example of tragedy; but "where Ritter spoke of 'disaster' and 'blindness,' Fischer saw only 'intent' and 'premeditation.' Everything that Fischer brought forward as evidence . . . to

14. Ritter, *The Sword*, II, 256.
15. Ibid., II, 254.
16. "Illogical" may be too mild a characterization of Ritter's views. Not only did the Schlieffen Plan "verge on the fantastic," but it created an incredible situation in which Germany began a war intended to save Austria-Hungary's position in the Balkans by invading a neutral country in northwestern Europe. Ritter, *The Sword*, II, 262–74. Gerhard Weinberg points out in *The Foreign Policy of Hitler's Germany*, vol. II (New York, 1980), that France followed in the footsteps of this unusual approach by assuring the British in 1938 that, in the event of war with Germany over Czechoslovakia, they would defend the Czechs by attacking the Italians in Libya.
17. Stone, "Gerhard Ritter," 160.

prove that Germany was striving for world power, was rejected by Ritter and interpreted as manifestations of an exaggerated, new German nationalism, which showed itself to be illiberal, conservative and militarist."[18] In other words, Ritter deplored the implications of Fischer's evidence no less sincerely than did the Hamburg school. But he considered that evidence reflective of a dangerous Wilhelmine divergence from the proven and stabilizing policies of Bismarckian *Staatsräson*. Surely, he felt, these attitudes were held by only a few admittedly highly placed Germans. Fischer, in contrast, argued that they were widespread, and that many (if not most) influential Germans were afflicted by "a collective megalomania which expressed itself in utterly unrealistic war aims and a grotesque inability to see the world as it actually was."[19] Ritter disagreed with this view but was unable to refute it.

He was more successful in pointing out Fischer's exaggerations and eagerness to see a "griff nach der Weltmacht" in everything the German government did in July 1914. Fischer's tendency to ascribe a cynical, calculated purposefulness to what most scholars now see as an aggressively inclined but not unequivocally warlike policy is one of the principal defects of his work. Another is his misunderstanding of the character and policies of Bethmann, who was both more belligerent than Ritter thought and less imperialistic than Fischer asserts. Ritter's work contributed to the consensus on these issues that has gradually emerged since his death, but the actual formulation of that consensus was left to others. For Ritter, despite his acceptance of some of Fischer's findings, never endorsed the theory of "calculated risk" which Fischer introduced and later disavowed. That theory now forms the foundation of contemporary scholarship on German policy during the crisis of July 1914.

Ritter could not accept this theory for several reasons. First, he had a theory of his own. "He believed that by giving a blank cheque to Austria-Hungary on 5 July – a free hand against Russia's Serbian ally – Germany was letting herself be led by Austria-Hungary."[20] This is also Sidney Fay's interpretation, and its chief limitation is that it does not appear to be supported by the documentary record, the Riezler diaries, or common sense. By the mid-seventies, nearly

18. Janssen, "Gerhard Ritter," 296.
19. Klaus Epstein, "Gerhard Ritter and the First World War," in Walter Laqueur and George L. Mosse, eds., *1914: The Coming of the First World War* (New York, 1966), 188.
20. Janssen, "Gerhard Ritter," 299.

all historians had abandoned it, including Ritter's own pupil, Karl-Heinz Janssen.

Second, Ritter did not consider Fischer's evidence conclusive. He put little stock in the declarations in favor of preventive war made by German generals; bellicose statements were this group's natural mode of expression, and they were no more meaningful than the Kaiser's outraged ramblings. "He also did not accept as proof the pretty definite reports of journalists and diplomats in the summer of 1914," probably because he considered them inconsistent with German policy as he understood it.[21] The Riezler diaries might have helped change his mind, but given his opinion of Riezler's lack of political sophistication, he might have discounted those as well. One item that would at least have caused him to reconsider his position was the advice of Moltke to Jagow in June 1914 that a preventive war should be launched soon because Germany had a good chance of winning before the Russian armaments buildup was completed. But this information was disclosed after Ritter's death.[22]

Finally, Ritter could not accept the idea that Germany deliberately risked a preventive war because he had made up his mind long before that this was a slanderous myth invented by the victors of Versailles. He was highly critical of the conduct of the German military before, during, and after July 1914, but he never abandoned Lloyd George's view that none of the civilian governments wanted war and that the nations had "slithered over the brink" inadvertently. For all of its respect for evidence, history remains essentially a collection of personal evaluations of past events, based not only upon factual data but upon value judgments, impressions, and subjective interpretations of that data. Ritter no more than Fischer could free himself from these limitations, which do not constitute defects of character or intellect. Ritter, after all, had grown up in the Second Reich and had volunteered in the Great War. Fischer had been too young for service in that conflict and grew up during the war and the first years of the Weimar Republic. His students, of course, were considerably younger and held worldviews reflective of the post-1945 period. Historians may strive for objectivity, but they bring to that quest attitudes and predilections derived from all of their experiences, not merely their assessments of historical evidence. Those attitudes and predilections in turn affect their

21. Ibid., 299.
22. Ibid., 299.

interpretations of such evidence.

Thus Ritter viewed the crisis of July 1914 from the perspective of a patriotic German who had served honorably in the Great War, who hated Nazism and risked his life in the struggle against it, who hoped that German self-respect might be rebuilt after 1945 on the firm foundations of the pre-Weimar era. This did not prevent him from recognizing some of the defects of Wilhelmine Germany: "The prewar Germany I describe is the Germany of my youth. For most of my life, as I looked back on it, it seemed to me to be bathed in a kind of radiance that did not begin to darken until the outbreak of war in 1914. Now, at the twilight of my life [1960], my probing eye finds shadows far deeper than my generation perceived."[23] But it did prevent him from accepting Fischer's interpretation which, in the words of Fischer's Australian proponent, "is inspired by a spirit of ruthless national self-examination and a consistent determination not to overlook any . . . facts which tend to besmirch the national image."[24]

To expect Ritter to abandon his long-standing beliefs in destiny, nemesis, and tragic fate as the chief actors in the German historical disaster in favor of Fischer's pitiless catalogue of evils perpetrated not by sinister forces but by ordinary human beings was to expect too much. We are all limited by our value systems just as we are liberated by them. *The Sword and the Scepter*, Ritter's beautifully written, perceptive treatment of the interaction of politics and militarism in Germany, deserves to be read as a chef d'oeuvre in its own right and as a complement and corrective to Fischer's equally valuable books. Truth is to be found in them all, and the individual reader cannot be absolved of the responsibility to consider both perspectives in his or her search for an acceptable interpretation of the crisis of July 1914.

Karl Dietrich Erdmann (University of Kiel)

Kurt Riezler's diaries brought Karl Dietrich Erdmann into the Fischer affair. Riezler was Bethmann's adviser, confidant, and in some respects alter ego, throughout the eight years of the latter's chancellorship. He kept a diary at sporadic intervals throughout his career as a public servant; after his death in Munich in 1955, the

---

23. Ritter, *The Sword*, II, 2.
24. Moses, *The Politics of Illusion*, 54.

manuscript passed into the custody of his brother Walter. Its importance as a historical source was recognized even before the outbreak of the debate over German war aims; in 1956, Theodor Heuß corresponded with Walter Riezler in the hope of obtaining his permission to edit and publish the document.[25] Walter Riezler proved reluctant and considered destroying the diaries, as Kurt had requested in his will. He was dissuaded by the combined efforts of Heuß, Erdmann, and Hans Herzfeld. In the process of this lengthy struggle, Erdmann was able to gain access to the diary entries pertaining to the July crisis and used them in 1964 as the basis for an important article which first made Riezler's observations known to a wide readership. That article, published with Walter Riezler's authorization, defended Bethmann Hollweg against the allegations made by the Hamburg school.[26]

Walter Riezler died in 1965, and control of the diaries passed to Kurt Riezler's daughter, Mary White, who lived in New York. Erdmann delivered a copy to her personally later that year so that she might reach a decision concerning publication. She returned the copy to Erdmann late in 1967 and the following year granted him permission to edit the diaries and publish them. During the time the copy was in her possession, the American historians Fritz Stern and Konrad Jarausch had obtained access to it and were permitted to publish articles based on it.[27] "All this took place not without a certain amount of misunderstanding between the German custodian of the original and his American colleagues."[28] As mentioned earlier, both Fritz Fischer and Gerhard Ritter were denied access to the total manuscript and were permitted to examine only small excerpts. Ritter concluded from his perusal that Riezler's rudimentary political sophistication rendered his observations suspect, while Fischer made full use of the small portions he was allowed to see by quoting those segments which substantiated his case.

25. Bernd Sösemann, "Die Tagebücher Kurt Riezlers: Untersuchungen zu ihrer Echtheit und Edition," *Historische Zeitschrift* 236 (1983): 337.

26. Karl Dietrich Erdmann, "Zur Beurteilung Bethmann Hollwegs," *Geschichte in Wissenschaft und Unterricht* 15 (1964): 525–40.

27. Fritz Stern, "Bethmann Hollweg and the War: The Limits of Responsibility," in Fritz Stern and Leonard Krieger, eds., *The Responsibility of Power: Historical Essays in Honor of Hajo Holborn* (New York, 1967), 252–85; Konrad H. Jarausch, "The Illusion of Limited War: Chancellor Bethmann Hollweg's Calculated Risk, July 1914," *Central European History* 2 (1969): 48–76.

28. John A. Moses, "Karl Dietrich Erdmann, the Riezler Diary, and the Fischer Controversy," *Journal of European Studies* 3 (1973): 241–42.

Finally, in 1972, Erdmann completed his work and published the Riezler diaries,[29] accompanying them with a 159-page introduction which contains a wealth of historiographical information pertinent to the entire controversy over German war aims. He had been in the midst of that dispute from the beginning, negotiating with the Riezler family, sharing platforms with Fritz Fischer and Gerhard Ritter, and serving as president of the German Historical Association in 1964, the year in which the epic Fischer-Ritter debate was held in Berlin. For our purposes, only his work on the July crisis itself is pertinent.

Prior to his acquaintance with the Riezler manuscript, Erdmann adhered to the conventional German view of Bethmann's role in July 1914. He believed with Ritter that the outbreak of war was a great tragedy which was not desired by the German leadership and which Bethmann had not foreseen when he and the Kaiser issued the blank check to Austria-Hungary. But the diaries changed his mind. Riezler considered any limitation of German aspirations to be an unfriendly act, and according to his writings, Bethmann shared this view. Riezler's diary entry for July 7 indicates that Bethmann was well aware of the possible consequences of the blank check – not merely European war but possibly world war.[30] Erdmann at once revised his position and agreed with Fischer that Bethmann had consciously and deliberately risked general war from the outset of the crisis. Had Fischer not radicalized his position by claiming in *War of Illusions* that the German government had planned war from December 1912, Erdmann (and, indeed, many of Fischer's opponents) might have endorsed the pricipal tenets of his argument.

But one of those tenets troubled Erdmann even before 1969: that was the contention that Bethmann had counted on British neutrality as the indispensable element in a German military victory. Only through keeping Britain neutral, Fischer asserted, could success against Russia and France in a continental war be assured. Ritter agreed with Fischer that British neutrality was the foundation of Bethmann's policy, although his interpretation of the essentially defensive character of that policy obviously contradicted Fischer. The difficulty with this position was that Riezler's diaries seemed to refute it. The July 7 entry suggested that Bethmann realized from

29. Kurt Riezler, *Tagebücher, Aufsätze, Dokumente*, ed. Karl Dietrich Erdmann (Göttingen, 1972).
30. Erdmann, "Zur Beurteilung," 536.

the beginning that Britain would oppose Germany in a war resulting from Austrian action against Serbia. But such a war would end
in Germany's defeat. Therefore Bethmann's policy in the July crisis
was designed to *avoid* war rather than to promote it. In addition
to the Riezler July 7 entry, Erdmann presents documentary information tending to prove that "neither the German Foreign Office,
nor the army, nor the navy, reckoned with the neutrality of
England."[31]

This contention formed the basis of a dispute within the overall
controversy which has continued to the present day, ironically
ranging Fischer and his late adversary Ritter against Erdmann and
Egmont Zechlin. The implications of Erdmann's assertion are significant. If Bethmann knew that a war resulting from Austrian
action against Serbia would end unfavorably for Germany because
of inevitable British intervention and therefore bent all his efforts to
avert such a catastrophe, then the image of the chancellor with
which we are left is not very different from his image prior to 1961:
as a conscientious, honorable civil servant, his actions in July 1914
were predicated on the belief that war would be disastrous for
Germany. Erdmann's writings thereby created a compromise position which many German historians could endorse. Having accepted Fischer's evidence demonstrating that Germany consciously
ran the risk of war in July 1914, they could at the same time
conclude that Bethmann, while taking that risk, had nonetheless
done everything in his power to preserve peace.

Riezler's entries offered support for such a conclusion. Bethmann, at least since 1911, had confided to Riezler that the international position of Germany was deteriorating. Encircled by a
hostile Entente, Germany watched helplessly as Russia upgraded
its armaments, France enacted the Three-Year Law, and Britain
initiated naval talks with Russia which in June 1914 seemed likely to
lead to the signing of an Anglo-Russian naval convention.[32] In fear
and despair, Bethmann had rolled the dice in July 1914, gambling on
Russian reluctance to oppose Germany (as in the Bosnian crisis of
1909) but realizing that if Russia and France *did* come in, Britain

31. Karl Dietrich Erdmann, "War Guilt 1914 Reconsidered: A Balance of New
Research," in H.W. Koch, ed., *The Origins of the First World War*, 2d ed. (London,
1984), 363.
32. Erdmann, "Zur Beurteilung," 532–36. Both Erdmann and Zechlin emphasized the ongoing naval talks between England and Russia as destructive of Bethmann's hopes for peace.

would intervene as well. This position, unacceptable to Ritter (who would have considered Bethmann "an irresponsible gambler and adventurer" for playing with Germany's fate in a hopeless game), bowed to Fischer's evidence while preserving Bethmann's reputation.[33]

Erdmann's role in preserving, editing, and publishing the Riezler diaries was of great value, and all historians of the period are in his debt. But there are difficulties with the diaries and with Erdmann's work as well. Riezler was an inconsistent diarist, going for months without making entries and then recording large blocks of information on certain days. Much of the information entered on those days appears to constitute distillations and summaries of conversations and impressions from a much earlier date. This may be the case with the July 7 entry, which purports to form a record of an after-dinner conversation between Riezler and Bethmann at Hohenfinow but which contains references to earlier occurrences and conversations. (It is also possible that this entry is merely the record of Bethmann's own recollection of such matters, uttered on that very evening.) The point is that the historian, being uncertain, must allow for both possibilities.

Second, Riezler's journal entries stop on July 27 and are not resumed until August 14, nearly two weeks after the outbreak of war. Riezler's statement in the August 14 entry in the published edition that he had had no time to record private observations during the previous eighteen days rings true, given what we know of that hectic period; but it did not prevent skeptics from postulating that Riezler *had* made entries which were later expunged from the manuscript, either by Riezler himself or by his family. In a 1983 article in *Historische Zeitschrift*, Bernd Sösemann called attention to the peculiar fact that the diary entries between July 7 and August 14 were written on a different sort of paper from that used by Riezler before and after that period. These entries were made on loose paper (called *Blockblatter*) and had been inserted at the appropriate places in the original manuscript.[34] Erdmann had not disclosed this in his 1964 article and had likewise neglected to mention it in his definitive edition of the diaries. Even more unusual was the report of Guido

33. Erdmann, "War Guilt," 363.
34. Sösemann, "Die Tagebücher," 340–65, including four photographic reproductions of pages of the handwritten diary. The similarity to the *faux Henry* forgery which helped to convict Alfred Dreyfus of treason was not pointed out by Sösemann, but could hardly be missed by the attentive reader.

Dessauer, an expert in the chemical analysis of paper, who according to Sösemann dated manufacture of the paper in question to *after* the Great War.[35]

Sösemann's arguments concerning the implications of this (and of a great deal of other highly technical evidence cited in his article) called into question Erdmann's scholarly integrity and the authenticity of the entries. Sösemann raised the possibility that Walter Riezler may have transcribed his brother's July 1914 entries (given certain alleged dissimilarities in handwriting) and in so doing may have altered them. Sösemann also pointed to the possibility that Kurt Riezler may have rewritten the entries after the war for reasons both political and personal. Finally, he criticized Erdmann for having contributed to this suspected falsification through his own editorial work.[36] Fritz Fischer pounced upon these suggestive findings, arguing in a provocative monograph that the original entries had been altered, either by Walter Riezler or by someone else, because they would have revealed Bethmann as a statesman bent on instigating a world war – a statesman, in other words, who fit very closely Fischer's portrayal of him.[37] Fischer's analysis of the fate of the manuscript in the years following Riezler's death in 1955 suggested that the document had been tampered with and that Erdmann, who must have known of the tampering, remained silent regarding its implications.

Erdmann defended himself in a lengthy and somewhat arcane response in the same volume of *Historische Zeitschrift*.[38] He refuted each of Sösemann's points in turn, citing studies by different chemists who concluded that the paper could have been manufactured at any time between 1900 and 1940, explaining Riezler's political views at considerable length, and offering a number of explanations for the alleged inconsistencies. Here the matter rests, with each side taking from the debate those elements that support its own position. On balance, it appears that Sösemann has succeeded in calling into question the authenticity of the July/August entries. After his work, no historian can use these entries with full confidence that they paint an accurate portrait of Bethmann. He has not demonstrated

35. Ibid., 357.
36. Ibid., 365–69.
37. Fritz Fischer, *Juli 1914: Wir sind nicht hineingeschlittert* (Hamburg, 1983). A rough translation would read "July 1914: we did not slither into it," an obvious reference to Lloyd George's remarks.
38. Karl Dietrich Erdmann, "Zur Echtheit der Tagebücher Kurt Riezlers: Eine Antikritik," *Historische Zeitschrift* 236 (1983): 371–402.

conclusively that Erdmann was part of a plan to manipulate the spurious entries for political purposes, but a careful reading of all items involved in the controversy leads this historian to conclude that Erdmann's performance as editor of the diaries fell far short of normal standards of historical objectivity and detachment.[39]

Finally, it is very difficult (and sometimes impossible) to separate Riezler's views from those he attributes to Bethmann. To what extent did he put Bethmann's words and actions into his own philosophical and political constructions? This issue is so confusing that Erdmann, the editor of the diaries, states baldly that "the policy of the German government during the July crisis corresponds to a theory of calculated war risk developed by Kurt Riezler before the war," while Wayne Thompson, Riezler's biographer (and an opponent of the Fischer thesis), states precisely the opposite.[40] Obviously the historian must use the Riezler diaries with prudence and care, recognizing their undeniable historical value while subjecting each entry to close scrutiny and comparison with external evidence. Even then, at least with respect to the July/August entries, no final judgment can be rendered with certainty.

Similarly, it is difficult for the historian of the July crisis to know what to make of Erdmann's findings. In some respects, they are clear-cut and convincing. His opinion that Bethmann ran a calculated risk beginning on July 6, a position first advocated by Fritz Fischer, is now accepted by virtually all historians of the period. Likewise, his disclosure that Bethmann shared the worldview of much of the German educated elite, a worldview riddled with social Darwinism and dreams of the domination of the weak by the strong, is shared by historians of the Hamburg school (Fischer, Geiss, Moses, and others), as well as by their opponents (Zechlin, Jarausch, Stern, and particularly H.W. Koch).[41]

39. This entire debate exists only in German. The lack of an English rendition is on the one hand regrettable and on the other understandable. Given the maddeningly intricate nature of this material, most English-speaking readers would find the text no more clear in English than in German.

40. Erdmann, "War Guilt," 367; Wayne C. Thompson, *In the Eye of the Storm: Kurt Riezler and the Crises of Modern Germany* (Iowa City, 1980), 94.

41. On this issue, Erdmann and Thompson confirm a substantial portion of Fischer's original thesis (the latter perhaps without knowing it). Thompson stresses that Riezler's repeated references to conquest, domination, expansion, and subjugation, although shocking to modern readers, were part and parcel of the ordinary dialogue of educated Germans in the Wilhelmine Reich. Fritz Fischer's contention that German elite opinion favored aggressive, expansionistic conquest could not have been more vigorously defended. See Thompson, *In the Eye of the Storm*, chap. 2.

These aspects of Erdmann's writings provide the basis for consensus, but his arguments concerning British neutrality do not. Here the documentary record appears to support Ritter and Fischer, both of whom were convinced that Bethmann was anxious to keep Britain neutral. Erdmann's allegation that substantial documentary evidence exists to indicate that the Foreign Office and the military and naval ministries never reckoned with British neutrality is correct. It is, of course, also correct to state that substantial documentary evidence, including but not restricted to portions of the Riezler diaries, points in the opposite direction. Jagow stated bluntly to Jules Cambon that he was certain of British neutrality; the Kaiser's marginalia insisted that Russia would be unsupported by England; and Bethmann himself attempted to secure British nonparticipation through his infamous offer of July 29 to respect the territorial integrity of metropolitan France should Britain remain out of a continental war. It strains credulity to conclude that these were the actions and remarks of men convinced that Britain would intervene.

Beyond this, the nature of the evidence argues against Erdmann's position. The opinion of the military and naval authorities regarding British neutrality is not conclusive with respect to the chancellor's views. Bethmann's statements concerning the likelihood of British intervention are limited to the July 7 entry in the Riezler diaries. Against this must be measured not only the statements of Jagow and Wilhelm II cited in the preceding paragraph, but Bethmann's own actions in late July. In addition to his attempt to secure British neutrality on July 29, his last-minute efforts early on the morning of July 30 were undertaken immediately upon receipt of Lichnowsky's telegram (DD 368) containing Grey's unmistakable warning of British intervention. The Kaiser's marginalia on this document are hysterical even for him and certainly do not lend credence to the supposition that he had counted on British opposition all along. Why did he write these things, and why did Bethmann frantically lobby Berchtold if the German government was simply following a consistent policy of hoping to avoid a European war at any cost, since they could not win such a war given British intervention? In that case, Bethmann should (and probably would) have acted much earlier to defuse the crisis. The proximity of his pleas for restraint to the unwelcome news regarding British neutrality does not substantiate Erdmann's thesis.

Yet the evidence presented by Erdmann is not inconsequential,

116

and the fact that some historians consider his conclusions unsatis-
factory does not relieve those scholars of the responsibility of
developing other conclusions consistent with that evidence. The
Hamburg school has held with its original findings, asserting that
the Riezler diaries testify "to the continuity of German aims and so
to the strengthening of the Fischer thesis."[42] A.J.P. Taylor's solution is admirably consistent with his view of the crisis: like the other
principal players in the July crisis, Bethmann simply did not know
what he was doing.[43] Norman Stone suggests that "German policy
was operating on two levels. Bethmann Hollweg did not consciously want war: privately he thought that a German victory
would be a great disaster for Germany. On the other hand, German
behaviour in the month of July 1914 could not reasonably be
expected to end in anything but a great war."[44] There is something
to be said for each of these positions, but none of them represents a
fully satisfactory response to the issues raised by the Riezler diaries.

Karl Dietrich Erdmann's interpretation of German policy during
the crisis legitimized the acceptance by the *Zunft* of several of the
claims set forth by Fritz Fischer. But Fischer, as we have seen, went
well beyond those claims with his assertion that Germany had
planned the war at least eighteen months before it broke out. This
precluded outright endorsement of his views by the majority of
German historians, and the ambiguous nature of the evidence found
in the Riezler diaries muddied the waters yet further. Others,
notably Wolfgang Mommsen, Andreas Hillgruber, and Egmont
Zechlin were meanwhile adding their contributions to the debate.

Wolfgang Mommsen (University of Düsseldorf)

In his early thirties when the Fischer controversy broke out, Wolfgang Mommsen was admirably suited to regard the dispute with
equanimity. Descended from a lengthy line of distinguished members of the *Zunft*, he was just embarking on his own scholarly career
and was not personally committed to the patriotic self-justification
which had influenced older generations so profoundly. Mommsen's

---

42. Moses, "Karl Dietrich Erdmann," 252.
43. Taylor, *War by Time-Table*. Taylor, in *The Struggle for Mastery*, 525, antici-
pates Erdmann by concluding that the General Staff "had always assumed that Great
Britain would enter the war." But he draws the line at extending this supposition to
Bethmann.
44. Stone, "Gerhard Ritter," 165.

work on the origins of the war revolves around a structural analysis of the Wilhelmine Reich and contains implications which reach far beyond the July crisis itself.

Two of Mommsen's writings are pertinent to this study. In *Das Zeitalter des Imperialismus* (1969), he argued that prior to June 1914, both Bethmann and Jagow "rejected decisively the idea of a preventive war."[45] But the news of the impending conclusion of a naval convention between England and Russia reached Germany in that month and transferred the initiative to those elements in the government which favored such a conflict. Bethmann, when faced with the July crisis, attempted to pursue a "policy of the diagonal" (one of his favorite images) by encouraging Austria-Hungary to undertake a local war against Serbia. This would demonstrate clearly the degree of Russian readiness for war. If Russia backed down, as Bethmann hoped would happen, Austria would emerge strengthened. If Russia intervened and a general war resulted, Bethmann would accept the consequences, which would necessarily include British intervention (bearing in mind the Anglo-Russian naval talks). Thus the chancellor willingly ran the risk of a world war, "but without explicitly aiming toward it."[46] This study, published just prior to the release of *War of Illusions* took a position that was compatible with the basic thrust of the Fischer thesis while differing from it on the issue of the likelihood of British intervention.

Mommsen's 1966 essay, "The Debate on German War Aims," held out an olive branch toward the Hamburg school by enumerating Fischer's achievements while identifying his shortcomings in terms that allowed for the possibility of compromise. At the same time, this article sketched the framework for a structural analysis of Imperial Germany, soon provided in *Das Zeitalter des Imperialismus*. Mommsen's utilization of analytic techniques commonly identified in Germany with the Hamburg school further signaled his willingness to embrace a number of Fischer's arguments. But the extension of the Fischer thesis to include the concept of premeditated war left Mommsen unimpressed. As John Moses pointed out, "Mommsen denies Fischer's basic thesis that the German Reich since its foundation was striving continuously to reach world power

45. Wolfgang J. Mommsen, *Das Zeitalter des Imperialismus* (Frankfurt, 1969), 269.
46. Ibid., 277.

status and that the First World War was a logical extension of this governing political will."[47]

In a 1973 article, "Domestic Factors in German Foreign Policy before 1914," Mommsen set forth his disagreements with Fischer and developed his own schematic for analysis of Germany's role in the July crisis (which, despite the title, is discussed in the concluding pages of the piece). He identifies four types of analysis currently being applied to Imperial Germany: the socio-Marxist approach, practiced by George W.F. Hallgarten; the moralistic approach used by the Hamburg school; the "Kehrite" approach, named for the late Eckart Kehr and utilized by Hans-Ulrich Wehler (among others); and the functional-structural approach, adopted by a variety of scholars including Gerhard Ritter, John C.G. Röhl (a defender of Fischer), and Mommsen himself.[48] The article is a superb combination of historiographic analysis and acute historical insight; it should be read and reflected upon by anyone interested in the history of Wilhelmine Germany. Only the portions dealing with the July crisis will be discussed here.

Mommsen's treatment of German policy prior to the delivery of the Austrian ultimatum demonstrates how far German scholarship had come in the twelve years since *Griff nach der Weltmacht*. Previously heretical contentions are now taken for granted: Bethmann and the Kaiser, far from being surprised by Austria's request of July 5, were ready for it and had made their decision before Hoyos ever arrived, "probably around the 2nd or 3rd [of July.]"[49] The chancellor was not bullied by the military (which played a very limited role on July 5–6), but recognized an opportunity to split the Entente by running the risk of a European war, unlikely though such an eventuality might be. Since neither France nor England would be interested in fighting for the Serbs, Russia would naturally cave in following a demonstration of diplomatic support for Serbia (as in 1909). Mommsen contends that Bethmann agreed to this course of action "only after some hesitation," since after all it constituted a "major shift in German policy."[50]

---

47. Moses, *The Politics of Illusion*, 90.
48. Wolfgang J. Mommsen, "Domestic Factors," 7–9.
49. Ibid., 39.
50. Ibid. Mommsen parts company with Fischer when he defends the sincerity of the German government's belief that the Austro-Serbian war could be isolated. He cites in substantiation an entry from the Riezler diaries suggesting that if the war were limited to Serbia and Austria-Hungary, Germany might then feel free to

So Bethmann gambled on Russian weakness – but he did not, as Fischer claims, gamble on British neutrality. Fischer's contention that the German government wanted Britain to stand aside so that France and Russia could be destroyed is, in Mommsen's opinion, contradicted by the available evidence. Bethmann's policy was not based on a cynical, undeviating lust for world power, but on muddled thinking and fear. While his plan of action "satisfied the request of the military establishment insofar as it did nothing to avoid war," it counted on a diplomatic solution of the crisis because of Bethmann's realization that Britain would back France and Russia if it came to war.[51]

For Mommsen, the Riezler diaries prove that the chancellor recognized that Britain could not allow France to be defeated by Germany. He did hope that Britain would preserve a watchful neutrality during the opening stages of a continental war while working toward a diplomatic settlement. This, in his mind, would not be so very different from the role Britain had played in helping to prevent the Balkan wars from engulfing all of Europe. But of course there *was* a difference: Germany and France had not been belligerents in the Balkans. Britain, even if neutral at the outset, would not stand aside forever if its peace initiatives failed. All the more reason for war to be avoided entirely, or, if it came, to be prosecuted vigorously and won quickly through the Schlieffen Plan, so that France would be defeated before Britain could intervene. Mommsen summarizes that "the assumption that Great Britain might remain neutral did not play a key role in German calculations on the eve of the First World War. Rather, the opposite is true. It was the startling news that Great Britain was apparently about to join the opposite camp that set things in motion."[52]

In such circumstances, Grey's reluctance to issue an unmistakable warning to Germany early in the crisis becomes inconsequential. Since Bethmann never assumed that Britain would remain neutral,

---

conclude an agreement with Russia – at Austria's expense! This contention renders laughable the usual justification for German policy, that Germany was forced to support Austria-Hungary in order to *defend* the latter's very existence.

51. Ibid., 41.

52. Ibid., 38–39. Mommsen's reasoning here is perplexing. Why would the news that Britain was about to join France and Russia be "startling" if Bethmann had assumed all along that Britain would intervene sooner or later? There were, after all, only three possible permutations: British support for the Central Powers, which was never considered likely; British neutrality, on which Mommsen and others say Bethmann never counted; or British support for the Entente.

an early commitment to France would only confirm his presuppositions. Indeed, it might have made war more certain by strengthening Moltke's "argument that . . . it was better to fight now, at a moment when in his opinion the war could still be won decisively within months, rather than later."[53]

Mommsen, like Erdmann and others whose work we will examine shortly, correctly identified the assumption that Germany counted on British neutrality as a cornerstone of the Fischer thesis. With the exception of Ritter, who agreed with Fischer on this point, all of the historians discussed in this chapter attacked Fischer by attacking this supposition. For Mommsen, then, the Great War was not the consequence of Germany's lust for world power or of a set of concrete expansionistic aims worked out over the previous decade. Instead, German policy in July 1914 was an opportunistic reaction to an unanticipated but not unwelcome crisis, a crisis which gave Bethmann and Wilhelm the chance to embark on a preventive war to break Germany's encirclement and redraft the European power constellation in a manner more favorable to German aspirations.

Andreas Hillgruber (University of Cologne)

Fischer, Geiss, Ritter, and Mommsen are familiar figures to American readers because of the appearance of many of their works in English translation. This is not the case with Karl Dietrich Erdmann, Egmont Zechlin, and Andreas Hillgruber, most of whose work remains accessible solely in the original German. Since only those publications by Erdmann and Zechlin that refer specifically to the Fischer controversy would normally be considered candidates for translation, the situation surrounding those works is less perplexing than that around Hillgruber's works, which paint in sweeping strokes and vivid colors the most gripping aspects of German history in the twentieth century.

Hillgruber was fascinated by the German *Sonderweg*, or "special path," of historical development. Why did Germany evolve so differently from France and England in the nineteenth and twentieth centuries? What elements of continuity and discontinuity are present in German foreign policy from Bismarck through Hitler? What role did Germany play in the outbreak of the two world wars

53. Ibid., 41.

of the twentieth century? What strategic principles were followed by Hitler in his conduct of World War II? What role has been played by the "German question" in the years since 1945? These provocative and extremely significant questions are of concern to anyone interested in the history of the past two centuries. Yet only one of Hillgruber's books, *Deutschlands Rolle in der Vorgeschichte der beiden Weltkriege* (1967) has been translated into English. Most American historians are familiar with his work only through references to it in standard histories (like Gerhard Weinberg's *Foreign Policy of Hitler's Germany*) or review articles (like Holger Herwig's assessment in *Central European History*).

Erdmann's 1964 disclosures concerning the Riezler diaries inspired Hillgruber to look into Kurt Riezler's published works in search of clues to German policy in 1914. In a famous 1966 article, he argued that the central motivating impulse of that policy was fear of Russia. Bethmann Hollweg indeed ran a calculated risk that July, but not out of ambition to "grasp for world power"; rather, he was trying to preserve intact the dominant continental position that Germany had enjoyed since 1871. In this sense Bethmann was the heir of Bismarck, not the forerunner of Hitler. These contentions were woven into the context of twentieth-century German history in a book published the following year.[54]

Following the pattern established by Fritz Fischer, Hillgruber concentrates on German policy in his writings on the July crisis. Bethmann's actions on July 5–6 put the policy of calculated risk into motion. Hopefully Russia would remain on the sidelines when Austria attacked Serbia, thanks to the tsar's affinity with the monarchical cause in Europe. Riezler noted in his diary on July 11, "A *fait accompli*, and then friendly toward the Entente, and the shock can be absorbed."[55] This would alter the Balkan power balance in a manner that, according to Riezler's earlier theoretical writings, could nonetheless be accepted by Russia. The pivotal question was this: would Russia be able to distinguish between its vital interests

54. Andreas Hillgruber, "Riezlers Theorie des kalkulierten Risikos und Bethmann Hollwegs politische Konzeption in der Julikrise 1914," *Historische Zeitschrift* 202 (1966): 333–51; *Germany and the Two World Wars*, trans. William C. Kirby (Cambridge, Mass., 1981).

55. Kurt Riezler, quoted in Hillgruber, *Germany*, 31. Interestingly, Hillgruber cites this remark *before* Riezler's oft-mentioned quotation of Bethmann's desire to "split the Entente." The latter phrase is disclosed on p. 32 and is never linked by Hillgruber to Riezler's July 11 entry. The result is a benevolent portrayal of Bethmann which is not entirely consistent with the Riezler entries.

and its prestige, as Bismarck always tried to do? If so, then it would acquiesce in Austria's chastisement of Serbia; if not, there would be war. "In either case, the choice between peace and general war was, in accordance with Riezler's conception, shifted to the enemy."[56]

Hillgruber does not minimize the degree of risk implicit in this decision. Bethmann gambled on an operation which in his own estimation had only minimal prospects for success and then only if Austria moved quickly. He ran the risk because he was convinced that Germany's chances of victory diminished with each passing day and that some sort of military confrontation was unavoidable if the encirclement strategy of the Entente was to be broken. All of this reasoning is, in Hillgruber's estimation, consistent with the theories set forth in Riezler's published writings prior to July 1914. German policy in the fateful days before the Great War followed a model designed by the chancellor's closest political counsellor.[57]

Why did the model not work? Hillgruber cites Bethmann's two chief aims: to support Austria-Hungary and to avoid a world war. His policy began to come apart when Russia refused to abandon Serbia. Now Germany had to deal quickly with France and Russia, but this involved implementation of the inflexible Schlieffen Plan, which would almost certainly bring England into the war because of the violation of neutral Belgium and the threat to the integrity of France. Hillgruber, like Erdmann, claims that Bethmann's policy "was not pursued with the goal of disengaging England from the Triple Entente in order to allow a continental war of Germany and Austria-Hungary against France and Russia."[58] He never believed in British neutrality, and when in the early hours of July 30 he urged restraint on Vienna, he was not motivated by fear of British hostility (since the Kaiser's *Halt in Belgrade* plan would be acceptable to London), but by the realization that the time had now arrived to settle the crisis through cooperation with the Entente. Unfortunately, he had not let Vienna in on his plans; Berchtold knew

56. Hillgruber, *Germany*, 30.
57. Hillgruber, "Riezlers Theorie," 337–41. If this view is correct, then the problem of distinguishing between Bethmann's thoughts and those of Riezler in the diaries is rendered moot: they thought as one and worked together in July 1914 to implement a policy on which they had agreed in advance. Wayne Thompson, *In the Eye of the Storm*, 94, disagrees, holding that "German control over events was relinquished too quickly for an effective application of the kind of calculated risk which Riezler had described."
58. Hillgruber, *Germany*, 26. Again, it is difficult to reconcile this interpretation with Riezler's July 7 quotation, "We have the prospect of splitting the Entente."

nothing of Riezler's theoretical model and failed to comprehend the reasoning behind Berlin's abrupt about-face. By the time Vienna was willing to be reasonable, continental war, and with it world war, could no longer be avoided. The military now stepped in, spurred on by the preliminary reports of Russian general mobilization. The calculated risk model had failed.[59]

German policy in July 1914 was thus free of any desire for aggressive territorial expansion, and in this sense, Fritz Fischer is wrong. But in a larger sense, only his timing is incorrect. Germany *did* shift from an essentially peaceful policy to one of conquest and domination; but this transformation occurred not on December 8, 1912, and certainly not earlier than that, but in the autumn of 1916, when command of the war effort passed to Paul von Hindenburg and Erich Ludendorff. Their desire for Teutonic expansion and for maneuvering space for future wars foreshadows Hitler's dreams; he and his movement are descended from them, not from Bethmann and the Kaiser. This does not absolve Germany of responsibility for the outbreak of war in 1914, a responsibility which Hillgruber contends is heavy indeed. But it puts that responsibility in the perspective constructed by Fritz Fischer in 1961 rather than in 1969. Germany risked a preventive, not premeditated, war out of apprehension rather than avarice.

This construction continued the *Zunft*'s efforts to portray Bethmann in a more favorable light than that cast upon him by the Hamburg school. Yet the Riezler diaries, as we have already seen, are not unambiguous. Do they really show that Bethmann ran a calculated risk? John C.G. Röhl has his doubts. The risk theory "holds that it was Germany's intention not to go to war but merely to use the threat of a major war to force Russia to break with her allies, France and Britain, and join the German bloc instead."[60] But Riezler's entries do not indicate that Bethmann believed that such a realignment could actually be achieved. Instead, they offer "a great deal of evidence . . . to show that a major war was regarded as necessary or even desirable by the German Chancellor. Indeed, such evidence seems quite to outweigh that pointing to the existence of hopes on his part for a peaceful outcome of the crisis."[61]

If Bethmann's mood was truly as bleak as the diaries seem to indicate (and there is no way to determine this with certainty), then

59. Hillgruber, "Riezlers Theorie," 346–48; *Germany*, 35–38.
60. Röhl, *1914*, 22.
61. Ibid., 24.

Röhl has a valid point. The diaries depict the chancellor as a man skeptical of Germany's chances of emerging from the unfolding crisis without a major war. He had a number of opportunities to disengage the plan he had set in motion, but ignored all of them until July 30 and then failed to cut loose in time. Gerhard Ritter would have called such conduct criminally reckless, and he would have been right. Röhl concludes that "German policy in July 1914 was either not calculated at all, or . . . it was calculated to produce war."[62]

Hillgruber's work raised as many questions as it answered, but the *Zunft* had one more champion to offer.

Egmont Zechlin (University of Hamburg)

Everyone who taught at Hamburg did not belong to the Hamburg school. Egmont Zechlin, several years older than Fischer and his colleague at Hamburg for two decades, remained unconvinced of the younger man's assessment of Germany's role in July 1914. Although agreeing with Fischer in many respects, he contended that Bethmann never counted on British neutrality and denied the plausibility of Germany's having planned for war as early as 1912. Zechlin's work remains little known in the United States, scattered as it is in a large number of articles in different German scholarly journals. Yet when read as a whole, his views represent the most systematic, consistent, and plausible of the various challenges to the Hamburg school emanating from the *Zunft*.[63]

Zechlin accepts many of Fischer's basic tenets. He has no doubt that Germany embarked deliberately on an extremely risky policy in July 1914. The widespread fear of Russian military improvements and of the tightening noose of encirclement led to a profound fatalism in German ruling circles. Bethmann was not the only high-ranking official who believed that if Germany must fight, it should do so sooner rather than later; but neither was he, as Ritter alleged, a peace-loving philosopher-statesman outmaneuvered by the shortsighted military elements surrounding the throne. The factor precipitating Bethmann's policy in the summer of 1914 was the unwelcome news that England and Russia were preparing to

---

62. Ibid., 27.
63. Only two of Egmont Zechlin's articles on July 1914 have thus far been translated into English. A fascinating collection of his most important work, unfortunately available only in German, is *Krieg und Kriegsrisiko: Zur deutschen Politik im Ersten Weltkrieg* (Düsseldorf, 1979).

sign a naval convention. This eroded Bethmann's conviction that England and Germany could continue to cooperate to preserve peace and led him to believe that action should be taken to split the Entente by driving England and Russia further apart.[64]

This was the context in which Bethmann made his decision to issue the blank check to the Dual Monarchy. That guarantee of German support was intended not merely as an effort to bail Austria out of its difficulties, but as "a reaction to the precarious developments within the European constellation which the Chancellor had been watching with growing concern since May."[65] Zechlin portrays this decision in terms that could easily have been drawn from *Griff nach der Weltmacht*. Germany expressly envisioned the possibility of Russian intervention in an Austro-Serb war: "Because of its traditional ties to the Balkan States, Russia would find it virtually impossible to stand by idly if Austria commenced hostilities against Serbia. To do nothing would risk an immense loss in prestige."[66] In these words, written in 1964, he shows little sympathy for the position taken by conservative German historians that Russia had no genuine national interests at stake and should have backed down. Bethmann was determined to exploit the Sarajevo crime to squeeze Russia until it squeaked; he knew that this might well lead to world war and said as much to Riezler.

So Germany consciously embarked on a policy likely to lead to a preventive war. But for Zechlin, as well as for others (including Fischer), the term preventive war seems inadequate. Fischer holds that in order for a war to be preventive, there must be at least the theoretical possibility of an attack by the other side. Since this possibility did not exist in July 1914, Germany's war was aggressive in nature. Zechlin too shuns the term preventive, but does so for a different reason. He sees Germany's policy as defensive rather than aggressive, based as it was on fatalism and fear rather than on overweening pride and expansionistic ambition. He uses the term "preventive defense" to describe the war Bethmann had in mind, a limited, "cabinet-style" war like the Seven Years' War of 1756–63, not a total war like the wars of the French Revolution. This war

64. Egmont Zechlin, "Cabinet versus Economic Warfare in Germany: Policy and Strategy during the Early Months of the First World War," trans. Heinz Norden, in H.W. Koch, ed., *The Origins of the First World War*, 2d ed. (London, 1984), 194–201.

65. Ibid., 202–3.

66. Ibid., 203.

would redraw the power balance in the Balkan peninsula (a limited objective designed to shore up the declining international position of the Central Powers); it would not signal the onset of a burst of German expansionism intended to achieve European domination as a stepping-stone to world-power status.

This is the crux of Zechlin's difference with Fischer, a difference of philosophy rather than action, of intentions rather than deeds. It is a nuanced difference that is not immediately evident in much of Zechlin's work. In a 1977 article, he writes that "this primarily and intentionally defensive objective, of securing and strengthening the international position of the Reich and its freedom of movement within world politics, was the main preoccupation of German policy in July 1914. To challenge this theory there are no indications at all . . . which could be produced to show that the German government . . . had been planning an expansionist war with conquests in the east and in the west with the intention of gaining the hegemony in Europe."[67] A number of scholars, including many from the Hamburg school, would find no contradiction between the positions expressed in these two sentences. Thus Imanuel Geiss wrote in 1966 that "the differences between him and the Fischer group, on that point at least, have been reduced to a few subtle shades of interpretation."[68]

There are, however, other differences between the two positions, the most significant one being the dispute over Bethmann's alleged belief in British neutrality. Zechlin takes a position identical to that of Erdmann, Mommsen, and Hillgruber, contending that Berlin took seriously the British concern for the viability of France and recognized that a German defeat of France would seriously impair Britain's national interests. This, he says, is proof that Germany did not will the Great War, for what government would work toward a conflict in which it would certainly be defeated? Rather it counted on the localization of the war between Austria and Serbia; keeping Russia out was the key to keeping Britain out.

British neutrality therefore emerges as the most vexing point at issue between the Hamburg school and its critics. Neither side's position appears satisfactory. Fischer's assumption that Bethmann hoped that England would remain uninvolved is grounded in two conclusions: first, that the available evidence points in that direc-

---

67. Egmont Zechlin, "July 1914: Reply to a Polemic," trans. Brian Follett, in H.W. Koch, ed., *The Origins of the First World War*, 2d ed. (London, 1984), 373–74.
68. Geiss, "The Outbreak," 76.

tion; and second, that if Bethmann were truly convinced that a war against the entire Entente could not be won, yet embarked on a policy designed to bring about such a war, his action "would have been nothing short of murder."[69] Unwilling to believe that Bethmann was either a lunatic or a vicious criminal, Fischer holds that Bethmann believed in and worked to assure British neutrality. This explains his frantic appeals to Vienna on July 30, when his hopes went aglimmering.

To accept Fischer's conclusion is to accept a precarious chain of reasoning. If Bethmann believed that Britain could be kept on the sidelines, then he must have believed one of two other things: (1) that British commitments to the viability of France were at least negotiable and at most bluff; or (2) that British commitments to France would never come into play because Russia would refrain from taking Serbia's side and the Franco-Russian alliance would remain inoperative. Yet how could he take either contention seriously? What gave either Germany or Austria the notion that after a century in which the Eastern question had been the subject of continual dispute and consultation among several powers, the map of the entire region could suddenly be redrawn without taking any other opinions into account? How could Russia grant Austria the exclusive right to solve the Serbian problem? And once Russia came in, as Bethmann (according to the Riezler diaries) considered probable, France would come in too, and how could Britain be kept out? Was it rational to assume that Whitehall would stand idly by as the Channel ports fell into the hands of the one nation which had since 1898 deliberately attempted to build a fleet that would rival Britain's? If Bethmann believed that he could obtain British neutrality, on what did he base his belief?

Similarly, Zechlin's position leaves many questions unanswered. Like Erdmann, he feels that the Riezler diaries, taken in concert with the evidence indicating that other branches of the German government were resigned to British intervention, prove that Bethmann was resigned as well. But many of his actions appear inconsistent with such a belief. Is it merely coincidental that his July 30 telegrams to Vienna followed so closely upon his receipt of Lichnowsky's account of Grey's unequivocal warning? Why did Bethmann chastise Goschen so severely on August 4? Did he think (as his comments imply) that England *caused* the Great War that he had

69. Fischer, *World Power*, 100.

wished to avoid? How could he have believed such a thing? Or was he bitterly disappointed that Britain had chosen to intervene despite his best efforts to convince it to remain neutral? Why did the Kaiser and Jagow, in private memoranda as well as in open conversations, express their conviction that Britain would stay out? In early August, Grand Admiral Tirpitz criticized the government for having gotten involved in a war with Britain before the fleet was ready. If it was assumed throughout the German government that Britain would enter any continental conflict, why did Tirpitz not intervene in early July in an effort to avoid such a disaster? If Bethmann sincerely wanted Britain as a negotiating partner in July 1914, why was it (as Zechlin himself writes) that "the German leadership insisted on maintaining its challenge to Russia, by consistently boycotting British mediation efforts and obstinately refusing to engage in any serious effort to restrain Austria from military action"?[70]

Those words could easily have been written by Fritz Fischer. Zechlin's view of German conduct in July 1914 is in many ways consistent with that set forth by the Hamburg school. With respect to British neutrality, neither of their positions is completely acceptable to those who examine the evidence in search of answers rather than excuses or support for preconceived notions. Perhaps this dissatisfaction is attributable to the efforts of both Fischer and his opponents to understand Bethmann's policy in exclusively rational terms. Certainly it leaves us without a fully suitable solution to a pivotal question.

For the *Zunft*, this has so far proven to be the end of the line. Its members formulated a coherent response to the challenge laid down by the Hamburg school, and neither response nor challenge has been substantively altered since the early seventies. That all this had been accomplished within little more than a decade is the true measure of Fischer's achievement. He and his adherents unraveled more than forty years of patriotic self-censorship and in so doing cleared the path for German historians who wished to come to grips with their country's history. Nearly all of them did so, to one degree or another, often at the cost of great personal anguish. This commitment to the pursuit of historical truth on the part of both the proponents and opponents of the Fischer thesis should not be lost sight of as younger generations of historians build on the insights and the struggles of their predecessors.

70. Zechlin, "Cabinet," 204.

6

The Debate outside Germany

The translation into English of Luigi Albertini's three volumes actually inhibited debate on the origins of the Great War. Albertini's erudition and ambition seemed overwhelming, and many scholars in Britain and the United States were prepared to accept his views as definitive, even if they had read only pieces of his work. His contention that the Central Powers bore primary responsibility for the outbreak of war coincided neatly with the assumptions of most historians outside Germany, and his strong criticism of Poincaré, Grey, and Sazonov was attractive to revisionists. Accordingly, the 1950s ended with the controversy apparently settled, as students of twentieth-century Europe turned their gaze to subjects such as the rise of Nazi Germany and the Russian Revolution.

Griff nach der Weltmacht had little immediate effect on this state of affairs. It caused an explosion in West Germany but only a muffled thud elsewhere. A few English- and French-language reviews appeared, and an occasional newspaper article referred to the acrimony stirred up in Germany by Fischer's views; but his work for the most part remained unknown to those unable or unwilling to read it in German.[1] Barbara Tuchman's best-selling *Guns of August* (New York, 1962) dealt only sparingly with the month of July, and her uncompromising anti-German tone was not derived

1. Hansjoachim Koch, in the introduction to his collection of readings on the Great War, contends that Fischer's book "was quickly translated into English," whereas "it took five years to find a publisher for Ritter's main work in the United States and only via that country did Ritter's work reach the shores of Britain." In fact, *Griff nach der Weltmacht*, published in 1961, was issued in translation in 1967; Ritter's *Staatskunst und Kriegshandwerk*, a multivolume work, was completed in 1967 and published in English between 1969 and 1972. It is true that the first of Ritter's volumes, published in German in 1954, was not issued in the United States until 1969 (in its third version); but this was due less to the fact that "both Great Britain and the United States are notorious for their disinclination to publish important historical monographs in any language" than to its newly attained significance as part of Ritter's response to Fischer.

from Fischer, of whose work she took no notice. The fiftieth
anniversary of the July crisis in 1964 resulted in a spate of summary
articles and potboilers, most of them warmed-over Albertini with a
dash of Fay or the reverse. Ludwig Reiners's *The Lamps Went Out
in Europe* (New York, 1965) is a good example of this sort of
writing, which broke no new ground and ignored the controversy
raging in Germany.

This situation changed in 1966. In Britain, James Joll's article in
Past and Present ("The 1914 Debate Continues: Fritz Fischer and
His Critics") exposed a wide readership to the renewed debate for
the first time. Joll's vivid writing style, cogent appraisal of the
conflicting views, and subtle defense of Fischer aroused considerable interest. Simultaneously, the British *Journal of Contemporary
History* issued a special number devoted to new research on the
Great War. Somewhat misleadingly entitled *1914: The Coming of
the First World War*, it contained articles covering events as late as
1916 and was immediately published as a book in Britain and the
United States. Oddly, Fischer and Ritter wrote nothing for the
volume, but the Hamburg school was defended by Imanuel Geiss
and the *Zunft* by Wolfgang Mommsen. Other valuable and provocative articles, including Norman Stone's "Hungary and the
Crisis of July 1914," Klaus Epstein's "Gerhard Ritter and the First
World War," I.V. Bestuzhev's "Russian Foreign Policy February-
June 1914," and Hans Rogger's "Russia in 1914" made the book
indispensable to an entire generation of researchers. It was quickly
translated into French and German and, in company with Joll's
article, stimulated a high level of interest in the Fischer debate. The
issuance of *Griff nach der Weltmacht* in English translation followed in 1967, making Fischer's thesis accessible to a wide audience.

Since that time, the historiography of the July crisis has evolved
through three stages, each of which will be dealt with in turn.

Stage One, 1966–1970

The first stage covers the period from the watershed year of 1966 to
the publication of Fritz Fischer's second book, *War of Illusions*, and
the dissemination of the revised Fischer thesis contained therein.
Renewed interest in the outbreak of the war stimulated some
important and innovative work, five examples of which are
analyzed here.

Vladimir Dedijer, a Yugoslav journalist, former partisan fighter, and editor in chief of the project to publish the Serbian documents from July 1914, addressed the first key to the crisis in *The Road to Sarajevo* (1966). His assessment of Serbian governmental complicity has not been seriously challenged and constitutes (at least in the absence of new evidence) the final word on the subject.

Dedijer cites the report of Jakov Milović, submitted between June 2 and 13, 1914, disclosing that Princip and his confederate Grabez had been guided by Milović across the border into Bosnia and had then proceeded to Sarajevo. Milović was an agent of Narodna Odbrana and of Serbian military intelligence. When Pašić received this report, he opened two investigations, one of Colonel Dimitrijević and one of the border authorities. Simultaneously, he "discussed the matter with some of the cabinet ministers" and took unspecified measures to intercept the group in Bosnia. The report did not mention Franz Ferdinand, but it did state that the two men were heavily armed.[2]

A power struggle between Pašić and Dimitrijević was apparently at the root of the latter's decision to permit one of his operatives, Voja Tankosić, to transmit weapons to Princip's band in Sarajevo. Dedijer contends that Dimitrijević "did not expect that Princip and his accomplices would succeed in killing the Archduke, although he did think their efforts might provoke a greater strain in relations between Pašić and the Austro-Hungarian government." This would strengthen Dimitrijević's position vis-à-vis Pašić, whom he considered an implacable enemy of the Black Hand, the secret society actually responsible for the archduke's murder. In corroboration, Dedijer cites Tankosić's comment upon his arrest, when he responded to an Austrian general's inquiry into his motivations with the laconic "to spite Pašić."[3]

Dedijer concludes that according to the archives of the Serbian foreign ministry, the Pašić government never informed Austria-Hungary in any official manner of its two investigations. He considers it probable that Jovan Jovanović, the Serbian minister in Vienna, "went to Count Bilinski and mentioned vaguely the dangers for the Archduke during his trip to Bosnia and Hercegovina."[4] Three inferences can be drawn with reasonable confidence: the Serbian government neither created nor approved of the plot; it

2. Dedijer, *Road to Sarajevo*, 390.
3. Ibid., 395.
4. Ibid.

failed to deliver a precise and explicit warning to the Austro-Hungarian authorities; and the actual perpetrators, the Black Hand, were motivated more by internal political disputes in Belgrade than by any real desire to alter the succession to the Austro-Hungarian thrones, let alone begin a Great War.

Our second key, German conduct prior to the delivery of the ultimatum, was analyzed in detail by the two American historians who were granted access to the Riezler diaries while Marie White was examining them in New York. In articles published in 1967 and 1969, Fritz Stern and Konrad Jarausch took issue with Fischer's characterization of Bethmann Hollweg. Stern, provost of Columbia University and author of a number of probing analyses of twentieth-century German history, argues that Bethmann's principal motive was not, as Fischer would have it, the lust for world power, but apprehension regarding the future of Germany. Sarajevo was merely a pretext: "Unrequited [it] would worsen Germany's situation; . . . properly exploited [it] might lead to a dramatic escape from that situation."[5]

Stern is very hard on Bethmann. The chancellor knew that his actions might result in a world war, which in turn would "result in the uprooting of everything that exists."[6] He intended at the very least to split the Entente, or if that failed, to wage war under the most favorable conditions possible. As early as July 23, he "envisioned the sequences of events that would lead up to a 'defensive' war, provoked by Russia, which alone could unite the nation and perhaps even deceive other nations."[7] Fischer is wrong in his analysis of Bethmann's motivations: "It is naive and excessively rationalistic to suppose that aggression must spring from lust of conquest. Fear, too, impels aggressive action."[8]

But Fischer's misreading of the evidence in no way exonerates Bethmann. He may have been motivated by fear of the future, but that fear was almost certainly misplaced. In a marvelous passage, Stern asks the fundamental questions that Bethmann should have asked himself (or that Riezler should have asked him): Why fear that after 1917 a powerful Russia would destroy Germany? What would convince England, the self-appointed defender of the

---

5. Stern, "Bethmann Hollweg," 263.
6. Kurt Riezler, quoted in Stern, "Bethmann Hollweg," 263.
7. Stern, "Bethmann Hollweg," 264.
8. Ibid., 268.

continental balance of power, to support the destruction of German domination of Europe in favor of Russian hegemony? In such circumstances, would not England have restrained Russia or, if worst came to worst, supported Germany? And if Austria-Hungary had broken with Germany because of lack of support over Sarajevo (another of Bethmann's apparently sincere phobias), would this not have opened the door to exactly what Bethmann said he wanted – a Russo-German alliance against Austria that would incidentally split the Entente? The chancellor may indeed have been apprehensive, but he feared ghosts and chimeras, not serious probabilities. Stern concludes that Bethmann, while not a rabid imperialist, nonetheless bears tremendous responsibility for the outbreak of war. "In a sense, the most damaging evidence that the Riezler Diary provides for the July crisis lies in what it does *not* say: it contains no hint or thought of any move by Bethmann to arrest the crisis, to save the peace."[9]

Konrad Jarausch (then of the University of Missouri, now at the University of North Carolina at Chapel Hill) was the other scholar who saw the Riezler diaries in New York. In an article in *Central European History* in 1969, followed four years later by a full-length biography of Bethmann Hollweg, he presented his own interpretation of German conduct. Jarausch recognizes that the Hamburg school has laid to rest the assertion that Szögyény's reporting from Potsdam was inaccurate; he characterizes Bethmann's statements of July 6 as "one of the most momentous assurances of European history."[10] The blank check was issued in cold blood, and it was considerably more than a check: it was explicit authorization for the breaking of the Entente through a diplomatic realignment in the Balkans, of which Austria's chastisement of Serbia would constitute only one component. The following day, Bethmann explained his conduct to Riezler in terms of Anglo-Russian naval conversations, the encirclement of Germany, and the declining strength of Austria-Hungary. The chancellor adopted this policy as a result of political pressure from the Kaiser's military advisers, buttressed by the fact that Wilhelm had already gone a long way toward committing German support before calling in Bethmann. His policy was a compromise, an effort to hammer out a course of action acceptable to the top decision makers: "The war party in Berlin seized upon

9. Ibid., 265.
10. Jarausch, "The Illusion of Limited War," 56.

the crime to force Bethmann to abandon his moderate *Weltpolitik* and to embark upon unabashed military imperialism."[11]

This was a policy of hideous risk, a policy of preventive war, but not a policy of premeditated aggression. Jarausch is skeptical of the argument of Erdmann and Zechlin that Bethmann never counted on British neutrality: "The intervention of Britain or any other great power would upset the carefully balanced odds" in favor of Bethmann's calculated risk.[12] Indeed, he asserts that Wilhelm von Stumm, the Wilhelmstraße's top British expert, "minimized the risk of London's intervention and strongly counselled Bethmann to act."[13] Jarausch formulates the central issue in this way: Did Germany embark on a world war with malice aforethought in order to attain the status of a world power, or did it simply attempt to shore up the declining position of its sole ally? He opts for the latter assessment, which he portrays as psychologically defensive. "But the means that were adopted, the diplomatic offensive in the Balkans, the encouragement of Austrian punitive action against Serbia, the effort to prevent the intervention of the great powers and the attempt to split the Entente were *offensive*."[14]

What about Bethmann's last-minute efforts to urge restraint on Vienna? The chancellor feared world war while planning for

11. Konrad H. Jarausch, *The Enigmatic Chancellor: Bethmann Hollweg and the Hubris of Imperial Germany* (New Haven, 1973), 181; idem, "The Illusion of Limited War," 73. Jarausch appears ignorant of Geiss's assertion that Bethmann and Wilhelm had worked out this policy in a series of meetings prior to July 5. In "The Illusion," 55, he states that Wilhelm "recalled Bethmann to Berlin" on July 5 – a partially accurate statement. His account also mentions the interesting coincidence that on July 4 Undersecretary of State Zimmermann received from the General Staff two studies, "The Completion of the Russian Railroad Network" and "The Growing Power of Russia." Anyone conversant with standard military efforts to sway decision makers will recognize the implications of the timing of the issuance of these reports.

12. Jarausch, "The Illusion of Limited War," 58. This implies that Russian intervention would also have "upset the odds"; one wonders how Bethmann could possibly have hoped to avoid *that*, and the Riezler diaries indicate that he did not. It is interesting to note that Jarausch, alone among major scholars discussed in this book, points out that Pourtalès, the German ambassador to Russia, was Bethmann's cousin ("The Illusion of Limited War," 53). It is surprising that those historians who make much of the schoolboy relationship between Poincaré and Paléologue seem to have overlooked this relationship and its implications for Bethmann's assessment of Pourtalès's rather sanguine diplomatic reportage.

13. Jarausch, "The Illusion of Limited War," 74, n. 90, quoting Werner von Rheinbaden, *Kaiser, Kanzler, Präsidenten* (Mainz, 1968), 96, 108, in which Rheinbaden in turn quotes Stumm to the effect that "I erred in 1914 and advised Bethmann falsely."

14. Jarausch, "The Illusion of Limited War," 75.

continental hostilities. Riezler wrote on July 25 that "for the last days the Chancellor has almost always been on the phone. Apparently [there are] preparations for all eventualities, conferences with the military about which nothing is being said. . . . The merchant marine is warned. . . . [T]he financial mobilization [has begun]. So far nothing could be done out in the open."[15] Once he realized that Britain would probably intervene, he tried to draw Berchtold back from the brink by "urgent long-distance phone calls"; but the military became anxious and claimed the final say. "The ambiguity of the original compromise had carried Bethmann to the brink of a world conflagration and had transferred the final decision to the military. Only in this manner can the confusion of the Wilhelm-strasse, the consternation of the Chancellor and the complete lack of diplomatic preparation for war with France, Russia, and England be understood."[16]

Jarausch's conclusions are more favorable both to Germany and to Bethmann than are Stern's, as Jarausch himself admits.[17] But it must be remembered that prior to 1961, even proponents of Albertini would have considered Jarausch's portrayal of Bethmann unbelievably harsh. The displacement of the locus of the debate through the work of Fischer and his critics could not be more obvious than in a comparison of Stern's and Jarausch's work with that of early antirevisionists like Renouvin and Schmitt. Today, two decades after publication of their interpretations, Stern's and Jarausch's explanations of the events have won broad support among students of the conduct of German policy in July 1914.

In the same collection that featured Fritz Stern's essay, Arno Mayer of Princeton University published an intriguing essay that accused policymakers of a willingness to embark upon foreign wars for domestic political reasons.[18] A scholar whose professed intention is to write Marxist history "from the top down," Mayer takes

---

15. Kurt Riezler, quoted in Jarausch, *The Enigmatic Chancellor*, 164–65.
16. Jarausch, *The Enigmatic Chancellor*, 172; idem, "The Illusion of Limited War," 75.
17. Jarausch, "World Power or Tragic Fate?" 77.
18. Arno J. Mayer, "Domestic Causes of the First World War," in Leonard Krieger and Fritz Stern eds., *The Responsibility of Power: Historical Essays in Honor of Hajo Holborn* (New York, 1967), 286–300. The use of foreign war for domestic purposes was first attributed (at least in the twentieth century) to Viacheslav K. Plehve, Russian minister of the interior 1902–4, who spoke this way concerning the Russo-Japanese War. See Edward H. Judge, *Plehve: Repression and Reform in Imperial Russia, 1902–1904* (Syracuse, 1983).

issue with the tendency of historians of July 1914 to concentrate on "the personal attitudes, motives, and objectives of the principal foreign-policy actors."[19] His essay discusses the interconnection of domestic politics and foreign policy, a relationship which he alleges is "exceptionally intense under prerevolutionary and revolutionary conditions."[20]

Mayer's perspective on Bethmann is necessarily quite different from that of other historians discussed in this book. Instead of a chancellor bent on splitting the Entente because of Germany's precarious encirclement, he takes one prong of Fischer's argument and gives us a leader whose supreme concern was that the Social Democrats support the war effort. Assured of this, Bethmann then "readily either yielded to or agreed with those of his civil and military advisers – and William II – who looked to a smashing diplomatic or military triumph to consolidate the monarchy, to perpetuate Prussia's three-class franchise, and to check both reformists and revolutionaries."[21] Similarly, those who have criticized Grey for waffling prior to July 29 have missed the point. The British foreign secretary failed to stand up to Berlin not because of diplomatic concerns, but because of domestic political considerations: the impending civil war over Ireland and the deeply divided cabinet.

For Mayer, the fear of revolution at home outweighed the fear of complications abroad in the minds of the statesmen of July 1914. His position was highly controversial and was attacked by many who read the same evidence with different eyes. Konrad Jarausch, for example, asserted that Bethmann's fear of revolution in Germany contradicted Mayer's theory: the chancellor, far from pursuing a warlike policy in order to preserve the existing order in the Wilhelmine Reich, regarded war with apprehension precisely *because* he was uncertain of Socialist support.[22] Mayer's conclusions, expressed since 1967 in a variety of accounts, have fascinated scholars while extending Eckart Kehr's concept of "the primacy of domestic politics" to one of its logical limits. But the lacunae in his

19. Mayer, "Domestic Causes," 286. A cogent summary of Mayer's methodology may be found in his *The Persistence of the Old Regime: Europe to the Great War* (New York, 1981), 3–15.

20. Mayer, "Domestic Causes," 287. His implication is that such conditions prevailed in Germany in 1914.

21. Ibid., 297. Mayer downplays the other prong of Fischer's argument, that Bethmann attempted to keep Britain neutral.

22. Jarausch, "The Illusion of Limited War,", 58, n. 31.

model have remained unfilled, and few historians have been willing to buy the total package.

Our survey of the first stage of the post-Fischer era concludes with a consideration of the work of L.C.F. Turner, professor of history at the Royal Military College of Australia. His views, as developed in articles in 1965 and 1968 and a monograph in 1970, restore the study of military questions in July 1914 to a position of utmost significance. Turner's analysis of the first five of our "keys" to the July crisis reflects the influence of a variety of historians, from Sidney Fay to Fritz Fischer; it is in his study of the sixth key, Russian general mobilization, that he makes an original contribution to the debate.

In his assessment of Serbian governmental complicity, Turner adopts a revisionist outlook. Pašić's government was certainly aware of the plot and may have tried to warn the Austrian authorities; but regardless of Serbian intentions, Geiss's assertion that Princip alone was responsible for the murders is ludicrous. Turner takes his stand on "an accepted principle of international law that a government is responsible for acts of violence which emanate from its territory."[23] His discussion of German conduct in the first stage of the crisis is, however, clearly antirevisionist. Bethmann and the Kaiser orchestrated the Potsdam meetings in advance and urged the Dual Monarchy to go to war. The Hamburg school is wrong when it alleges that war with Russia and France was actively desired, but Bethmann's hopes for localization were unrealistic at best: "If Germany and Austria had been able to crush Serbia their military position would have been very significantly improved, but for this reason the prospects of their being permitted to do so were exceedingly slight."[24]

Turner identifies himself with Albertini when discussing the third key. Poincaré clearly assured Sazonov that French support would be forthcoming no matter what Austria did against Serbia, but Barnes's contention that the French and Russians cooked up the war between them is plainly foolish. Albertini's view of Grey's conduct is likewise correct: had he said on July 24 what he said on July 29, Bethmann might have come to his senses and called off Berchtold. In any case, Grey did not need cabinet approval to issue an early warning, any more than he needed it to issue a later one.

23. Turner, *Origins*, 80.
24. Ibid., 85.

With his survey of the fifth key, Turner approaches what he considers the key issue in the entire crisis. He does not accept Zechlin's contention that Bethmann never counted on British neutrality. Here his position is clearly Fischerite. Bethmann's behavior on July 27 constitutes "the gravest indictment against German policy in July 1914"; two days later, he had accepted the likelihood of war with France and Russia "and was gambling on British neutrality."[25] He tried to pin the blame on Russia so that British opinion would turn against the Entente and the Social Democrats would support the continental war. Without question, his messages to Vienna on July 30 were sincere expressions of desperation. Turner makes clear that the historian's position on the fifth key is determinative of his or her stand on the sixth: if Bethmann *was* sincere on July 30, then Russian mobilization was catastrophic because it derailed a peace effort which would probably have worked; if Bethmann was merely trying to shift the blame to Russia, then Kantorowicz is right and Russian mobilization was a technical consideration of minor significance. Turner says that Bethmann was insincere on July 27 and sincere on July 30, thus foreshadowing his approach to the vexing question of Russian general mobilization.

Turner tips his hat to the Hamburg school for its insistence on the importance of social and economic factors in the prewar period. He parts company with them on questions concerning military strategy, asserting that they have largely ignored such considerations (a valid objection also raised by Gerhard Ritter). Turner attempts to rectify this in his articles and book. In his opinion, Sazonov was an ignoramus in military matters. He urged partial mobilization as a means of exerting pressure on Austria, apparently failing to realize that Austria would then respond with general mobilization and that the Austro-German alliance would force Germany to declare general mobilization as well. As if this were not enough, Jagow did not realize it either, as his July 27 conversation with Goschen proves. Pathetically, all of this was bootless anyway. "It must be stressed that for Russia to bring diplomatic pressure to bear on Austria, it was unnecessary for her to mobilize; all that was required was that she should threaten to do so."[26]

Furthermore, although it is commonly believed among historians

25. Ibid., 100–101.
26. Turner, "Russian Mobilization," 74.

of the crisis that the technical problems associated with partial mobilization forced the Russian General Staff and the tsar into general mobilization, this perception is inaccurate. Despite the absence of a detailed plan for partial mobilization, such action would have been possible, albeit accompanied by certain unavoidable delays in general mobilization if that option were selected later. Yet – and this is Turner's most original and compelling insight – partial mobilization would have led to a major war no less certainly than general mobilization. Since "some of the army corps detailed for operations against Austria would have to enter the Warsaw military district," Germany itself would be threatened even by partial mobilization and would be forced to mobilize in turn.[27] Therefore, rivers of ink have been spilled in vain over the tsar's dithering and Sazonov's melodramatic instructions to Yanushkevich to "smash your telephone." This made excellent bathos, but played no role in the outbreak of continental war. That was assured by the tsar's *initial* decision in favor of partial mobilization.

It is difficult to see why not only Sazonov and Jagow, but even Moltke, failed to understand this connection. The chief of the Great General Staff stated as late as the morning of July 30 that Russian partial mobilization did not require German general mobilization. But that afternoon he abruptly changed his mind and pressed Bethmann to proclaim the *Kriegsgefahrzustand* and, having failed, sent his famous telegram to Vienna undercutting the chancellor's policy there. Turner's speculation concerning the reason for this about-face is revealing. It appears that Moltke panicked upon receipt of "news from Vienna that Conrad intended to adhere rigidly to Plan B [an initial attack against Serbia] and did not propose to abandon that plan in the light of Russian partial mobilization. . . . [T]he implications for Germany were catastrophic. Unless Austria fully committed herself to Plan R [an initial attack against Russia] and launched a great offensive in Poland, the German Eighth Army in East Prussia would be overwhelmed by the Russian masses and the prospects for the success of the Schlieffen Plan would be hopelessly compromised."[28]

Russian general mobilization, which followed closely upon Moltke's change of mind, was therefore crucial – not because it altered

27. L.C.F. Turner, "The Role of the General Staffs in July 1914," *Australian Journal of Politics and History* 11 (1965): 319.
28. Turner, *Origins*, 108–9.

the military realities, but because it helped Moltke persuade Beth-mann that there was no alternative to European war. In his early work, Turner is severely critical of the Russian action. He calls Russian mobilization, either partial or general, "an act of irresponsible folly" and "the most important decision taken in the history of Imperial Russia," which "effectively shattered any prospect of averting a great European war."[29] Two years later he was less convinced: "Russian and Austrian general mobilization made a great war inevitable."[30] But in either case, Russian mobilization is for Turner not a military technicality but a tragic, devastating factor in the July crisis. His overall assessment, partly revisionist, partly antirevisionist, partly Hamburg, partly *Zunft*, is solid if unexceptional; it is his unwavering conviction that military matters *counted heavily* in July 1914 that marks the significance of his contribution.

Stage Two, 1970–1977

With the publication of *War of Illusions* in 1969, the Fischer controversy was transformed from a debate over allegations that Germany had waged a preventive war (which by that time were accepted by nearly everyone) into a dispute over premeditation (in which few endorsed Fischer's position). Some felt that the affair which had ushered in the decade of the sixties was ending with the onset of the seventies. Joachim Remak of the University of California at Santa Barbara, author of *The Origins of World War I, 1871–1914* (New York, 1967), began his 1971 lead article in the *Journal of Modern History* with these lines: "Fritz Fischer's decade has ended. It began, neatly enough, in 1961 with *Der Griff nach der Weltmacht*, and drew to a close, in 1969, with *War of Illusions*. In between, there has been more discussion, scholarly and otherwise, than has been caused by any other single historian in our lifetime."[31]

In 1971 Remak was ready to move beyond the Fischer dispute. He could not support the conclusions drawn by the Hamburg school, primarily because of their nearly exclusive emphasis on German policy. For Remak, the war that began in 1914 was the third Balkan war, another in a series of crises in that part of the

29. Turner, "Russian Mobilization," 86–87.
30. Turner, *Origins*, 109.
31. Joachim Remak, "1914 – The Third Balkan War: Origins Reconsidered," *Journal of Modern History* 43 (1971): 353.

world, "the one gamble, or rather series of gambles, that did not
work out, the one deterrent that did not deter. It happens."[32] His
article was essentially a rewritten version of the final chapter of his
previously published book, rearranged into subdivisions designed
to assess the degree of responsibility of each of the participants, à la
Sidney Fay.

In the tradition of Fay, Remak explains the outbreak of war in
classic revisionist terms. Austria-Hungary and Serbia share primary
responsibility for the war; on a secondary level, Russia and Germany; then England, and finally France. The Serbian government
must be held responsible for failing to prevent the Sarajevo murders,
which they probably had learned of in advance, and for failing to
crack down on the Black Hand, which they certainly knew all too
well. German conduct prior to the delivery of the ultimatum was
indeed a calculated risk, but in taking this risk Germany had no
intention of assuming world-power status. It was a simple operation
to shore up Austria and split the Entente – a diplomatic maneuver,
nothing more. The problem was that Bethmann miscalculated,
assuming that Austria would act quickly and that Britain would stay
out. "Germany's guilt lies, not in dream of world domination . . .
[but] in risks taken that were immeasurably too high; in allowing
military planners to dictate policy; and beyond that, in the general
amateurishness that marked the nation's diplomatic behavior in the
quarter-century before Sarajevo. These things were quite bad
enough. There is no need to add imaginary sins to real ones."[33] But
even here, Remak tips his hat to Fay: "Austria was setting the
course, and neither friend nor foe had been allowed an honest look
at its direction."[34]

When dealing with France and England, Remak departs from the
conventional revisionist posture. France may have been guilty of
indiscreet conduct and an excess of enthusiasm in its dealings with
Russia, but to have altered this would have altered nothing. Germany would still have attacked France, and the French would have
been forced to fight back. "History can be very simple at times."[35]
And can anyone believe today that Germany would have behaved
differently had the British warned them sooner? The nation that had

32. Ibid., 366.
33. Ibid., 361.
34. Ibid., 362.
35. Ibid., 355. For a refutation of this line of thinking, see Albertini, *The Origins*,
esp. III, 164.

signed the Treaty of 1839 and concluded the Entente Cordiale had already given ample notice: "It was a matter of vital interest to Great Britain whether France survived as a power, and who would control the channel ports of Belgium and France."[36] Any German statesman who failed to recognize this probably should have been barred from any influence over foreign policy. True, England itself had upset the world-power balance after 1870 with the attainment of a far-flung empire; but Belgium was invaded not by the British navy, but by the German army. Basic facts should not be forgotten.

As for Russia, it is not true that its mobilization made war inevitable. Only German general mobilization was designed to lead directly and irrevocably to war. Russia's responsibility stems from its pre-1914 foreign policy of expansion in southeastern Europe; Austria had more to fear from Russia than the reverse. But the fundamental problem, even more important than Austria's fear of Russia, was Austria's fear of Serbia's desire to unite all South Slavs and, in doing so, to destroy the Habsburg monarchy. This situation, which could not be solved by negotiation, was worsened immeasurably by the Balkan wars of 1912–13, which strengthened Serbia and emboldened it to act more forcefully against Austria. The Great War, or "the third Balkan war," was the result.

Remak's approach is avowedly old-fashioned. Although he purports to be commemorating the end of the Fischer decade, his article emphasizes pure diplomatic history and pays little attention to the social and economic factors identified by the Hamburg school. He asks the question, What have the sixties taught us? but the answer is not immediately obvious. By restating the problem in classical terms in a cheerfully written, eminently readable article, Remak at the very least succeeded in wresting it free from a purely Fischer-esque emphasis on German policy; but beyond this, his approach satisfied few historians familiar with the debate as it had evolved since 1961.

One such scholar was Paul Schroeder, professor of history at the University of Illinois and a skilled practitioner of diplomatic history in his own right. In his opinion, Remak was asking the wrong question. A series of diplomatic crises had afflicted Europe since 1914: Morocco (1905), Bosnia-Hercegovina, Morocco (1911), Tripolitania, the Balkan wars of 1912 and 1913, and even the flap over the appointment of German General Otto Liman von Sanders as

36. Remak, "1914," 356.

head of the German Military Mission in Constantinople in 1913. Each of these had appeared dangerous to the peace of Europe, yet each had been settled without a continental war. For Schroeder, the proper question is not, Why did the Great War break out in 1914? but Why was the Great War not avoided in 1914? In addition to having asked the wrong question, Remak provided the wrong answer: "Remak's view of July 1914 as the one gamble that did not succeed overlooks the fact that those who gambled in Germany and Austria did not expect to succeed in avoiding general war."[37]

Schroeder tips his hand from the outset, contending that Fritz Fischer is essentially correct in his assessment of Germany's drive for world power. But Fischer is not entirely fair to Bethmann and is far too concerned with Germany's quest for *Weltpolitik* to notice the presence of other motives in German policy. His central thesis, that Germany from 1890 to 1914 consciously pursued an aggressive foreign policy rooted in domestic political, social, and economic conditions and concerns has survived the attacks of his critics.

> The difficulty arises in accepting the notion, implicit in all of Fischer's work and explicitly drawn by many historians as the chief lesson of it, that Germany's bid for world power was the *causa causans*, the central driving force behind the war. Fischer never demonstrates this convincingly. . . . [H]e cannot assume, as he constantly does, that German policy was decisive for other powers without a great deal more investigation than he has done. Moreover, Fischer's own principle of the *Primat der Innenpolitik* (the primacy of domestic politics) should have led him to assume that other powers would, like Germany, act mainly from their own indigenous drives, rather than mainly react to what Germany did, as he depicts them doing.[38]

This is trenchant criticism, and Schroeder does not hesitate to follow it with his own explanation of the events of 1914. Comparing the European state system to the Tacoma Narrows Bridge, he contends that in both instances, exceptional stress caused built-in supports to become destructive elements, bringing their respective structures crashing down – the one in 1914, the other in 1940.[39] Thus the European state system itself, which Bismarck so admired

37. Paul W. Schroeder, "World War I as Galloping Gertie: A Reply to Joachim Remak," *Journal of Modern History* 44 (1972). 321–22.
38. Ibid., 320.
39. The Tacoma Narrows Bridge collapsed "when winds induced pressures on supporting members sufficient in turn to cause the supports to generate destructive

and respected, was destroyed by some of the very devices that had for decades preserved its stability and coherence. When these devices were placed under intense pressure, they became destructive rather than stabilizing elements.

Europe's pre-1914 crises were in this sense danger signals. For Schroeder "they . . . indicate a general systemic crisis, an approaching breakdown,"[40] rather than a healthy relationship among powers that should have prevented war indefinitely. This is the context for his question, Why not war in 1914? War was not a departure from the norm, but a perfectly acceptable recourse to exceptional means for solving exceptional problems. "Until 1914 peace did not just happen, but was caused. The wars that did not occur seem to me harder to explain than the one that did."[41] But the one that did is, after all, the subject under discussion, and to explain it we need to understand the structures built into the European system, which until 1914 had prevented war, but which finally broke down and destroyed the peace.

Central to Schroeder's conception of stresses and balances is the position of Austria-Hungary within the system. More than any other element, it was Austria which destroyed the system as a result of the incredible pressures to which its position was subjected. For centuries, Austria had been a guarantor of the system, a stabilizing influence in a region of Europe once menaced by the Turks and was now threatened by the centripetal forces of nationalism. From whence did these pressures emanate? From Austria's own internal decay? From Germany's aggressive expansionism? Partly, but only partly. Even more important as a source of pressure on Austria, in Schroeder's view, was Britain's failure to recognize the importance of Austria as a stabilizing factor.

Certainly Britain, whose policy had long been predicated on the maintenance of the European balance of power against all efforts by any single nation to tip the balance, had no reason to consciously weaken one of the major supports of that balance. But that is what was done in the years prior to 1914. "The immediate threat to the balance in 1914 was not German power . . . but Austrian weakness."[42] Germany could not afford to let Austria, its last viable

---

forces within the bridge." Ibid., 321, n. 8. The bridge's nickname, "Galloping Gertie," explains the reference in the title of Schroeder's article.
40. Ibid., 321.
41. Ibid., 323.
42. Ibid., 335.

ally, wither on the vine; it was likely that Germany would go to war to prevent such a calamity; so Entente policy should have been directed toward preserving Austria as a stabilizing force, as Turkey had long been preserved, even after its debility had become apparent to everyone. Such a policy would have maximized Europe's chances of holding Germany's admittedly aggressive attitudes in check and maintaining peace.

What was done instead? Austria, not Germany, was encircled by the Entente. The Balkan League strengthened Serbia, the greatest threat to the integrity of the Dual Monarchy. Vienna's Balkan allies, Romania and Bulgaria, were being wooed by Russia and France. Britain supported these moves as perfectly consistent with the Anglo-Russian Convention of 1907, which represented a mortal threat to Austria by directing Russia's attention away from Persia and toward the Balkans. "Even the Anglo-French and Anglo-Russian naval talks were directed as much against Austria in the Mediterranean as against Germany in the North and Baltic Seas."[43] The British treated Germany with respect, but they treated Austria with contempt. "Britain undermined Austria's position before the war . . . and assisted in her destruction during it, in a fit of absence of mind. . . . Let Austria go under, and a great war for the mastery of Europe became almost mathematically predictable. . . . The basic point is that everyone saw the central threat to the European system in the decline of Austria, and no one would do anything about it."[44]

The Remak-Schroeder exchange moved the debate on the July crisis into a different dimension. After more than a decade of nearly exclusive concentration on Germany, scholars would once again examine the motives, ambitions, and mistakes of other participants in the crisis. But Fischer's impact was ineradicable. Germany's chief responsibility for the outbreak of war was now assumed by nearly everyone; what remained was to analyze all other aspects of the crisis not with the purpose of determining responsibility, but of explaining more subtle factors. Schroeder's ingenious metaphor called attention to the importance of Austria within the European state system. Others would now address July 1914 not in terms of a recapitulation of the diplomatic documents, but in more imaginative terms, some laid down by Fischer, some by his opponents, and some, like Schroeder's, of the historian's own making.

43. Ibid., 338.
44. Ibid., 341–45.

This work began in the early seventies and did not bear fruit until years later. Contributions to the debate between 1972 and 1980 had been envisioned prior to the Remak-Schroeder exchange and were largely conditioned by the Fischer dispute and the issues it raised. Thus Volker R. Berghahn, now professor of history at Brown University, inaugurated a projected series of volumes for St. Martin's Press on the roles of individual nations in the prewar period with *Germany and the Approach of War in 1914*. While challenging Fischer on some points, he used the basic theses of the Hamburg school to develop a comprehensive explanation of German conduct in Europe during the years following Bismarck's fall.

For Berghahn, traditional diplomatic history in the style of Fay, Schmitt, and Albertini cannot provide a thorough understanding of the issues involved in the outbreak of the war. Yet Eckart Kehr's assertion of the primacy of domestic policy is likewise flawed. What is needed is a judicious blending of the effects of foreign and domestic considerations on the formulation of policy by all the principal actors in the July crisis. Concentrating on the role of Germany, Berghahn provides a model for the sort of analysis undertaken on a country-by-country basis by James Joll in 1984.[45]

Berghahn's view of Germany's aims in the July crisis resembles Fischer's in several respects. The impetus for Austrian action against Serbia came not from Vienna but from Berlin; in Austria, swift retribution was advocated only by Conrad, and it took German pressure on July 5–6 to convince Berchtold that such action was warranted. The German government realized that Russian intervention was likely and that such intervention would lead to a major war. Berghahn cites the Riezler diaries in support of his assertion that Bethmann understood what he was getting into; in addition, he holds that Bethmann was under pressure from the Kaiser, who had resolved to demonstrate that he could be relied upon to pursue a forceful foreign initiative without losing heart.

Yet Fischer is not correct on all points, for according to Berghahn "the available evidence . . . seems to suggest that the Chancellor genuinely hoped for a German victory short of a great war."[46] Bethmann wanted exactly what Riezler's diaries indicate – a short, victorious war against Serbia to shore up the crumbling position of

---

45. Volker R. Berghahn, *Germany and the Approach of War in 1914* (New York, 1973), 2–3. See below for a discussion of Joll's work.
46. Ibid., 193.

the Central Powers, followed by reconciliation with the Entente from a position of strength. Germany had not been planning a major war since the so-called War Council of December 1912, and did not want one even in mid-July 1914. Berghahn points out that the desire for a limited war became wishful thinking almost immediately since the Potsdam assurances of July 5–6 were predicated upon swift Austrian action, which the Ministerial Council of July 7 prevented by the adoption of Tisza's proposal. "It may be that it was this virtual coincidence of the decision to wage war against Serbia at the conscious risk of a world war on 5 July and the practical inevitability of such a major war as a result of the procedure adopted only two days later, which induced Fritz Fischer to assume that the Central Powers wanted a *world* war all along."[47]

For Berghahn, this is "too linear an interpretation of German and Austrian intentions."[48] The evidence demonstrates that Germany continued to hope for localization of the conflict well beyond July 7. Once it became apparent that this was unlikely, the intervention of Great Britain was reckoned with unflinchingly by the army, which had known all along that the British would not stand by and watch the destruction of France but had underestimated seriously the impact of such intervention.[49] Nevertheless, Bethmann continued to hope that the Entente would back down and that full-scale war could be avoided.

Russian mobilization put an end to those hopes, but its significance has been exaggerated. For Berghahn, Fischer's analysis of the reasoning of the Russian government demonstrates incontrovertibly that St. Petersburg was not bent on war and intended to keep on negotiating without invading either Germany or Austria. But "to Germany, the Tsar's mobilization order was the last straw only because the Central Powers were by then bent on waging a European war and were, for domestic reasons, merely waiting to be given a pretext for starting it."[50]

Berghahn's book made the chief issues in the Fischer controversy more easily accessible to readers lacking the energy and patience to read the original volumes, and its publication in 1973, two years before the English translation of *War of Illusions* appeared, made it

47. Ibid., 196.
48. Ibid.
49. Ibid., 200.
50. Ibid., 207.

doubly appreciated by English and American readers. The following year, Michael Gordon of the University of California at Santa Barbara blended Fischer's conviction that Germany consciously sought world-power status with the concept of the primacy of domestic policy espoused by Fischer, but taken much farther by Hans-Ulrich Wehler and others who have rediscovered the work of Eckart Kehr. Gordon's article in the *Journal of Modern History* followed some of the suggestions of Arno Mayer by investigating the relationship between domestic conflict in Britain and Germany and the outbreak of war in 1914.

Gordon finds Fischer's work deficient in two areas. First, it is not always clear that Fischer selects his material according to a consistent set of criteria (in other words, he may have selected material to fit his thesis), and the conclusions he draws from that material are not always logical. Second, he fails to compare German ambitions and policies to those of other countries, leaving himself open to the charge of unfairly persecuting his own country. Gordon proposes to attempt such a comparison, based upon current theories of political modernization and economic development and modeled on the principle of the primacy of domestic policy.[51]

The result is a stimulating essay in comparative history. Britain and Germany are contrasted with respect to electoral reform, left-wing political movements, governmental institutions, national identities, tariff policies, rate and forms of industrialization, and a variety of other items. But Gordon's conclusions agree fully with neither Fischer nor Mayer. The latter's contention that nations use foreign adventures as a means of solving domestic difficulties, "illuminating though it is in the German case, goes astray in the British."[52] And although Fischer has displaced the debate from concepts of German guiltlessness and the equal guilt of all parties and has relocated it in the sphere of preventive war, he places too much emphasis on the deliberate, calculated nature of German policy. Here other members of the Hamburg school, like Geiss, are closer to the truth with their concentration on psychological, emotional, political, economic, and military factors in German life "as the propellant behind the plunge into war."[53]

---

51. Michael R. Gordon, "Domestic Conflict and the Origins of the First World War: The British and the German Cases," *Journal of Modern History* 46 (1974): 193.
52. Ibid., 202, n. 42.
53. Ibid., 195.

Gordon's comparisons are illuminating, but even he returns to German policy as a focal point, probably because there is little in British policy to indicate a drive toward war, preventive or otherwise. In a persuasive paragraph, he calls attention to the tentative nature of Germany's borders and the presence of millions of German-speaking people outside them. Gordon argues that Germany's power structure was faced with three choices in attempting to shore up the Wilhelmine Reich's position in Europe: sustain Bismarck's *Kleindeutschland* (smaller or lesser Germany), dominated by Prussia and marked by instability; create *Grossdeutschland* (greater Germany) by absorbing Austria and the German-speaking portions of its empire; or "go further and seek a German-dominated *Mitteleuropa* (central Europe) running from the North Sea to the French Alps, from Alsace-Lorraine into Western Russia."[54] He agrees with Fischer that *Mitteleuropa* was the choice made by most German elites before 1914 and that the result was a decision by the leadership to grasp for world power as a means of achieving it.

The work of Remak, Schroeder, Berghahn, and Gordon, like many of the most important contributions of the 1980s, concentrates on factors operative prior to 1914 as conditions precedent to the July crisis. Fischer not only displaced the debate from equivalent responsibility to preventive war; he also focused it on such factors rather than solely on the events of the five weeks between June 28 and August 4. But occasional pieces have found something new to say about the crisis itself. One of these is the suggestive article by Ulrich Trumpener, "War Premeditated? German Intelligence Operations in July 1914," based largely upon the previously unused draft of an internal history of the German army intelligence service.

Trumpener begins with a discussion of the Potsdam interviews of July 5–6. Most prominent military and naval officers were on leave or absent from Berlin, and the few who were consulted were not among Moltke's closest confidants.[55] No alteration in the "sleepy" routine of the General Staff took place, and Fischer is wrong when he states that by July 18 the army was fully prepared for mobilization (although the measures initiated by the government around

54. Ibid., 212.
55. Ulrich Trumpener, "War Premeditated? German Intelligence Operations in July 1914," *Central European History* 9 (1976): 62–63. Trumpener fails to mention the presence at Potsdam of Prussian war minister von Falkenhayn, a figure of some significance who would replace Moltke as chief of the General Staff later that year.

that time are not mentioned in the sources used by Trumpener). Special surveillance of Russia was not ordered until after the delivery of the ultimatum on July 23, and even then the General Staff appears to have believed that although war with the Entente might result, it would be unlikely to occur prior to a lengthy diplomatic crisis which would afford plenty of time for military preparations.

Gradually this comforting illusion faded. On the evening of July 24, the Königsberg radio station monitored "an 'unusually long' exchange of coded messages between the Eiffel Tower and the Russian wireless station at Bobruysk."[56] Two days later, reports of Russian military preparations began to arrive. Now the General Staff developed an acute interest in Russian developments, unmatched as yet by an equivalent preoccupation with France (probably because both the French mobilization schedule and Joffre's Plan XVII were already known to the Germans). By July 28 the situation had become sufficiently alarming for Moltke to draft his infamous memorandum on the political situation and forward it to Bethmann. Trumpener holds that these warnings "were not simply intended to put pressure on the civilian leaders in Berlin. Rather, they reflected a genuine concern at the Great General Staff over the head start the Russians were getting with their 'premobilization' program."[57] But Bethmann refused to authorize proclamation of the *Kriegsgefahrzustand* (requested by Falkenhayn on the morning of July 29), and this made the General Staff nervous because the rigid timetables of the Schlieffen Plan were dependent on the slowness of Russian military measures.

By that afternoon, the generals' anxiety had eased, and Moltke failed to support strongly Falkenhayn's renewed request for emergency measures. Why? Probably because new intelligence information had arrived that morning, indicating that Russian preparations were not very far advanced and that French reservists had not been called up. Shortly thereafter, however, the Foreign Office

56. Ibid., 67. This is a fascinating piece of information. Certainly the Russian government communicated extensively with Serbia on the morning of July 25; was Sazonov seeking advice from Paris prior to offering it to Belgrade? If so, from whom was he receiving it, Poincaré and Viviani being at sea and out of touch with Paris? Is it possible that some of this traffic was being relayed to the French leaders via a Russian station that was close enough to their location to reach them? If so, then the Russians could have communicated with Poincaré and Viviani on their own. Until the French government releases the texts of these coded messages, another of the mysteries of July 1914 will remain undeciphered.
57. Ibid., 74.

was informed officially of Russian partial mobilization against Austria. This, coupled with disturbing intelligence reports that the Belgians were calling up their reserves and preparing for the defense of Liège, once again brought the Schlieffen Plan to the fore. Trumpener contends that this explains the sudden hardening of Moltke's attitude around noon on July 30.

Russia's decision to declare general mobilization on the afternoon of July 30 was not officially confirmed in Berlin until 11:45 A.M. the following day, but German military intelligence had been reporting it since late on the evening of July 30, and one of their freelance agents, a Polish tradesman named Pinkus Urwicz, actually smuggled one of the red mobilization placards across the border on the morning of July 31. Trumpener concludes that because of intelligence work, Moltke and Falkenhayn possessed "considerably more, and better, information on the scope and tempo of Russia's 'premobilization' measures than is reflected in the various collections of diplomatic documents and other civilian government records from that period which were published after the war."[58] This in turn renders the military's escalating demands for countermeasures more readily comprehensible.

Trumpener's analysis of this newly unearthed evidence casts doubt on Fischer's contention that the Great General Staff was preparing for war well before the ultimatum, in conjunction with a decision taken at the War Council of December 8, 1912. The last of the works of the 1970s which we will examine also takes issue with aspects of Fischer's thesis, particularly the concept of the *Primat der Innenpolitik*. Zara Steiner's *Britain and the Origins of the First World War* was the second volume in the St. Martin's series and the first in-depth appraisal of its subject to be published since the appearance of the relevant chapters in Albertini. She stands firmly behind the primacy of foreign policy in British diplomacy, arguing "that diplomatic decisions tended to be a response to outward events and external situations."[59] Steiner does attempt to meet Fischer partway by conceding that domestic politics affected the

58. Ibid., 85.

59. Zara S. Steiner, *Britain and the Origins of the First World War* (New York, 1977), 248. H.W. Koch takes note of Steiner's claim that Fischer's thesis does not hold for Britain, calling it "simply misleading because the author does not proceed from methodological and theoretical premises identical with those of Fischer. Economic, social and institutional analysis receive only very marginal attention whereas in Fischer's work they represent its very core." Koch, *Origins*, 18.

perceptions of British statesmen, but her overall tone minimizes the impact of this modification.

Steiner is also skeptical of Zechlin's assertion that news of the Anglo-Russian naval talks threw Bethmann into a fatalistic depression. If this is true, it was the result of gross overestimation of the likelihood of a meaningful agreement. The fact is that England and Russia were farther apart in the spring of 1914 than they had been since the Russo-Japanese War, largely because of acrimonious disputes over Asian interests. Grey feared that England would have to choose between a friendlier or more distant relationship with Russia, and he was agonizing over this problem when the July crisis hit. According to Steiner, the conventional portrayal of Grey's early indifference to a quarrel between Austria and Serbia does not stand up to scrutiny. Lichnowsky warned the foreign secretary on July 6 that Austria would take severe measures and would be supported by Germany; "there is every indication that Grey took the ambassador's warnings seriously."[60]

Did Germany hope for British neutrality? Steiner says yes, contending that Bethmann laid the groundwork for the war by making a bid for British cooperation in localizing the conflict. "It was . . . in keeping with his character that he should have hoped for British neutrality while knowing it was improbable."[61] Grey grew alarmed when it became evident that Germany would cooperate with England only over localization of the dispute, not with the intention of preventing war altogether. This would destroy the strategy that had worked so effectively in 1912; like Bethmann, Grey continued to hope for German assistance while recognizing its improbability. He informed Lichnowsky on July 9 of his intention to replicate the 1912 procedures and attempted to exercise a calming influence in Paris and St. Petersburg.

From the beginning, Grey was reluctant to provoke Berlin. His suggestion that Austria and Russia discuss the Serbian issue after the delivery of the ultimatum was not what Poincaré and Sazonov had in mind; their call for a joint Entente demarche at Vienna was anathema to Grey at this juncture. As it turned out, Grey's cautious policy did not prevent a deepening of the crisis. "The working

---

60. Steiner, *Britain*, 200.
61. Ibid., 126. Later she qualifies this assertion, writing on p. 226 that "Bethmann and Jagow may have hoped that Grey would delay long enough to allow the German army time to make its intended break through Belgium."

partnership of the Balkan Wars was not revived because the Central Powers had other goals in mind."[62] The problem was that Grey had no alternative strategy in reserve. He hoped that by denying British support to either side, he would make the opposing alliances think twice before escalating the crisis. This did not happen, and when it was clear that his strategy had failed, all that Grey could consider doing was to approach the cabinet on July 27 and ask if Britain would support France should the latter be attacked by Germany.

The response was anything but encouraging: five ministers threatened to resign if the cabinet went to war for France. Two days later, Grey openly urged just such a policy and found the majority of the cabinet against him. His unequivocal warning to Lichnowsky was delivered *after* this session of the cabinet had concluded and was taken entirely on his own initiative. Steiner doubts that such a warning would have deterred Berlin even had it been issued much earlier. Germany "was too strong to accept a final check on her ambitions without at least trying to break out of her enclosed position unless that check was powerful enough to make all hope of success futile. Britain, even in alliance with France and Russia, could not pose that kind of threat."[63]

Grey's warning, unauthorized by a divided cabinet, could have been issued at any time during the crisis. Steiner implies that Grey deferred such a warning not because of opposition from within the government, but because until late in the crisis he clung to the hope that Germany would renew its cooperative stance of 1912. Only when it became clear to him that Germany was backing Austria to the hilt – a fact of which he had been apprised on July 6 but had never fully accepted – did he fling down the gauntlet in desperation. "What followed [his warning] was shadow-boxing rather than diplomacy."[64] By July 30 Bethmann was convinced that war with France and Russia was unavoidable and that Britain must be kept out as long as possible. But his efforts to throw the blame on Russia missed the point. It was true that Britain would be skeptical of participation in a war started by Russia, but it was not possible for Britain to remain on the sidelines and watch as France was destroyed. What was decisive for British policy in July 1914 was the belief that a strong France was essential to the European balance of power.

62. Ibid., 224.
63. Ibid., 256.
64. Ibid., 226.

This survey of the scholarly output of the 1970s demonstrates the continuing concentration of the debate on the issues raised by the Hamburg school. The Remak/Schroeder exchange had planted seeds which had not yet borne fruit and would not do so until the eighties.

Stage Three: Since 1980

In this decade, historians have moved beyond the limits of the Fischer controversy, attempting to blend diplomatic, political, economic, social, cultural, and psychological insights into a modern view of what went wrong seventy-five years ago. As of this writing, no one has produced a cohesive new treatment in monographic format, although James Joll has come close. But the building blocks for such a treatment are being manufactured in a variety of forms. We will examine some of them in the concluding portion of this chapter.

The role of Austria-Hungary in the July crisis is reexamined by Samuel R. Williamson Jr., president of the University of the South and author of *The Politics of Grand Strategy: Britain and France Prepare for War, 1904–1914* (1969) and, more recently, of *Austria-Hungary and the Coming of the First World War* (1990). Prior to 1961, Austrian responsibility for the coming of the war was taken for granted. Few contested the roots of complicity: Austria had determined to use the archduke's murder as a pretext to crush Serbia; had intentionally prepared an unacceptable ultimatum with a short time limit; had quickly severed diplomatic relations and, equally quickly, declared war; and the Austro-Hungarian foreign minister, Berchtold, had ignored repeated German pleas for moderation and mediation. Germany's blank check of support had been used in a cynical and treacherous effort to prove that the Habsburg Empire was still a great power.

Fritz Fischer departed from this commonly held position, not by exonerating Austria, but by ignoring it. His copious denunciations of German intentions bleached Austrian actions into a colorless record of unswerving submission to the wishes of Berlin. Far from denying Austrian complicity, he simply understated it to such an extent that it no longer attracted the attention of most historians (Schroeder being the most prominent exception). Even Remak, who accepted the pre-Fischer view of Austrian responsibility, spent so much time refuting Fischer's assertion of German aggression and

155

propounding his own thesis of Serbian responsibility that he mentioned Austria's role only in passing.

Williamson attempts to rectify this imbalance. For him, Vienna's part in the crisis was central. Berchtold's policy was not that of a timid, second-rate power egged on by the impulsive and aggressive rulers in Berlin; rather, it was that of "a great power capable of independent action and decision," a multinational state determined to exercise influence over the Balkans and to preserve its own integrity against the Serbian challenge.[65] Williamson tells us that the famous visit of Wilhelm II to Franz Ferdinand's estate at Konopischt on June 13, 1914, was far less significant than Berchtold's visit the following day. Their conversation convinced the foreign minister that a bold, forceful step was required if Vienna was to regain the initiative in the Balkans. On his return to the Ballhausplatz, Berchtold authorized senior section chief Franz von Matscheko "to draft a memorandum for his use with Berlin in proposing a new, more dramatic *Balkanpolitik*."[66] This document was completed on June 24 and formed the basis for the revised memorandum that Hoyos carried to Potsdam on July 5. Thus the Austrian request for the blank check was framed in terms drafted *before* Sarajevo, terms originally intended to justify diplomatic action rather than military force.[67]

Behind Berchtold's initiative lay a broadly based foundation of support. Chief of Staff Conrad von Hötzendorf, who had advocated preventive war with Serbia for years, naturally felt that his hour had struck. But Berchtold's supporting cast also included Minister of War Alexander von Krobatin, Austrian Prime Minister Count Karl Stürgkh, Finance Minister Bilinski, and Emperor Franz Josef himself – in fact, virtually every prominent political figure in the Dual Monarchy except Tisza. These men had made their decision and had done so without any pressure from Germany.

---

65. Samuel R. Williamson Jr., "Vienna and July 1914: The Origins of the Great War Once More," in Samuel R. Williamson Jr. and Peter Pastor, eds., *Essays on World War I* (New York, 1983), 9, 29.

66. Samuel R. Williamson Jr., *Austria-Hungary and the Coming of the First World War* (New York, 1990), 9–3 (forthcoming, page references are to the manuscript).

67. Ibid., 9–24. Yet Matscheko's proposals, even in their original form, were vigorous. A demonstration of strength was necessary to convince the Serbians and the Russians that Austria-Hungary "had the capacity to determine its own future . . . . The monarchy must pursue an aggressive diplomatic policy . . . . The diplomatic policies of the Central Powers, when the war actually came, were already forecast by Matscheko's assessment."

This was the context of the Potsdam meetings. Bethmann, like Wilhelm II, endorsed the monarchy's request for support for its planned action against Serbia. "From Berlin's standpoint, it had agreed to Vienna's request. But the initiative had been Vienna's, not Berlin's. The steps that pushed Europe toward war were taken in Vienna."[68] What if Berlin had refused its backing? Perhaps Berchtold would have backed down. Perhaps he would have repeated his actions of October 17, 1913, when Austria-Hungary had dispatched an ultimatum to Serbia with only perfunctory warning to Berlin. In any event, Williamson declares, the chief significance of the blank check was the leverage it provided Berchtold for use in converting Tisza to the idea of military action.

Williamson concurs with Fay's well-known comment concerning Germany's putting a noose around its neck and handing the rope to a clumsy adventurer: "What happened was a fateful meshing of aggressive German *Weltpolitik* with an even more aggressive, irresponsible Habsburg *Balkanpolitik*."[69] If Austria was Germany's client, it was a most assertive client indeed.

The key to this situation was, in more than one respect, the assassination of the archduke, and Williamson restores this event to its previously held pivotal position in the history of the crisis. Princip's crime not only provided a pretext for action; more significantly, it removed from the scene the one Austrian policymaker who could have resisted war. Franz Ferdinand, as portrayed by Williamson, was fearful of war with Russia because of three potential results: defeat, excessive dependence on Germany, and the probability that war would inhibit constitutional reform.[70] He was Conrad's sworn enemy and just the man to urge caution on Berchtold. His death assured that a powerful critic of the military would be unable to advise against an invasion of Serbia, and when Berchtold sided with Conrad in the early days of July, Austria began to act "as if Russia did not exist."[71]

This casual attitude toward a powerful foe prevailed at the meeting of the Common Ministerial Council on July 7. Russian

68. Ibid., 10–10.
69. Williamson, "Vienna and July 1914," 24.
70. Ibid., 22.
71. Ibid., 25. This peculiar aberration is addressed at some length in another article in the anthology edited by Samuel R. Williamson Jr. and Peter Pastor, by William Jannen Jr., "The Austro-Hungarian Decision for War in July, 1914," *Essays on World War I* (New York, 1983), 55–74.

intervention was considered likely, but no attention was paid to the adoption of measures which might induce Russian tolerance of a swift, limited operation that would not jeopardize Serbian sovereignty. German backing was disclosed but was not used to pressure Tisza until *after* the meeting; no one present spoke of any necessity to act in order to please Berlin. Italy's position was barely considered. Williamson displays for us a government resolved on military action against Serbia irrespective of diplomatic considerations.[72]

Tisza remained an obstacle, and his opposition was finally overcome not by Berchtold but by Baron Stephen von Burian, the Hungarian minister in Vienna. "Burian warned Tisza that failure to resolve the Serbian problem might exacerbate the Rumanian issue in Transylvania," and it was this domestic concern that at last overcame the Hungarian premier's resistance.[73] But Tisza was not the sole cause of the seventeen-day delay in dispatching the timed note. In an effort to placate the monarchy's agrarian interests, Conrad had sent entire units on harvest leave between July 6 and 25. If he revoked those orders, the harvest would be jeopardized, the railways would be clogged, and everyone in Europe would know something was up. On top of those considerations, the presence of Poincaré and Viviani in St. Petersburg through July 23 meant that "ironically, the Habsburg resolve to act decisively demanded delay, not expedition."[74]

Given this lengthy postponement, why did Berchtold not disclose the note's full contents to Bethmann? Because, says Williamson, the German Foreign Office was leaky. Jagow had indeed learned the gist of the proposed action on July 11 and promptly communicated it to his ambassador in Rome, who told the Italian foreign minister, who told his ambassadors in Russia, Serbia, and even Austria-Hungary itself, where the incoming telegram was deciphered by Austrian codebreakers! No wonder Berchtold clamped the lid down after that. But the damage was even more extensive: Vienna assumed that St. Petersburg could also read Italian codes and that Belgrade would learn of Austrian intentions through this channel.[75] Pašić's actions on July 18 bear out this

72. Williamson, *Austria-Hungary*, 10–14.
73. Ibid., 10–16.
74. Ibid., 10–15.
75. "While neither the recently published Serbian documents nor the Russian documents give any indication of messages from St. Petersburg, indirect evidence

speculation, for he informed his missions abroad that "Belgrade would resist any Habsburg demand that infringed upon its sovereignty."[76] As if this were not enough, Poincaré's remarks to Szápáry on July 22 were clearly meant as a warning to Vienna and suggested that the Russians had naturally shared their information with the French.[77]

Once the ultimatum was delivered and the Serbian response rejected, what would Vienna do about it? Williamson gives us no indication that Germany pressed for a quick declaration of war. Conrad's hopes for delay until the completion of partial mobilization on August 12 were dashed by the insistence of Berchtold and Hoyos that such postponement would result in tremendous international pressure on the monarchy to negotiate rather than fight. Some of that pressure, as we know, eventually came from Berlin, but Williamson dismisses it in three sentences. True to its reading of the crisis situation from beginning to end, Vienna pursued a consistently belligerent policy which Germany could not deflect with last-minute reservations.[78]

Williamson's work is of great value in correcting a distortion resulting from the Hamburg school's emphasis on German policy. He has restored Austria-Hungary to its proper role as a leading belligerent in July 1914: "In 1914 Austria-Hungary was not an innocent, middle-level government pressured into war by its more aggressive, ambitious northern ally. . . . Certainly it is incorrect to focus all attention on Berlin, or to suggest that Vienna was merely a marionette in the July crisis."[79] In some respects, his analysis *understates* German involvement; but given the vast attention paid to Berlin since 1961, this represents a helpful corrective rather than a dangerous distortion. His trenchant critique of Berchtold's policy, set in the context of Austro-Hungarian foreign and domestic concerns and buttressed by extensive archival research, gives Williamson (at least for the foreseeable future) the final word on the role of the Dual Monarchy in July 1914.

If Austria was not a puppet, was Germany a puppeteer? David Kaiser of Carnegie-Mellon University has his doubts. In a 1983

from the Serbian documents suggests that Belgrade learned of the Habsburg intentions." Ibid., 10–17 – 10–18.

76. Ibid., 10–18.
77. Ibid., 10–20.
78. Ibid., 10–24.
79. Williamson, "Vienna and July 1914," 29–30.

article in the *Journal of Modern History*, he takes a fresh look at Germany's role in the outbreak of war. Kaiser, while lauding Fischer's methodological concern with the relationship between German domestic and foreign policy, contends that the nature of this relationship has not been explored adequately. Fischer merely paralleled the two while failing to proffer any evidence for a link between them. More recent writings by Berghahn, Wehler, Eley, and Paul Kennedy have concluded that the twin terrors of socialism and democracy backed the German government into a corner and encouraged it to adopt a belligerent foreign policy and to view war as a desirable alternative to the revision of traditional elite rule.[80] Kaiser considers this inadequate. "On the whole," he says, "recent literature has distorted the domestic aims which foreign policy was designed to achieve before 1914, misunderstood the goals of *Weltpolitik* as originally adopted in 1897, and obscured the real reasons for the 1914 decisions that helped unleash a world war."[81]

According to Kaiser, those who developed *Weltpolitik* never intended to use it to maintain the exclusive political control of the conservative elite. It was a combination of bargains designed to keep various interest groups in balance – a practice common to coalition as well as monarchical governments. Bethmann and his predecessor Bülow both feared the domestic impact of a major war; they never pursued a belligerent foreign policy on the assumption that internal difficulties would thereby be ameliorated. "Bethmann in 1914 risked war because of a mistaken belief that Germany's international position demanded it."[82] This explains Fischer's failure to demonstrate a causal link between domestic and foreign policy in prewar Germany: such a link, if it exists, is both weaker and less significant than Fischer would have it. We must search for the roots of German foreign policy not at home but abroad.[83]

Kaiser, like Williamson, points out that the July crisis was not solely the work of the German government. The assassination was the work of Serbian nationalists, while the Austrian decision to

---

80. See Berghahn, *Germany and the Approach of War in 1914*; Hans-Ulrich Wehler, *The German Empire, 1871–1918* (Birmingham, U.K., 1985); Geoff Eley, *Reshaping the German Right: Radical Nationalism and Political Change after Bismarck* (New Haven, 1980); and Paul M. Kennedy, *The Rise of the Anglo-German Antagonism, 1860–1914* (London, 1980).

81. David E. Kaiser, "Germany and the Origins of the First World War," *Journal of Modern History* 55 (1983): 444.

82. Ibid., 445.

83. The compatibility of this argument with Steiner's position is evident.

confront Serbia predates the Hoyos visit to Potsdam. But Bethmann's July policy was rooted in neither of these considerations,
but in his own despair over Germany's allegedly deteriorating
position. He was convinced that Germany must expand or perish
(Fischer is correct here), and he decided to take a calculated risk for
his own reasons, without any pressure from the military; "the
argument of Wolfgang Mommsen and Konrad Jarausch that the
military forced Bethmann into a compromise policy likely to lead to
war is not supported by the evidence."[84] Indeed, if Bethmann had
felt cornered by belligerent soldiers, he could have called upon his
allies for support. Tirpitz had consistently opposed war for at least
six years, while the Kaiser could be relied on to back off as soon as
the scent of cordite reached his nostrils. Yet Bethmann encouraged
both men to remain away from Berlin in July and subverted the
emperor's efforts to preserve peace. Kaiser maintains that "war took
place only because Bethmann *circumvented* the decision-making
structure of the German government."[85]

So the war of 1914 was, as Fischer claimed, "grasping at world
power." But it is clear that Kaiser's views, if borne out by further
research, would constitute an extensive modification of Fischer's
critique of German foreign policy. His analysis of Bülow's aims is
both cogent and persuasive; although it covers an area that Fischer
did not address in his books, it contains a number of elements that
call his arguments into question. The evidence which Kaiser presents to support his assertion that Bethmann actually profited from
the 1912 election results seems to me conclusive, and his explanation
of the origins and purposes of *Weltpolitik* both indicates that
Fischer's assumptions may have been to facile and opens a previously "settled" matter to future research and exposition. Kaiser's
willingness to question some of Fischer's fundamental contentions
while endorsing his central thesis that Germany sought world
power in an active and aggressive manner foreshadows the eventual
revision of much of Fischer's work.

Kaiser raises and discusses a number of provocative questions; he
does not, however, solve them all, at least not to my satisfaction.
One example must suffice – his interpretation of the extent of the

---

84. Kaiser, "Germany," 468–69.
85. Ibid., 469. Throughout his article, Kaiser convincingly maintains that Bethmann was in every respect in charge of German foreign policy during the duration of
the crisis. Postwar efforts to throw the blame onto the Kaiser or the military lack
supporting evidence.

German military's influence over Bethmann's policy. Granted that Moltke was absent from Berlin through most of July, his role thereafter was not as pacific as Kaiser implies. Specifically, his July 28 memorandum to Bethmann did nothing to encourage the chancellor to depart from his risky path. Moltke declared that Russia's intention to mobilize against Austria would force war between the two, which for Germany would constitute a *casus foederis*. By contrast, Jagow had assured British and French diplomats the day before that Russian mobilization against Austria would *not* be sufficient to involve Germany in war. Moltke's intervention in the diplomatic snarl may not, as Geiss argues, have "placed a diametrically opposed interpretation on Russian mobilization";[86] a good case can be made for the contention that he was simply correcting Jagow's mistake. But to term this communication "most temperate in tone" is to interpret Moltke's action in the most favorable light possible and to misconstrue its likely effect on German policy.[87]

The contributions of Williamson and Kaiser to a deeper understanding of the roles of the Central Powers in the outbreak of war have been matched by a renewed interest in the policies of the Entente. Dominic Lieven of the London School of Economics reinterpreted Russian actions in his 1983 contribution to the St. Martin's series. Lieven's aim is twofold: to furnish an examination of Fischer's assertion of the primacy of domestic factors in foreign policy as that assertion might apply to Russia and to discuss the extent to which Russian foreign policy was influenced by its governmental structure. He holds that although domestic concerns certainly bore heavily on the termination of the Russo-Japanese War in 1905, Russian foreign policy was in essence conditioned by external factors, chief among them distrust of German ambitions in Europe. Internal groups impelling Russia toward aggression enjoyed less popular support than in Germany; the more perceptive Russian rightist leaders feared revolution at home in the event of war; and Russia, unlike Germany, controlled tremendous natural resources without recourse to aggression. Further, he contends that the isolation of the Russian government from the pressures and interest groups characteristic of mass politics made it possible for that government to concentrate a disproportionate share of the

86. Geiss, *July 1914*, 266.
87. Kaiser, "Germany," 469.

nation's wealth on the pursuit of external objectives. Russia could not have pursued such an expensive foreign policy to the detriment of internal conditions without the presence of authoritarian rule.

The stimulus of Lieven's book derives from its almost exclusive concentration on the Entente side of the 1914 equation. He accepts without hesitation the evidence of Serbian complicity in the Sarajevo crime while remaining skeptical of Barnes's contention that Russian diplomats in Belgrade knew of the conspiracy from the beginning. Ambassador Hartwig and military attaché Artamonov "were unsympathetic to the Black Hand's struggle against Pašić and were well aware that Serbia needed a long respite before running the risks of involvement in any further external crises."[88] Had Russian officials learned of the plot, they would surely have reported it to Pašić and advised him to act against it. Sazonov himself certainly knew nothing either before or after June 28 about Serbian involvement; confronted with unsubstantiated Austrian allegations directed at the Narodna Odbrana and cognizant of Vienna's propensity for concocting anti-Serbian complaints on a foundation of forgeries, he naturally reacted with incredulity.

Russia's contacts with its allies in July are covered sketchily. Lieven correctly points out that no written record of conversations between Poincaré and Sazonov on July 20–23 has been discovered, but he finds it unlikely that Paléologue would have taken such a "self-confidently vigorous line" had Poincaré not authorized it. In any case, the position taken by the French ambassador was perfectly consistent with France's attitude at least since 1912. As for Britain, Grey's noncommittal attitude left Sazonov as much in the dark as Bethmann was. At the crucial meeting of the Common Ministerial Council on July 24, the foreign minister called attention to the danger of running a serious risk of war with Germany in the absence of firm support from London.

Certainly Russia was not blameless in the crisis. War Minister Sukhomlinov was reluctant to tell the Common Ministerial Council that Russia was not ready for a lengthy war, although he consoled himself with the notion that the necessity for Germany to prevail quickly would preclude any such eventuality.[89] The Russian government's inability to deal with domestic dissent may have led

88. Dominic Lieven, *Russia and the Origins of the First World War* (New York, 1983), 139.
89. Ibid., 113, 143. Lieven correctly points out that a long war was in the interests of the Entente and that the Russian military should therefore have prepared for one.

the Austrians to conclude erroneously that the tsar could not risk a continental conflict. And, peculiarly, the leading foreign affairs experts of the centrist parties in the Duma were far more belligerent and unreasonable than the "sinister forces" surrounding the Imperial court, which (taking their cue from Rasputin) opposed war with Germany. But having said all this, Lieven leaves no doubt in the reader's mind that, unlike Turner, he holds Russia essentially guiltless in the outbreak of war.

For Lieven, Russian mobilization was not the decisive step in the crisis. Admittedly, Chief of Staff Yanushkevich blundered in failing to inform the Common Ministerial Council on July 24 that partial mobilization would seriously impede future progress toward general mobilization, should this become necessary (one wonders if Yanushkevich realized this). But, Turner and others to the contrary, for the Russian army mobilization was not the equivalent of a declaration of war. Those who contend that partial mobilization would not have hindered subsequent general mobilization underestimate the complexity of the Imperial Russian system of reserve call-ups. Finally, Lieven asserts that the entire question of the impact of Russian mobilization is moot. A European conflict was likely even without it, given "Russia's key decision . . . on 24/25 July to support Serbian independence even at the risk of war."[90] Combined with the unwavering commitment of Austria to war with Serbia and the concomitant unwillingness of Germany to permit Russia to crush Austria, this leads Lieven to conclude with Fischer that "the major immediate responsibility for the outbreak of war rested unequivocally on the German government."[91]

This detailed and knowledgeable treatment is not without obstacles for the student of the July crisis. Lieven mentions Sazonov's supportive attitude toward Serbia, citing a telegram from Serbian ambassador Spalayković to Belgrade on the evening of July 24. But he appears unaware of another such telegram, dispatched the next day and containing Spalayković's enthusiastic description of military measures taken by the Common Ministerial Council at 11:00 A.M. on July 25. Gale Stokes believes that this document is the "missing telegram" whose existence was inferred by Albertini and others and which was responsible for hardening Serbia's attitude toward the Austrian ultimatum on the afternoon of July 25.[92]

90. Ibid., 146.
91. Ibid., 151.
92. Gale Stokes, "The Serbian Documents from 1914: A Preview," *Journal of*

Knowledge of this document might have sharpened Lieven's characterization of Sazonov's mood on July 25, a description which seems to owe a bit too much to the foreign minister's own apologia for his role.[93]

Within the St. Martin's series, Lieven's analysis of the Russian role in the coming of the war is complemented by that of John F.V. Keiger of the University of Salford, who supplies the first detailed reexamination of France's role in the crisis since Albertini's account appeared in the early forties. Aided by several collections of private papers of French diplomats and ambassadors only recently opened to historical scrutiny, his book views with skepticism the impact of *revanche* and attempts a systematic rehabilitation of the reputation of Raymond Poincaré.

Even those, like Remak and Schroeder, who disagreed with Fischer's belief in the overriding responsibility of Germany still relegated France to a position of comparative insignificance befitting an unlucky nation which happened to be, through no fault of its own, on the receiving end of the Schlieffen Plan. This attitude contrasts sharply with that of the early revisionists, who tended to place a large share of the blame on France, due to the supposedly bellicose sentiments of the displaced Lorrainer, Poincaré. Fischer's strong emphasis upon German guilt turned the focus of the debate eastward and made France the forgotten belligerent of July 1914. Keiger's view is that French policy in July is indeed worthy of attention, if only to rebuke Albertini and reinforce the growing consensus in support of French passivity.

Much of Keiger's account covers familiar ground. He notes with accuracy that during the 1890s many inhabitants of the lost provinces became disenchanted with the protectionism and anticlericalism of the French government and enamoured of the prosperity offered by membership in the economically dynamic German Empire.[94] On the subject of the nationalist revival, he observes that

---

Modern History 48 (1976): on-demand supplement, 73–74. Stokes believes that a telegram sent from St. Petersburg at noon could have reached Belgrade by 4:00 P.M., in time to affect the Serbian government's decision on the reply to be delivered two hours later. But if it did arrive so rapidly, what explains the mobilization of the Serbian army at 3:00 P.M.?

93. On this point see John W. Langdon, "Emerging From Fischer's Shadow: Recent Examinations of the Crisis of July 1914," *The History Teacher* 20 (1986): 80–81.

94. Keiger, *France*, 15. But see the opposite conclusions drawn by Dan P. Silverman, "The Economic Consequences of Annexation: Alsace-Lorraine and

the widely accepted belief in a strong resurgence of French patriotism between 1905 and 1914 is contradicted by Jean-Jacques Becker's demonstration that such a revival, if it existed at all, was not shared by the rural majority of the country and that post-1905 patriotism was far less aggressive than its counterpart of twenty years earlier.[95] The originality of his narrative lies in its novel view of Poincaré, who emerges from these pages not as a fire-breathing revanchist, but as a realistic Germanophobe whose personal experience of war's destruction led him to adopt a cautious foreign policy aimed at safeguarding France against a repetition of 1870.

Seeing himself as a manager rather than an innovator, Poincaré retained control over foreign affairs, even after his election as president, by the simple expedient of appointing as foreign ministers inexperienced, submissive men who would be forced to turn to him for guidance and direction. He believed in military readiness and a strong Entente, but refused to provoke Germany unnecessarily and pursued a conciliatory policy toward Germany on colonial issues. As the July crisis opened, Poincaré constituted, in Keiger's opinion, a force for peace and stability rather than war and revenge.

This attitude persisted throughout July. Albertini contends that Viviani's failure to compose minutes of Poincaré's talks with Sazonov must have been deliberate, to hide the fact that France was urging Russia to stand firm on Balkan matters. But Keiger makes the valid point that Sazonov's July 29 telegram to the Russian ambassador in Paris, Aleksandr Isvolsky, refers only to the promises of support offered by Paléologue and not to any prior understanding with Poincaré and Viviani. This, coupled with his analysis of Poincaré's policy toward Russia during the previous two years, leads Keiger to conclude that any pledge of unconditional backing for Russia would have been inconsistent with Poincaré's methods and goals. Further, he disagrees profoundly with the contention shared by Albertini and Jules Isaac that, throughout the crisis, Viviani exercised a conciliatory, moderating influence on the volatile Poincaré: "It should now be clear that during the July crisis Poincaré was the principal decision-maker in [French] foreign policy, with Viviani acting as a mere puppet."[96] Those who consider

Imperial Germany, 1871–1918," *Central European History* 4 (1971): 34–53.
95. Jean-Jacques Becker, *1914: Comment les français sont entrés dans la guerre* (Paris, 1977).
96. Keiger, *France*, 164.

France's policy in late July to have been prudent and proper have Poincaré to thank for it. To Keiger, even Albertini's judicious verdict – that Poincaré simply exploited German and Austrian blunders in order to regain the lost provinces – is unfair to the French president, a much more passive diplomat than most historians suggest.

Clearly, Keiger lacks sympathy for the Hamburg school's insistence upon the primacy of domestic politics in the making of foreign policy. He notes the unequivocal importance of external considerations in Poincaré's view of France's role in the world, and since the president retained control of foreign policy in his own hands, those considerations shaped that policy. Keiger has produced a serious, balanced (though not uncontroversial) reappraisal of French conduct in July which should render impossible any return to a revisionist view of Poincaré.

Certain aspects of Keiger's treatment of the crisis nonetheless present difficulties. He is certainly correct in claiming that "for French public opinion in 1914 the July Crisis, as we know it today, never really existed."[97] But what of it? As he himself recognizes, London and St. Petersburg were equally ignorant of the impending catastrophe, and they did not have a sensational scandal like the murder trial of Mme Caillaux to keep other news off the front pages. For that matter, once the blank check had been issued, Berlin was kept only erratically informed of the progress of things in Vienna, and German and Austrian public opinion were no more enlightened than French. Secrecy was what gave the July crisis its unique character among all the other major prewar imbroglios which developed gradually, were subjected to intense public scrutiny, and were all settled without recourse to general war. July 1914, had it been permitted to unfold in a similar way, might also have been settled peacefully. But it wasn't.

Keiger may also go too far in exculpating Poincaré. He is right in condemning Paléologue's duplicity, but he understates the implications of the lifelong friendship between the president and the ambassador. Paléologue's reputation as an emotionally high-strung, gossipy representative was already established when he was appointed ambassador in February 1914. Poincaré may not be to blame for his friend's excessive zeal, but he is clearly culpable for having appointed such a character to a highly sensitive diplomatic

97. Ibid., 145.

post in the first place. Beyond this, the two men doubtless exchanged views off the record on July 20–23. It is difficult to believe that even an enthusiast like Paléologue would seriously distort his friend's policy after having been reminded of it so recently and so personally. Keiger himself contends that Paléologue's failure to inform Paris in a timely fashion of the steps toward Russian mobilization constituted an effort to mislead the bureaucrats at the Quai d'Orsay, who were likely to stand against him. He carefully refrains from alleging that Poincaré would have joined that opposition.

Reservations concerning Keiger's interpretation are also held by Gerd Krumeich, whose 1980 book on French armaments and foreign policy in 1913–14 was translated into English one year after *France and the Origins of the First World War* appeared. Krumeich, a doctoral student under Wolfgang Mommsen at the University of Düsseldorf, analyzed at length the diaries of Raymond Poincaré in the Bibliothèque Nationale in Paris. Those diaries, which differ in a number of instances from Poincaré's published memoirs, helped Krumeich to lay the groundwork for a new interpretation of the motivations behind the Three-Year Law of 1913 and of French behavior during the July crisis.

Krumeich is unimpressed with Keiger's view of Poincaré, not least because Keiger, while quoting liberally from the Poincaré diaries, failed to utilize in any way Krumeich's analysis of them (published in German in 1980, three years before publication of Keiger's book). Accordingly, Krumeich takes pains in the English edition of his book to call attention to differences between the two interpretations. His overall objective is to challenge the Fischerite emphasis on the primacy of domestic politics, which he considers inadequate for a theoretical explanation of French policy in the two years prior to the Great War. Krumeich contends that "the theory, based on the preeminence of domestic policy, that the three-year law was a vehicle of socially conservative policy, cannot be substantiated. On the other hand, there is no reason to conclude a primacy of foreign policy."[98] French decision making was heterogeneous and took both foreign and domestic concerns into account.

In the waning months of the prewar period, these concerns manifested themselves in the context of the law to increase the term of military service from two years to three. Krumeich asserts that the decision to introduce this bill, far from being motivated by

98. Krumeich, *Armaments and Politics*, 18.

domestic political strategy, was actually taken in response to the German 1913 army bill which expanded both the line army and, more significantly, the officer corps. French military leaders did not anticipate an impending German attack, but realized that the increase in the size of the German army threatened their own strategic planning, which since 1911 had been based on an immediate offensive in the first days of a war. To change this line of thinking (epitomized by Plan XVII, adopted in 1913) would spook the Russians, whose rapid intervention in East Prussia would be vital to French military action against Germany and would thereby "jeopardise the entire network of French foreign and security policy."[99] But the French government realized that public opinion and the left wing of the National Assembly would never accept arguments based on the Russian alliance as reasons for altering the French term of service. For this reason, the Three-Year Law was sold to the nation as an indispensable measure to defend France against an imminently belligerent Germany.

Thus the decision to restructure the French army was attributable in large measure to external political and military considerations. Having said this, Krumeich also recognizes the domestic and social conditions which operated simultaneously with foreign concerns to shape French policy. In particular, he argues that "research to date [has] tended to neglect internal developments in France on the eve of the European crisis, although these developments had a considerable influence on decision-making in foreign policy."[100] Poincaré, who liked to appoint foreign ministers who would let him dictate foreign policy, had been boxed in by domestic political considerations following the June 1914 elections, which indicated a weakening of support for continuation of the three-year term. He was forced to accept as premier René Viviani, a Radical Socialist acceptable to the Left whose commitment to the Three-Year Law was not as solid as Poincaré's. As the two men left for Russia in mid-July, it was obvious that Poincaré's hopes of maintaining "national unity as a means of backing up an energetic foreign policy" were disappearing.[101] French diplomacy in the July crisis must be understood in this context.

Krumeich, armed with the Poincaré diaries, reassesses the St.

---

99. Ibid., 18.
100. Ibid., 217.
101. Ibid., 215.

Petersburg discussions of July 20–23. Contrary to Albertini's view, the Serbian problem was not raised in Poincaré's July 20 conference with Nicholas II. The tsar was concerned about the June elections, which had imperiled the Three-Year Law, and about his difficulties with Britain over a railway line in Anatolia, which threatened to negate the progress made toward an Anglo-Russian naval agreement. Anxious to reassure the Russian government, Poincaré hastened to provide pledges of French support for Russia in the Balkans; his July 21 remarks to Austrian ambassador Szápáry must be understood in this light.

Once the two statesmen were apprised of the terms of the Austrian ultimatum, they instructed their ambassadors at St. Petersburg and London to ask for an extension of the forty-eight-hour time limit, to advise Serbia to accept whatever portions of the ultimatum were consistent with its sovereignty, and to substitute an international inquest into the Sarajevo crime for the proposed Austro-Serb investigation.[102] Krumeich characterizes Poincaré's attitude as strongly supportive of Russian backing for Serbia, while Viviani signed the telegram without realizing that its effect would be to cast the dispute in international terms and thereby involve the Franco-Russian alliance. Over the next several days, Paléologue deliberately delayed or withheld from the two leaders information concerning Russian military measures, not because he doubted Poincaré's commitment to the alliance, but because he feared Viviani's reaction and was unable to communicate with Poincaré separately, given the shipboard proximity of the two men.

Once the *France* docked and liberated its passengers, Viviani's doubts concerning Poincaré's actions began to surface. He supported Grey's mediation proposals with far more vigor than Poincaré and on July 30 warned Russia against further escalation of the situation. Krumeich maintains that Keiger's opinion that Viviani, bored by foreign affairs, was merely Poincaré's puppet in July is not supported by the evidence. Poincaré's diaries indicate to him that the president dealt with Viviani gingerly, working around him when possible and at all costs avoiding an open confrontation in which "it can by no means be taken for granted that Poincaré's line would have come out on top."[103] Even when, at Poincaré's insistence,

102. Ibid., 219. Krumeich contends that Albertini's conclusion (*The Origins*, II, 590) that this telegram never existed is improbable, given its reproduction in full in Poincaré's diaries.
103. Krumeich, *Armaments and Politics*, 226.

general mobilization was ordered on August 1, Viviani attempted to have the decision rescinded only a few minutes after it was issued. But he lacked the autocratic authority of the tsar, who earlier had temporarily substituted partial mobilization for general, and the French government's decision stood.

For Krumeich, Poincaré's conduct in July 1914 was not that of the passive, prudent chess player portrayed by Keiger. Rather, it was that of a firmly committed supporter of the Franco-Russian alliance who feared that Germany's bluff, if not called, would succeed in splitting the Entente. Yet like Keiger, Krumeich disavows any return to a revisionist interpretation of French policy: "A point stressed by Isaac which cannot be over-emphasised is that the ultimate reason for [Poincaré's support for Russia] was not irresponsible 'playing with fire' or 'warmongering,' but years of fear of Germany's world-wide aspirations and aggression."[104]

One of the most helpful components of Krumeich's analysis is its frank assertion that it is inexact to speak of a "primacy" of either foreign or domestic policy when dealing with the outbreak of the Great War. The heterogeneous nature of decision making which he postulates offers the student of the July crisis freedom from both the tunnel vision of the purely diplomatic historians and the overly rigid categorizations of the Hamburg school. Building upon this insight, James Joll of the University of London, a student of the war's origins for more than two decades, summed up his views on the subject in *The Origins of the First World War*, a provocative monograph filled with paths for future historians to follow.

Joll, one of the most articulate and certainly the most reasonable of Fritz Fischer's defenders,[105] examined the background to the Great War in a number of venues, beginning with his 1966 article in *Past and Present* assessing the state of the Fischer controversy to that point. His 1968 inaugural lecture for the Stevenson Chair of International History at the University of London was reprinted as a pamphlet and was widely recognized as breaking new ground in the study of the conflict's origins.[106] In 1984, he blended many of the observations expressed in that lecture with further reflections on research after 1968 in a treatment of the subject that offers not only a fresh look at the July crisis but also, for the first time since Sidney

104. Ibid., 228.
105. This in no way implies that Fischer's attackers were any more reasonable than his defenders.
106. James Joll, *1914: The Unspoken Assumptions* (London, 1968).

Fay, an original interpretation of the underlying causes of the war.

Some of Joll's fundamental causes are similar to those isolated by Fay: imperialism, militarism, and the system of secret alliances. To these he adds the international economy, the primacy of domestic politics, armaments and strategy, and "the mood of 1914" in an effort to reach a more modern understanding of the forces making for war. Against this background, in which his most innovative ideas are developed, Joll's description of the July crisis appears professionally crafted but ordinary. He provides a few details absent from other accounts covered in this book – for example, the fact that the Russians "had broken the cipher used by the Austro-Hungarian Foreign Ministry and were presumably aware of the contents of the telegrams between Vienna and the embassy at St. Petersburg" throughout the month of July.[107] But a careful reading of Joll's chapter on July leaves the impression that Fischer and his opponents have between them constructed a workable version of what happened and where the responsibility lies. There is considerable material for future research and analysis, but most of it lies in the years prior to 1914.

Here Joll's monograph, by encapsulating the most significant findings of the past two decades and adding to them his own shrewd insights, points out a number of paths for eventual assessment. In his interpretation, the competing alliance systems were the products of fear of one's own friends as well as one's enemies. Thus Germany would go to the wall for Austria-Hungary not only out of desire to preserve the Habsburg Empire as an ally, but out of dread of having to absorb fifteen million German-speaking Catholics should the Dual Monarchy break apart (in which case Protestants would then constitute a minority within the Reich). England would back up France, not only because of a reluctance to see Germany dominate the continent by defeating France, but out of a suspicion that if France felt abandoned, that nation would come to some sort of understanding with Germany at London's expense. There was a growing belief in Britain that Russia was a greater threat than Germany anyway, while the Triple Entente was a paper tiger, designed to present a solid front in peacetime but useless should war ensue.

With respect to military matters, Joll views with skepticism Egmont Zechlin's conviction that an Anglo-Russian naval agreement would have posed an intolerable threat to Germany. He

107. Joll, *Origins*, 12.

quotes Grey on the subject: "To my lay mind it seemed that, in a war against Germany, the Russian Fleet could not get out of the Baltic and the British Fleet would not get into it."[108] Serbia, with an army still exhausted from the Balkan wars, was in no position to provoke a conflict with Austria in 1914, and there is no evidence to indicate that Dimitrijević or anyone else connected with Serbian military intelligence had the slightest idea that such a predicament might follow the assassination of the archduke. German plans to seize Liège as part of the first few days of the Schlieffen Plan had been kept a secret even from the Kaiser, and not until the last day of July did Bethmann recognize their implications. Joll goes further than most historians in endorsing the essence (although not all particulars) of Fischer's argument concerning the War Council of December 1912; but in his opinion "what is more important than the immediate responsibility for the actual outbreak of war is the state of mind which was shared by all the belligerents, a state of mind which envisaged the probable imminence of war and its absolute necessity in certain circumstances."[109]

In his chapter on the primacy of domestic politics, Joll sanctions Krumeich's contention that domestic and foreign concerns operated simultaneously in the calculations of all the powers. He finds no connection between domestic difficulties and foreign policy in Britain, agrees with Krumeich that their mixture in France was complex and bilateral, and confesses bewilderment at trying to assess their respective degrees of importance in the mind of the "vacillating and fatalistic Tsar."[110] With respect to Germany, the problem with the concept of the *Primat der Innenpolitik* is that acceptance of it precludes any recognition that statesmen occasionally mean what they say. Many of the ideas expressed by Bülow, Tirpitz, and Bethmann are so thoroughly consistent with Leopold von Ranke's idea of the primacy of foreign policy that to ignore them would constitute prima facie evidence of reductionism and bias. Similar difficulties afflict prevalent interpretations of imperialistic and economic reasons for war, which Joll finds shot through with facile reductionism and advanced categorosclerosis.[111] Finally,

---

108. Sir Edward Grey, quoted in Joll, *Origins*, 70.
109. Joll, *Origins*, 88.
110. Ibid., 108.
111. "Hardening of the categories," a disease first named by David Hackett Fischer of Brandeis University in his engaging book, *Historians' Fallacies* (Boston, 1966).

Joll's chapter on the mood of 1914 demonstrates in detail the "willingness to risk or accept war as a solution to a whole range of problems . . . . [I]t is still in an investigation of the mentalities of the rulers of Europe and their subjects that the explanation of the causes of the war will ultimately lie."[112]

Joll's assessment, by summarizing and building upon much of the best research developed during the past generation, challenges future historians to search for explanations for the outbreak of the Great War in both familiar and unfamiliar locations. Its publication in 1984 marked the completion of sixty-five years of analysis of the crisis of July 1914 and leads us to a consideration of the significance of those years of controversy and consensus.

112. Joll, *Origins*, 196.

Conclusion: 1990

It would be easy to look at the spectrum of historical accounts analyzed in this book and conclude that our knowledge of the crisis of July 1914 is mired in a hopeless relativism and that no consensus is possible. But this is not the case. After seventy years of research and writing, historians have reached tacit agreement on most aspects of the issue, a fact which their continuing disputes should not be allowed to obscure. This makes possible a plausible assessment of the keys to the crisis which have provided a framework for this book.

Serbian complicity in the Sarajevo assassination is indisputable but limited. The conspirators were recruited and dispatched by the Black Hand, an organization with extensive influence in Serbian life. The chief of Serbian military intelligence, Colonel Dragutin Dimitrijević, planned the attempt and arranged safe passage into Bosnia for the would-be assassins. The government itself knew nothing of these plans until early in June, when one of its informers filed a routine report. At this point it was too late to intercept the seven conspirators.

Nikola Pašić's government could not risk an open confrontation with the Black Hand, given its strength in the country and the imminence of a general election. The prime minister's efforts to extract an explanation from Dimitrijević proved unavailing. Conspiracies and plots were not uncommon in the Balkans, and many of them came to nothing; perhaps this one would also prove unproductive. But a successful attempt would plunge an unprepared Serbia into an immediate confrontation with Austria-Hungary. Pašić therefore alerted the Serbian minister to Vienna, Jovan Jovanović, and probably asked him to convey a discreet warning to the proper authorities. Jovanović went to Leon von Bilinski, the Austro-Hungarian finance minister (who was responsible for Bosnian affairs), and carried out his instructions. Unfortunately the

175

warning was so generalized and vague that no responsible official could have been impressed with its gravity to an extent sufficient to justify formal intervention with Potiorek. The governor of Bosnia's regrettable failure to implement adequate security precautions, coupled with his astonishing willingness to let the visit proceed following the near-miss bomb attack on Sunday morning, doomed the archduke and his wife. As a result, the attempt (which could easily have been frustrated with minimal police surveillance) succeeded.

The Serbian government did not inspire the plot and made well-intentioned but ineffective efforts to forestall it. The argument that governments are responsible for terrorist actions launched from their jurisdictions is technically correct but hopelessly abstract. Certainly neither Dimitrijević nor the Serbian cabinet wanted a military confrontation with Austria-Hungary, much less a world war. But the conclusion that Princip alone was guilty of the murders is equally untenable. We are all acquainted with the paving materials used to construct the road to hell, and as has often been observed with respect to the July crisis, results count more than intentions. Serbia bears responsibility, in the limited sense just outlined, for the Sarajevo crime. It does not bear responsibility for the outbreak of a general war, for which the murder of Franz Ferdinand was only a pretext.

German conduct between the assassinations and July 23 has (especially since 1961) been analyzed more thoroughly than any other aspect of the crisis. This attention has paid dividends. The revisionist contention that Austria blackmailed a feckless, unwilling Germany into an indefensible surrender of its own freedom of action will not stand up to scrutiny. Nor will the comforting view of Bethmann Hollweg as the heroic yet indecisive civilian leader gradually overridden by a reckless military establishment.

Prior to the arrival of Hoyos on July 5, the German government had considered its position and had decided to exploit the archduke's unfortunate demise to alter the balance of power in the Balkans, shore up Austria's position as a great power, and possibly split the Entente in the process. These intentions coincided with those of the Austrian government. There is no evidence to support the supposition that either party had to work hard to convince the other of the merits of its case, although Berchtold did have trouble with Tisza because of internal Hungarian concerns. Once agreement was reached, Tisza's recalcitrance forced the Austrians to move more slowly than the Germans wished, but it is difficult to imagine any of the Entente powers adopting a disinterested attitude had the ultimatum been delivered a week or two earlier. The crucial element was not one of timing but of impact. Simple Austrian chastisement of Serbia could have been swallowed by any Entente nation, even Russia; but the destruction of Serbian sovereignty and the resulting alteration of the Balkan power balance would have been no more palatable on July 9 than on July 23.

As for German foreknowledge of the ultimatum, documentary evidence indicates strongly that this was an excuse fabricated after the fact. Between July 10 and 22, Berlin was informed consistently of substantive developments, although not of the precise wording of the document. When the ultimatum itself arrived on July 22, the German government took no action to demonstrate disapproval. Jagow's claim that he considered the document too harsh is not supported by any contemporary document or statement. Throughout the early stages of the crisis, Chancellor Bethmann Hollweg deliberately ran the risk of a major European war, a war that he considered preventive in nature. Fritz Fischer's assertion that this war had been planned as early as December 1912 is unproven and probably unprovable; his regrettable insistence on this dubious proposition has distracted attention from the mountain of compelling evidence he has presented as proof of Germany's desire to grasp for world power. The calculated risk theory, despite its inherent absurdity in the context of the alignment facing Germany in July 1914, is accepted by most historians as a reasonable explanation of Bethmann's less than reasonable conduct. The more that is known about his role in July, the more one is drawn to endorse the conclusion, proposed sardonically by Gerhard Ritter, that the chancellor was a reckless, irresponsible adventurer gambling the lives of millions and the future of European civilization on one throw of a set of dice that were loaded against him. Hamlet he may have been, but this in no way excuses his conduct since even the indecisive Hamlet left the stage drenched in blood.

French policy toward Russia was very controversial in the twenties and thirties. Luigi Albertini's praise of Viviani and measured criticism of Poincaré laid the issue to rest until Gerd Krumeich and John Keiger resurrected it several years ago. No one today would accept Harry Barnes's argument that France and Russia conspired to force war on an unsuspecting Germany, but Albertini's description of the good René Viviani also seems unlikely to endure. In

177

addition, the Kehrite argument for the primacy of domestic politics appears only marginally applicable to France, where Poincaré pursued a consistent foreign policy in spite of internal obstacles.

That policy was predicated upon cold-blooded mistrust of German objectives rather than upon a superpatriotic desire to regain the lost provinces. The Russian alliance was the cornerstone not merely of French diplomacy but of French survival. France could not hope to defeat Germany without Russia, and Russia would not fight for Alsace and Lorraine. This excluded a war against Germany in which France was the aggressor. It also required France to support Russian aspirations in the Balkans, failing which St. Petersburg might strike a deal with Germany at the expense of Austria-Hungary, leaving France friendless. When Poincaré and Viviani visited the tsar on July 20–23, these considerations could not have been far from their minds.

There is no reason to believe that Poincaré's conversations with Sazonov and Nicholas II were either overly aggressive or pacifistic; after all, the precise nature of Austrian action against Serbia was not yet known, so specific countermeasures could hardly have been proposed. The fragmentary evidence available leads to the conclusion that the French statesmen reaffirmed their country's commitment to the Franco-Russian alliance and assured Sazonov of their cooperation against any outlandish Austrian claims. French ambassador Paléologue was no doubt briefed extensively on the ramifications of these commitments, and his encouragement of a firm stand, of which he made no secret, was consistent with what he perceived to be Poincaré's intentions. His undeniable duplicity in concealing from Paris news of Russian military measures was based not upon a fear that France would desert Russia, but upon a fear that French reluctance to sanction mobilization measures would spook Sazonov and result in a repetition of the diplomatic defeat of 1909. Paléologue feared that neither Poincaré nor Viviani would approve of precipitate Russian action, and he was probably correct.

Keiger and Krumeich have given us different portrayals of the Viviani/Poincaré relationship than that presented by Albertini. Viviani unquestionably was poorly prepared to influence French foreign policy, especially when accompanied by as forceful a personality as Poincaré. But the evidence is unfriendly to Keiger's characterization of the premier as the president's puppet. Viviani took a more cautious line than Poincaré throughout the crisis, although Albertini's dichotomizing of their positions appears overdrawn. Neither was willing to believe in the purity of Germany's intentions for very long, and there is no indication that after Viviani replied to the German ultimatum with the formula "France will act in accordance with her interests," that he went out and wept bitterly. Differences of opinion between French leaders were to be expected, as were disputes between Moltke and Bethmann, Berchtold and Conrad, Sazonov and Nicholas II, Grey and Sir Eyre Crowe; it was, after all, a major crisis with which they were dealing. That does not mean that one manipulated the other in order to reorient national policy in an aggressive direction.

Grey's reluctance to warn Germany was central to the thesis that the Great War began through misunderstanding. That position was somewhat discredited after 1939, when the Second World War began because the contending powers understood each other all too well. Today it is generally believed that Grey's defense of his inaction, the split within the British cabinet, explains little. A clarification of a nation's position is not equivalent to a declaration of war; it is an action which falls within the day-to-day job description of any foreign minister. Grey had no difficulty in issuing such a clarification on July 29, at a time when he had only four votes in the cabinet for taking Britain into a war on the side of France. Certainly he could have delivered such a warning much earlier, had he been so inclined. Why did he not do so? Probably because he counted on Germany's willingness to work with Britain toward a repetition of the 1912 cooperation that had localized the Balkan wars. The July crisis did not (at least at first) look very different from previous disputes which had been settled without general war. Only when Grey realized that Germany was backing Austria-Hungary to the finish did he snap to attention and attempt to call Berlin to order.

Regrettably, it didn't work – but that may not have been Grey's fault. Would Germany have pursued an aggressive course even if British intervention had been assured from the beginning? No consensus exists in this area. Those who hold that Bethmann hoped for British neutrality are obliged to answer the question negatively, while those who believe that British participation meant nothing to Berlin must respond in the affirmative. Fritz Fischer, in a dazzling display of logical incoherence, contends that Germany's policy would have been undeviatingly aggressive *and* that Bethmann hoped to keep London out of it! My own assessment of the evidence and arguments leads to the conclusion that earlier action by Grey would have convinced Bethmann that it was impossible to split the Entente over the Serbian question and that Germany faced a war it was unlikely to win. Had this conviction been developed prior to July 27, the Austrian declaration of war on Serbia could have been forestalled and Sazonov would not have pressed for Russian general mobilization. The entire course of the July crisis would have been altered, although war might still have eventuated.[1]

Bethmann's last-minute efforts to restrain Vienna were perfectly sincere. Those who hold that he was working to keep Britain neutral see in these actions the panic-stricken flailings of a desperate man who had just recognized the bankruptcy of his policy. Those who accept the version of the calculated risk theory based on the Riezler diaries also consider his efforts sincere; the crisis was to be intensified until it had exposed the divisions within the Entente, at which time mediation and a step back from the brink would be undertaken. The problem was that Berchtold had not been let in on the game and failed to respond to Berlin's entreaties until Russia had jumped into the fray. By that time it was too late, but this was not entirely Bethmann's fault.

In either scenario, the chancellor's efforts, while undoubtedly straightforward, were poorly conceived. They ran contrary to the line of policy which Germany had followed consistently since July 5, and they gave Berchtold too little time in which to respond.[2] Bethmann's rather pathetic attempts to keep the stone from rolling down the hill had no effect on the course of the crisis and in no way mitigate the actions that created the dangerous situation in which he found himself by July 29.

Russian general mobilization, our sixth and final key, no longer occupies its customary place of dishonor as the one action that made a great war inevitable. Few historians would go as far as Kantorowicz and contend that it was a mere technicality which exerted no influence on the development of the crisis; but not many more

1. This is not to say that Grey was in any way responsible for the worsening of the crisis. He was merely reacting to German and Austrian initiatives and was in no way attempting to deceive Berlin (as some revisionists alleged). The German government, in failing to anticipate correctly London's probable course of action, was guilty of criminal stupidity. They should have known all along that the sort of alteration of the balance of power which they had in mind could not be accepted passively by Grey or the cabinet.

2. It is revealing that some historians who allege that Berchtold gave Bethmann too little time to modify the text of the ultimatum nonetheless believe that Bethmann gave Berchtold ample time to reverse the entire course of Austrian policy, which by July 29/30 included a declaration of war. In each case, the time available was less than twenty-four hours.

would accept the contention that without it, war would have been avoided. It is now generally accepted that mobilization meant war only for Germany, because of the Schlieffen Plan, and that the Russian government saw mobilization as a negotiating tool (and believed that everyone else saw it in the same light). Sazonov responded to the Austrian bombardment of Belgrade and the German demand that Russia cease all military preparations by raising the pot and calling the bluff of the Central Powers. Only when Germany mobilized in turn and invaded Belgium did he realize the extent of his miscalculation.

Turner's important work must be considered in this context. He is correct in asserting that Russian partial mobilization, no less than general, would have required an escalatory response from Germany. Yet to expect Russia to refrain even from partial mobilization when faced with an apparent Austrian determination to undermine Serbian sovereignty and alter the Balkan power balance was to expect the impossible. For Russia it was not German but Austrian action that was determinative. Since Austria rejected mediation and seemed bent on a course of action clearly opposed to Russian interests in eastern Europe, the only alternative to some sort of mobilization was capitulation.

Russian general mobilization clearly was not evidence of aggressive designs. Despite the confusion over the potential effects of partial mobilization, the dissembling of Sukhomlinov, the incompetence of Yanushkevich, the emotionalism of Sazonov, and the vacillations of the tsar, it is difficult to conceive of an acceptable alternative path for Russia. In this area, as in the rest of the July crisis, we return to the central questions: Who initiated the confrontation? What did they expect to gain? How flexible were their positions and attitudes? What were the chances that general war might be avoided? The responses to these questions, in the light of seventy years of research, are not favorable to the Central Powers.

The differences and disagreements between historians over responsibility for the outbreak of the Great War are both understandable and defensible. Wegerer and Montgelas defended their country against perceived injustice; Barnes indicted those whom he saw as the aggressors in a fit of passion and righteous indignation; Fischer attacked the myopia of his own country, while Ritter attacked a man he considered a traitor. Each of these authors, and all of the others whose work is analyzed in this book, strove for scholarly objectivity (although some strove more persistently than others).

Yet the historian, when judging the past, has nowhere to stand save the present. No scholar can rest immune to the disputes, controversies, and political necessities of his or her own day. Historical objectivity is a goal to reach for but one never to be fully attained, and no one should be astonished to learn that none of those who have puzzled over the crisis of July 1914 have possessed it completely.

Just as no one can attain pure objectivity, so no one author has a monopoly over the truth. The interpretations assessed in these pages contain fragments of the truth which each reader must assemble into what seems to him or her a plausible reconstruction of the July crisis. Ironically, we know much more of the truth today than anyone did then. Participants in the events of July 1914 were harried and beleaguered men, wrestling with a situation which did not develop as any of them had expected. Each concentrated on his own corner of the problem, the challenges facing his own country; none saw the overall picture with the clarity we possess today. Further work remains to be done, but a reasonable range of explanations of the crisis is now available.

Those explanations, those reconstructions built from fragments of the truth, are as important today as they were in the twenties. Some of the earlier questions have been answered: Was Germany solely to blame? Should Germany pay reparations? Others have been formulated in our own day: Can war be avoided by studying crises of the past? Should Germany be reunified? Was Nazism an aberration or a logical culmination of German history? In attempting to answer these questions, those who analyze the recent past are not merely writing history, but making it. It is this sobering consideration that makes the crisis of July 1914 and the interpretations surrounding it more than matters of historical curiosity.

Select Bibliography

Albertini, Luigi. *Le origini della guerra del 1914*. 3 vols. Milan, 1942–43. English edition: *The Origins of the War of 1914*. Translated by Isabella M. Massey. 3 vols. New York, 1952–57.

Barnes, Harry Elmer. *The Genesis of the World War*. New York, 1925.

Berghahn, Volker R. *Germany and the Approach of War in 1914*. New York, 1973.

Dedijer, Vladimir. *The Road to Sarajevo*. New York, 1966.

Dehio, Ludwig. *Deutschland und die Weltpolitik im 20. Jahrhundert*. 2d ed. Frankfurt, 1961. English edition: *Germany and World Politics in the Twentieth Century*. Translated by Dieter Pevsner. New York, 1967.

Droz, Jacques. *Les causes de la Première Guerre Mondiale: Essai d'historiographie*. Paris, 1973.

Epstein, Klaus. "Gerhard Ritter and the First World War." In Walter Laqueur and George L. Mosse, eds., *1914: The Coming of the First World War*. New York, 1966, 186–203.

——. "German War Aims in the First World War." *World Politics* 15 (1962): 163–85.

Erdmann, Karl Dietrich. "Kurt Riezler – Ein politisches Profil." Introduction to Kurt Riezler, *Tagebücher, Aufsätze, Dokumente*. Edited by Karl Dietrich Erdmann. Göttingen, 1972, 3–161.

——. "War Guilt 1914 Reconsidered: A Balance of New Research." In H.W. Koch, ed., *The Origins of the First World War*. 2d ed. London, 1984, 343–70.

——. "Zur Beurteilung Bethmann Hollwegs." *Geschichte in Wissenschaft und Unterricht* 15 (1964): 525–40.

——. "Zur Echtheit der Tagebücher Kurt Riezlers: Eine Antikritik." *Historische Zeitschrift* 236 (1983): 371–402.

Faulenbach, Bernd. *Ideologie des deutschen Weges: Die deutsche Geschichte in der Historiographie zwischen Kaiserreich und Nationalsozialismus*. Munich, 1980.

Fay, Sidney Bradshaw. *The Origins of the World War*. Rev. ed. 2 vols. New York, 1930.

Fischer, Fritz. *Griff nach der Weltmacht*. Düsseldorf, 1961. English edition: *Germany's Aims in the First World War*. Translated by Fritz

Fischer. New York, 1967.
——. *Juli 1914: Wir sind nich hineingeschlittert.* Hamburg, 1983.
——. "Kontinuität des Irrtums: Zum Problem der deutschen Kriegszielpolitik im Ersten Weltkrieg." *Historische Zeitschrift* 190 (1960): 83–101.
——. *Krieg der Illusionen.* Düsseldorf, 1969. English edition: *War of Illusions.* Translated by Marion Jackson. New York, 1975.
——. *Weltmacht oder Niedergang.* Frankfurt, 1965. English edition: *World Power or Decline.* Translated by Lancelot Farrar, Robert Kimber, and Rita Kimber. New York, 1974.
——. "Weltpolitik, Weltmachtstreben und deutsche Kriegsziele." *Historische Zeitschrift* 199 (1964): 265–346. English translation: "World Policy, World Power, and German War Aims." Translated by H.W. Koch. In H.W. Koch, ed., *The Origins of the First World War.* 2d ed. London, 1984, 128–88.
Florinsky, Michael T. "The Russian Mobilization of 1914." *Political Science Quarterly* 42 (1927): 203–27.
Gasser, Adolf. "Der deutsche Hegemonialkrieg von 1914." In Imanuel Geiss and Bernd Jürgen Wendt, eds., *Deutschland in der Weltpolitik des 19. and 20. Jahrhunderts.* Düsseldorf, 1974, 307–39.
Geiss, Imanuel. "Kurt Riezler und der Erste Weltkrieg." In Imanuel Geiss and Bernd Jürgen Wendt, ed., *Deutschland in der Weltpolitik des 19. and 20. Jahrhunderts.* Düsseldorf, 1974, 398–418.
——. "The Outbreak of the First World War and German War Aims." In Walter Laqueur and George L. Mosse, eds., *1914: The Coming of the First World War.* New York, 1966, 71–87.
——, ed. *Julikrise und Kriegsausbruch, 1914.* 2 vols. Hanover, 1963–64. English edition: *July 1914: The Outbreak of the First World War – Selected Documents.* Translated by Imanuel Geiss. New York, 1967.
Geiss, Imanuel, and Bernd Jürgen Wendt, eds. *Deutschland in der Weltpolitik des 19. und 20. Jahrhunderts.* Düsseldorf, 1974.
Gordon, Michael R. "Domestic Conflict and the Origins of the First World War: The British and the German Cases." *Journal of Modern History* 46 (1974): 191–226.
Heinemann, Ulrich. *Die verdrängte Niederlage: Politische öffentlichkeit und Kriegsschuldfrage in der Weimarer Republik.* Göttingen, 1983.
Herwig, Holger H. "Clio Deceived: Patriotic Self-Censorship in Germany after the Great War." *International Security* 12 (Fall 1987): 5–44.
Herzfeld, Hans. "Zur deutschen Politik im Ersten Weltkriege: Kontinuität oder permanente Krise?" *Historische Zeitschrift* 190 (1960): 67–82.
Hillgruber, Andreas. *Deutschlands Rolle in der Vorgeschichte der beiden Weltkriege.* Göttingen, 1967. English edition: *Germany and the Two World Wars.* Translated by William C. Kirby. Cambridge, Mass., 1981.
——. "Die deutsche Politik in der Julikrise 1914." *Quellen und For-*

schungen aus italienischen Archiven und Bibliotheken 61 (1981): 191–215.

——. "Riezlers Theorie des kalkulierten Risikos und Bethmann Hollwegs politische Konzeption in der Julikrise 1914." *Historische Zeitschrift* 202 (1966): 333–51.

Isaac, Jules. *Un débat historique, 1914: Le problème des origines de la guerre.* Paris, 1933.

Jager, Wolfgang. *Historische Forschung und politische Kultur in Deutschland: Die Debatte 1914–1980 über den Ausbruch des Ersten Weltkrieges.* Göttingen, 1984.

Janssen, Karl-Heinz. "Gerhard Ritter: A Patriotic Historian's Justification." In H.W. Koch, ed., *The Origins of the First World War.* 2d ed. London, 1984, 292–318.

Jarausch, Konrad H. *The Enigmatic Chancellor: Bethmann Hollweg and the Hubris of Imperial Germany.* New Haven, 1973.

——. "The Illusion of Limited War: Chancellor Bethmann Hollweg's Calculated Risk, July 1914." *Central European History* 2 (1969): 48–76.

——. "World Power or Tragic Fate? The *Kriegsschuldfrage* as Historical Neurosis." *Central European History* 5 (1972): 72–92.

Joll, James. "The 1914 Debate Continues: Fritz Fischer and His Critics." *Past and Present* 34 (1966): 100–113.

——. *The Origins of the First World War.* London, 1984.

Kaiser, David E. "Germany and the Origins of the First World War." *Journal of Modern History* 55 (1983): 442–74.

Kantorowicz, Hermann. *Der Geist der englischen Politik und das Gespenst der Einkreisung Deutschlands.* Berlin, 1929.

——. *Gutachten zur Kriegsschuldfrage, 1914.* Edited by Imanuel Geiss. Frankfurt, 1967.

Keiger, John F.V. *France and the Origins of the First World War.* New York, 1983.

Koch, H.W., ed. *The Origins of the First World War.* 2d ed. London, 1984.

Krumeich, Gerd. *Aufrüstung und Innenpolitik in Frankreich vor dem Ersten Weltkrieg.* Wiesbaden, 1980. English edition: *Armaments and Politics in France on the Eve of the First World War.* Translated by Stephen Conn. Birmingham, U.K., 1984.

Langdon, John W. "Emerging From Fischer's Shadow: Recent Examinations of the Crisis of July 1914." *The History Teacher* 20 (1986): 63–86.

Lieven, Dominic. *Russia and the Origins of the First World War.* New York, 1983.

Marczewski, Jerzy. "German Historiography and the Problem of Germany's Responsibility for World War I." *Polish Western Affairs* 12 (1971): 289–308.

Mayer, Arno J. "Domestic Causes of the First World War." In Leonard Krieger and Fritz Stern, eds., *The Responsibility of Power: Historical*

Essays in Honor of Hajo Holborn. New York, 1967, 286–300.

Mommsen, Wolfgang J. *Das Zeitalter des Imperialismus*. Frankfurt, 1969.

——. "The Debate on German War Aims." In Walter Laqueur and George L. Mosse, eds., *1914: The Coming of the First World War*. New York, 1966, 45–70.

——. "Domestic Factors in German Foreign Policy before 1914." *Central European History* 6 (1973): 3–43.

Montgelas, Count Max. *Leitfaden zur Kriegsschuldfrage*. Berlin, 1923. English edition: *The Case for the Central Powers*. Translated by Constance Vesey. New York, 1925.

Moses, John A. "Karl Dietrich Erdmann, the Riezler Diary, and the Fischer Controversy." *Journal of European Studies* 3 (1973): 241–54.

——. *The Politics of Illusion: The Fischer Controversy in German Historiography*. New York, 1975.

Remak, Joachim. "1914 – The Third Balkan War: Origins Reconsidered." *Journal of Modern History* 43 (1971): 353–66.

Renouvin, Pierre. *Les origines immédiates de la guerre*. Paris, 1925. English edition: *The Immediate Origins of the War*. Translated by Theodore Carswell Hume. New York, 1927.

Ritter, Gerhard. "Eine neue Kriegsschuldthese?" *Historische Zeitschrift* 194 (1962): 646–68. An English translation of the final twelve pages is available: "A New War-Guilt Thesis?" Translated by Dwight E. Lee and Stewart A. Stehlin. In Dwight E. Lee, ed., *The Outbreak of the First World War: Causes and Responsibilities*. 4th ed. Toronto, 1975, 97–107.

——. *Staatskunst und Kriegshandwerk: Das Problem des Militarismus in Deutschland*. 2d ed. 4 vols. Munich, 1965–68. English edition: *The Sword and the Scepter*. Translated by Heinz Norden. 4 vols. Coral Gables, Fla., 1970.

Röhl, John C.G., ed. *1914: Delusion or Design?* New York, 1973.

Schmitt, Bernadotte Everly. *The Coming of the War, 1914*. 2 vols. New York, 1930.

Schollgen, Gregor. "Griff nach der Weltmacht? 25 Jahre Fischer-Kontroverse." *Historische Jahrbücher* 106 (1986): 386–406.

Schroeder, Paul W. "World War I as Galloping Gertie: A Reply to Joachim Remak." *Journal of Modern History* 44 (1972): 319–45.

Sösemann, Bernd. "Die Tagebücher Kurt Riezlers: Untersuchungen zu ihrer Echtheit und Edition." *Historische Zeitschrift* 236 (1983): 327–69.

Steiner, Zara S. *Britain and the Origins of the First World War*. New York, 1977.

Stern, Fritz. "Bethmann Hollweg and the War: The Limits of Responsibility." In Fritz Stern and Leonard Krieger, eds., *The Responsibility of Power: Historical Essays in Honor of Hajo Holborn*. New York, 1967, 252–85.

Stokes, Gale. "The Serbian Documents from 1914: A Preview." *Journal of Modern History* 48 (1976): on-demand supplement, 69–83.

Stone, Norman. "Gerhard Ritter and the First World War." *Historical Journal* 13 (1970): 158–71.

Sywottek, Arnold. "Die Fischer-Kontroverse: Ein Beitrag zur Entwicklung historisch-politischen Bewußtseins in der Bundesrepublik." In Imanuel Geiss and Bernd Jürgen Wendt, eds., *Deutschland in der Weltpolitik des 19. und 20. Jahrhunderts.* Düsseldorf, 1974, 19–47.

Taylor, A.J.P. *The Course of German History.* London, 1945.

——. *The Struggle for Mastery in Europe, 1848–1918.* New York, 1954.

——. *War by Time-Table: How the First World War Began.* New York, 1969.

Thompson, Wayne C. *In the Eye of the Storm: Kurt Riezler and the Crises of Modern Germany.* Iowa City, 1980.

Trumpener, Ulrich. "War Premeditated? German Intelligence Operations in July 1914." *Central European History* 9 (1976): 58–85.

Turner, L.C.F. *Origins of the First World War.* New York, 1970.

——. "The Role of the General Staffs in July 1914." *Australian Journal of Politics and History* 11 (1965): 305–23.

——. "The Russian Mobilization in 1914." *Journal of Contemporary History* 3 (1968): 65–88.

Ullrich, Volker. "Das deutsche Kalkül in der Julikrise 1914 und die Frage der englischen Neutralität." *Geschichte in Wissenschaft und Unterricht* 34 (1983): 79–97.

Wegerer, Alfred von. *Der Ausbruch des Weltkrieges.* 2 vols. Hamburg, 1939.

——. *Die Widerlegung der versailler Kriegsschuldthese.* Berlin, 1928. English edition: *A Refutation of the Versailles War Guilt Thesis.* Translated by Edwin H. Zeydel. New York, 1930.

——. "The Russian Mobilization of 1914." *Political Science Quarterly* 43 (1928): 201–28.

Williamson, Samuel R. Jr. *Austria-Hungary and the Coming of the First World War.* New York, 1990.

——. *The Politics of Grand Strategy: Britain and France Prepare for War, 1904–1914.* Cambridge, Mass., 1969.

——. "Vienna and July 1914: The Origins of the Great War Once More." In Samuel R. Williamson Jr. and Peter Pastor, eds., *Essays on World War I.* New York, 1983, 9–36.

——, ed. *The Origins of a Tragedy: July 1914.* Arlington Heights, Ill., 1981.

Zechlin, Egmont. "Deutschland zwischen Kabinettskrieg und Wirtschaftskrieg: Politik und Kriegsführung in den ersten Monaten des Weltkrieges 1914." *Historische Zeitschrift* 199 (1964): 347–458. An English translation is available: "Cabinet versus Economic Warfare in Germany: Policy and Strategy during the Early Months of the First World War." Translated by Heinz Norden. In H.W. Koch, ed., *The Origins of the First World War.* 2d ed. London, 1984, 189–291.

———. *Krieg und Kriegsrisiko: Zur deutschen Politik im Ersten Weltkrieg.* Düsseldorf, 1979.

———. "July 1914: Reply to a Polemic." Translated by Brian Follett. In H.W. Koch, ed., *The Origins of the First World War.* 2d ed. London, 1984, 371–85.

Index

189

Index

Pourtalès, Count Friedrich von (German ambassador in St. Petersburg), 47, 57, 69, 91, 135 n. 12

Princip, Gavrilo, 1, 8, 88, 132, 138, 157, 176

Reiners, Ludwig (historian), 131

Remak, Joachim (historian), 6 n. 7, 89, 141–44, 146–47, 150, 155, 165

Renouvin, Pierre (historian), 4, 39–45, 47, 50, 52, 54, 73, 79, 98, 136

revisionism, 3–5, 18–35, 42, 50, 61, 64, 68, 73, 84, 100, 130, 141–42, 165, 171, 176, 180 n. 1

Riezler, Kurt (adviser to Bethmann Hollweg), 71 n. 9, 104 n. 11, 107–17, 121–24, 127–28, 133–34, 136, 147, 180

Riezler, Walter, 110, 114

Ritter, Gerhard (historian), x, 66–67, 73–75, 77, 79–85, 89, 96–98, 101–13, 116, 119, 121, 125, 130 n. 1, 131, 139, 177, 181

Rogger, Hans (historian), 131

Röhl, John C.G. (historian), 119, 124–25

Rothfels, Hans (historian), 26, 73, 79, 100

Russia

Common Ministerial Council (July 24), 15, 163–64

diplomatic documents, 17–19

mobilization, 15, 29–30, 34, 38, 43, 49, 57–59, 72, 87, 90–91, 96–98, 105–06, 139–41, 143, 152, 162, 164, 168, 178, 180–81

Sarajevo, 1, 8, 10, 37, 45, 51–52, 62, 88, 91, 103, 127, 132–34, 142, 156, 163, 170, 175–76

Sazonov, Sergei (Russian foreign minister), 11, 12 n. 6, 15, 28–30, 34, 39, 42, 49, 55, 57–60, 63, 69, 72, 88, 91, 96, 130, 138–40, 151 n. 56, 153, 163–66, 178–80

Schlieffen Plan, 43 n. 17, 59–60, 64, 82, 101, 106, 120, 123, 140, 151–52, 165, 173, 181

Schmitt, Bernadotte Everly (historian), 4, 44–50, 52, 54, 66, 73, 79, 98, 136, 147

Schoen, Hans von (Bavarian chargé d'affaires in Berlin), 89

Schröder, Gerhard (West German foreign minister), 77, 84

Schroeder, Paul W. (historian), 6 n. 6, 143–47, 150, 155, 165

Seeberg, Erich, 66

Serbia

diplomatic documents, 17, 19, 132

reply to Austro-Hungarian ultimatum, 13

responsibility for assassination, 8, 10, 24, 27, 31, 37, 40, 45, 52, 62, 88, 103, 132–33, 138, 142, 163, 175–76

Sösemann, Bernd (historian), 113–14

Spalayković (Serbian minister in St. Petersburg), 164

Stegmann, Dirk (historian), 86, 93

Steiner, Zara S. (historian), 152–54

Stern, Fritz (historian), 110, 115, 133–34, 136

Stokes, Gale (historian), 164

Stone, Norman (historian), 101, 117, 131

Stresemann, Gustav (German foreign minister, 1923–29), 36

Stumm, Wilhelm von (political director in the German Foreign Office), 98, 135

Stürgkh, Count Karl (Austrian

194

prime minister), 156
Südekum, Albert, 72
Sukhomlinov, Vladimir
Alexandrovich (Russian minister
of war), 163, 181
Szápáry von Szapar, Count
Friedrich (Austro-Hungarian
ambassador in St. Petersburg),
159, 170
Szögyény-Marich, Count
Ladislaus (Austro-Hungarian
ambassador in Berlin), 9, 21, 31,
41, 45, 48, 53–54, 56, 88, 95,
134

Tankosić, Voja, 132
Taylor, A.J.P. (historian), 4,
61–65, 117
Thompson, Wayne C. (historian),
115, 123 n. 57
Tirpitz, Alfred von (grand admiral
and German secretary of state
for the navy), 59, 129, 161,
173
Tisza de Böros-Jeno, Count Istvan
(Hungarian prime minister), 10,
13, 71, 148, 156–58, 176
Triple Entente, 11, 22–24, 26–27,
33, 42, 49, 51, 53, 56–57, 60, 69,
82, 87–88, 92–95, 112–19, 120 n.
52, 122–23, 126, 128, 133–35,
137, 139, 142, 146, 148, 153,
162–63, 171–72, 176–77, 180
Trumpener, Ulrich (historian),
150–52
Tschirschky und Bogendorff,
Count Heinrich Leopold von
(German ambassador in Vienna),
25, 53–54, 71, 87, 89, 91, 97–98,
104–5
Tuchman, Barbara, W. (historian),
7 n. 8, 130–31
Turner, L.C.F. (historian), 87, 98,
138–41, 164, 181

Versailles treaty, 1–4, 18, 21, 30,
34, 50, 61, 84
Viviani, René (French premier and
foreign minister), 11–12, 24, 39,
42, 54–56, 63, 151 n. 56, 158,
166, 169–71, 177–79
Vogel, Barbara (historian), 86
Volkmann, Erich, 67

Wegerer, Alfred von (historian), 3,
21–24, 26, 36, 50, 53, 68, 181
Wehler, Hans-Ulrich (historian),
78 n. 28, 86, 93, 100 n. 1, 119,
149, 160
Weinberg, Gerhard L. (historian),
ix, 106 n. 16, 122
Weltpolitik, 135, 144, 157, 160–61
White, Marie, 110, 133
Wiesner, Friederich von, 10
Wilhelm II (emperor of Germany),
1, 4, 9 n. 14, 28, 31–33, 39, 41,
43, 45, 53, 58–59, 62–63, 68–69,
71–72, 88, 91, 93, 95, 108, 111,
116, 119, 121, 123–24, 129, 134,
137–38, 147, 156–57, 161, 173
Wilhelmstraße, 18, 31, 91, 136
Williamson, Samuel R., Jr.
(historian), ix, 51 n. 32, 155–60,
162
Witt, Peter-Christian (historian),
86, 93

Yanushkevich, Nikolai
Nikolaievich (Russian chief of
staff), 15, 57, 87, 140, 164, 181

Zechlin, Egmont (historian),
73–74, 79–81, 84–85, 96, 112,
115, 117, 121, 125–29, 135, 139,
153, 172
Zenker (captain, German naval
staff), 41
Zimmermann, Alfred (under
secretary of state, German